THE ROMAN RITUAL
REVISED BY DECREE OF THE
SECOND VATICAN ECUMENICAL COUNCIL
AND PUBLISHED BY AUTHORITY OF POPE PAUL VI

RITE OF PENANCE
STUDY EDITION

Approved for Use in the Dioceses of the United States of America
by the United States Conference of Catholic Bishops
and Confirmed by the Holy See

With readings from the Revised Lectionary for Mass

English translation prepared by the
International Commission on English in the Liturgy

United States Conference of Catholic Bishops
Washington, D.C.

Concordat cum originali
✠ Most Reverend Gregory M. Aymond
Chairman, USCCB Committee on Divine Worship
after review by Reverend Monsignor Anthony F. Sherman
Executive Director, USCCB Secretariat of Divine Worship

RITE OF PENANCE

SACRED CONGREGATION FOR DIVINE WORSHIP

Prot. n. 800/73

Decree

Reconciliation between God and his people was brought about by our Lord Jesus Christ in the mystery of his death and resurrection (see Romans 5:10). The Lord entrusted the ministry of reconciliation to the Church in the person of the apostles (see 2 Corinthians 5:18ff.). The Church carries out this ministry by bringing the good news of salvation to people and by baptizing them in water and the Holy Spirit (see Matthew 28:19).

Because of human weakness, however, Christians "leave [their] first love" (see Revelation 2:4) and even break off their fellowship with God by sinning. The Lord therefore instituted a special sacrament of penance for the pardon of sins committed after baptism (see John 20:21-23) and the Church has faithfully celebrated the sacrament throughout the centuries—in varying ways, but retaining its essential elements.

Vatican Council II decreed that "the rite and formularies for the sacrament of penance are to be revised so that they may more clearly express both the nature and effect of this sacrament."[1] In view of this the Congregation for Divine Worship has carefully prepared the new *Rite of Penance* so that the celebration of the sacrament may be more fully understood by the faithful.

In this new rite, besides the *Rite for Reconciliation of Individual Penitents*, a *Rite for Reconciliation of Several Penitents* has been drawn up to emphasize the relation of the sacrament to the community. This rite places individual confession and absolution in the context of a celebration of the word of God. Furthermore, for special occasions, a *Rite for Reconciliation of Several Penitents with General Confession and Absolution* has been composed in accordance with the Pastoral Norms on General Sacramental Absolution, issued by the Congregation for the Doctrine of the Faith, 16 June 1972.[2]

The Church is deeply concerned with calling the faithful to continual conversion and renewal. It desires that the baptized who have sinned should acknowledge their sins against God and their neighbor and have heartfelt repentance for them; it takes pains to prepare them to celebrate the sacrament of penance. For this reason the Church urges the faithful to attend penitential celebrations from time to time. This Congregation has

---

1   Second Vatican Council, constitution *Sacrosanctum Concilium*, no. 72: AAS 56 (1964) 118.
2   See AAS 64 (1972) 510-514.

therefore made regulations for such celebrations and has proposed examples or models that conferences of bishops may adapt to the needs of their own regions.

Pope Paul VI has by his authority approved the *Rite of Penance* prepared by the Congregation for Divine Worship and ordered it to be published. It is to replace the pertinent titles of the Roman Ritual hitherto in use. The *Rite* in its Latin original is to come into force as soon as it is published; vernacular versions, from the day determined by the conferences of bishops, after they have approved the translation and received confirmation from the Apostolic See.

Anything to the contrary notwithstanding.

From the office of the Congregation for Divine Worship, December 2, 1973, the First Sunday of Advent.

By special mandate of the Pope

✠ Jean Cardinal Villot
Secretary of State

✠ Annibale Bugnini
Titular Archbishop of Diocletiana
Secretary of the Congregation for Divine Worship

INTRODUCTION

I. MYSTERY OF RECONCILIATION
IN THE HISTORY OF SALVATION

1. The Father has shown forth his mercy by reconciling the world to himself in Christ and by making peace for all things on earth and in heaven by the blood of Christ on the cross.[1] The Son of God made man lived among us in order to free us from the slavery of sin[2] and to call us out of darkness into his wonderful light.[3] He therefore began his work on earth by preaching repentance and saying: "Repent and believe the Gospel" (Mark 1:15).

This invitation to repentance, which had often been sounded by the prophets, prepared people's hearts for the coming of the kingdom of God through the voice of John the Baptist, who came "preaching a baptism of repentance for the forgiveness of sins" (Mark 1:4).

Jesus, however, not only exhorted people to repentance so that they would abandon their sins and turn wholeheartedly to the Lord,[4] but welcoming sinners, he actually reconciled them with the Father.[5] Moreover, he healed the sick in order to offer a sign of his power to forgive sin.[6] Finally, he himself died for our sins and rose again for our justification.[7] Therefore, on the night he was betrayed and began his saving passion,[8] he instituted the sacrifice of the New Covenant in his blood for the forgiveness of sins.[9] After his resurrection he sent the Holy Spirit upon the apostles, empowering them to forgive or retain sins[10] and sending them forth to all peoples to preach repentance and the forgiveness of sins in his name.[11]

The Lord said to Peter: "I will give you the keys of the kingdom of heaven, and whatever you bind on earth will be bound in heaven, and whatever you loose on earth will be loosed also in heaven" (Matthew 16:19). In obedience to this command, on the day of Pentecost Peter preached the forgiveness of sins by baptism: "Repent and let every one of you be baptized in the name of Jesus Christ for the remission of sins" (Acts 2:38).[12] Since then the Church has never failed to call people from sin to conversion and through the celebration of penance to show the victory of Christ over sin.

2. This victory is first brought to light in baptism where our fallen nature is crucified with Christ so that the body of sin may be destroyed and we may no longer be slaves to sin, but rise with Christ and live for God.[13] For this reason the Church proclaims its faith in "one baptism for the forgiveness of sins."

In the sacrifice of the Mass the passion of Christ is again made present; his body given for us and his blood shed for the forgiveness of sins are offered to God again by the Church for the salvation of the world. For in the eucharist Christ is present and is offered as "the sacrifice which has made our peace"[14] with God and in order that "we may be brought together in unity"[15] by his Holy Spirit.

Furthermore, our Savior Jesus Christ, when he gave to his apostles and their successors power to forgive sins, instituted in his Church the sacrament of penance. Its purpose is that the faithful who fall into sin after baptism may be reconciled with God through the restoration of grace.[16] The Church "possesses both water and tears: the water of baptism, the tears of penance."[17]

II. RECONCILIATION OF PENITENTS IN THE CHURCH'S LIFE

The Church Both Holy and Always in Need of Purification

3. Christ "loved the Church and gave himself up for it to make it holy" (Ephesians 5:25-26) and he united the Church to himself as a bride.[18] He filled it with his divine gifts,[19] because it is his Body and his fullness; through the Church he spreads truth and grace upon all.

The members of the Church, however, are exposed to temptation and often fall into the wretchedness of sin. As a result, "whereas Christ, 'holy, harmless, undefiled' (Hebrews 7:26), knew no sin (see 2 Corinthians 5:21) but came solely to seek pardon for the sins of his people (see Hebrews 2:17), the Church, having sinners in its midst, is at the same time holy and in need of cleansing, and so is unceasingly intent on repentance and reform."[20]

Penance in the Church's Life and Liturgy

4. The people of God accomplish and perfect this continual repentance in many different ways. They share in the sufferings of Christ[21] by enduring their own difficulties, carry out works of mercy and charity,[22] and adopt ever more fully the outlook of the Gospel message. Thus the people of God become in the world a sign of conversion to God. All this the Church expresses in its life and celebrates in its liturgy when the faithful confess that they are sinners and ask pardon of God and of their brothers and sisters. This happens

in penitential services, in the proclamation of the word of God, in prayer, and in the penitential parts of the eucharistic celebration.[23]

In the sacrament of penance the faithful "obtain from God's mercy pardon for having offended him and at the same time reconciliation with the Church, which they have wounded by their sins and which by charity, example, and prayer seeks their conversion."[24]

Reconciliation with God and with the Church

5. Since every sin is an offense against God that disrupts our friendship with him, "the ultimate purpose of penance is that we should love God deeply and commit ourselves completely to him."[25] Therefore, the sinner who by the grace of a merciful God embraces the way of penance comes back to the Father who "first loved us" (1 John 4:19), to Christ who gave himself up for us,[26] and to the Holy Spirit who has been poured out on us abundantly.[27]

"The hidden and gracious mystery of God unites us all through a supernatural bond: on this basis one person's sin harms the rest even as one person's goodness enriches them."[28] Penance always therefore entails reconciliation with our brethren and sisters who remain harmed by our sins.

In fact, people frequently join together to commit injustice. But it is also true that they help each other in doing penance; freed from sin by the grace of Christ, they become, with all persons of good will, agents of justice and peace in the world.

Sacrament of Penance and Its Parts

6. Followers of Christ who have sinned but who, by the prompting of the Holy Spirit, come to the sacrament of penance should above all be wholeheartedly converted to God. This inner conversion embraces sorrow for sin and the intent to lead a new life. It is expressed through confession made to the Church, due expiation, and amendment of life. God grants pardon for sin through the Church, which works by the ministry of priests.[29]

a. Contrition

The most important act of the penitent is contrition, which is "heartfelt sorrow and aversion for the sin committed along with the intention of sinning no more."[30] "We can only approach the kingdom of Christ by *metanoia*. This is a profound change of the whole person by which we begin to consider, judge, and arrange our life according to the holiness and love of God, made manifest in his Son in the last days and given to us in abundance" (see Hebrews 1:2; Colossians 1:19 and passim; Ephesians 1:23 and passim).[31] The genuineness of penance depends on this heartfelt contrition. For conversion should affect a person from within toward a progressively deeper enlightenment and an ever-closer likeness to Christ.

b. Confession

The sacrament of penance includes the confession of sins, which comes from true knowledge of self before God and from contrition for those sins. However, the inner examination of heart and the outward accusation must be made in the light of God's mercy. Confession requires on the penitent's part the will to open the heart to the minister of God and on the minister's part a spiritual judgment by which, acting in the person of Christ, he pronounces his decision of forgiveness or retention of sins in accord with the power of the keys.[32]

c. Act of Penance

True conversion is completed by expiation for the sins committed, by amendment of life, and also by rectifying injuries done.[33] The kind and extent of the expiation must be suited to the personal condition of penitents so that they may restore the order that they have upset and through the corresponding remedy be cured of the sickness from which they suffered. Therefore, it is necessary that the act of penance really be a remedy for sin and a help to renewal of life. Thus penitents, "forgetting the things that are behind" (Philippians 3:13), again become part of the mystery of salvation and press on toward the things that are to come.

d. Absolution

Through the sign of absolution God grants pardon to sinners who in sacramental confession manifest their change of heart to the Church's minister; this completes the sacrament of penance. For in God's design the humanity and loving kindness of our Savior have visibly appeared to us[34] and so God uses visible signs to give salvation and to renew the broken covenant.

In the sacrament of penance the Father receives the repentant children who come back to him, Christ places the lost sheep on his shoulders and brings them back to the sheepfold, and the Holy Spirit resanctifies those who are the temple of God or dwells more fully in them. The expression of all this is the sharing in the Lord's table, begun again or made more ardent; such a return of children from afar brings great rejoicing at the banquet of God's Church.[35]

Need and Benefit of This Sacrament

7. Just as the wounds of sin are varied and multiple in the life of individuals and of the community, so too the healing that penance provides is varied. Those who by grave sin have withdrawn from communion with God in love are called back in the sacrament of penance to the life they have lost. And those who, experiencing their weakness daily, fall into venial sins draw strength from a repeated celebration of penance to reach the full freedom of the children of God.

a. To obtain the saving remedy of the sacrament of penance, according to the plan of our merciful God, the faithful must confess to a priest each and every grave sin that they remember after an examination of conscience.[36]

b. Moreover, the frequent and careful celebration of this sacrament is also very useful as a remedy for venial sins. This is not a mere ritual repetition or psychological exercise, but a serious striving to perfect the grace of baptism so that, as we bear in our body the death of Jesus Christ, his life may be seen in us ever more clearly.[37] In confession of this kind, penitents who accuse themselves of venial faults should try to be more closely conformed to Christ and to follow the voice of the Spirit more attentively.

In order that this sacrament of healing may truly achieve its purpose among the faithful, it must take root in their entire life and move them to more fervent service of God and neighbor.

The celebration of this sacrament is thus always an act in which the Church proclaims its faith, gives thanks to God for the freedom with which Christ has made us free,[38] and offers its life as a spiritual sacrifice in praise of God's glory, as it hastens to meet the Lord Jesus.

III. OFFICES AND MINISTRIES IN THE RECONCILIATION OF PENITENTS

Role of the Community in the Celebration of Penance

8. The whole Church, as a priestly people, acts in different ways in the work of reconciliation that has been entrusted to it by the Lord. Not only does the Church call sinners to repentance by preaching the word of God, but it also intercedes for them and helps penitents with maternal care and solicitude to acknowledge and confess their sins

and to obtain the mercy of God, who alone can forgive sins. Further, the Church becomes itself the instrument of the conversion and absolution of the penitent through the ministry entrusted by Christ to the apostles and their successors.[39]

Minister of the Sacrament of Penance

9. a. The Church exercises the ministry of the sacrament of penance through bishops and priests. By preaching God's word they call the faithful to conversion; in the name of Christ and by the power of the Holy Spirit they declare and grant the forgiveness of sins. In the exercise of this ministry priests act in communion with the bishop and share in his power and office as the one who regulates the penitential discipline.[40]

   b. The competent minister of the sacrament is a priest who has the faculty to absolve in accordance with the provisions of the code of Canon Law, canons 967-975. All priests, however, even though not approved to hear confessions, absolve validly and lawfully any penitents without exception who are in danger of death.

Pastoral Exercise of This Ministry

10. a. In order that he may fulfill his ministry properly and faithfully, understand the disorders of souls and apply the appropriate remedies to them, and act as a wise judge, the confessor must acquire the needed knowledge and prudence by constant study under the guidance of the Church's magisterium and especially by praying fervently to God. For the discernment of spirits is indeed a deep knowledge of God's working in the human heart, a gift of the Spirit, and an effect of charity.[41]

   b. The confessor should always show himself to be ready and willing to hear the confessions of the faithful whenever they reasonably request this.[42]

   c. By receiving repentant sinners and leading them to the light of the truth, the confessor fulfills a paternal function: he reveals the heart of the Father and reflects the image of Christ the Good Shepherd. He should keep in mind that he has been entrusted with the ministry of Christ, who accomplished the saving work of human redemption by mercy and who by his power is present in the sacraments.[43]

   d. Conscious that he has come to know the secrets of another's conscience only because he is God's minister, the confessor is bound by the obligation of preserving the seal of confession absolutely unbroken.

Penitents

11. The parts that penitents themselves have in the celebration of the sacrament are of the greatest importance.

When with proper dispositions they approach this saving remedy instituted by Christ and confess their sins, their own acts become part of the sacrament itself, which is completed when the words of absolution are spoken by the minister in the name of Christ.

In this way the faithful, even as they experience and proclaim the mercy of God in their own life, are with the priest celebrating the liturgy of the Church's continual self-renewal.

IV. CELEBRATION OF THE SACRAMENT OF PENANCE

Place of Celebration

12. The sacrament of penance is ordinarily celebrated in a church or oratory, unless a legitimate reason stands in the way.

The conferences of bishops are to establish the norms pertaining to the confessional, which will include provision for clearly visible confessionals that the faithful who wish may readily use and that are equipped with a fixed screen between the penitent and the confessor.

Except for a legitimate reason, confessions are not to be heard outside a confessional.[44]

Time of Celebration

13. The reconciliation of penitents may be celebrated in all liturgical seasons and on any day. But it is right that the faithful be informed of the day and hours at which the priest is available for this ministry. They should be encouraged to approach the sacrament of penance at times when Mass is not being celebrated and preferably at the scheduled hours.[45]

Lent is the season most appropriate for celebrating the sacrament of penance. Already on Ash Wednesday the people of God hear the solemn invitation, "Turn away from sin and be faithful to the Gospel." It is therefore fitting to have several penitential services during Lent, so that all the faithful may have an opportunity to be reconciled with God and their neighbor and so be able to celebrate the paschal mystery in the Easter triduum with renewed hearts.

Liturgical Vestments

14. With respect to liturgical vestments in the celebration of penance, the norms laid down by the local Ordinaries are to be followed.

A. RITE FOR RECONCILIATION OF INDIVIDUAL PENITENTS

Preparation of Priest and Penitent

15. Priest and penitents should prepare themselves above all by prayer to celebrate the sacrament. The priest should call upon the Holy Spirit so that he may receive enlightenment and charity; the penitents should compare their own life with the example and commandments of Christ and then pray to God for the forgiveness of their sins.

Welcoming the Penitent

16. The priest should welcome penitents with fraternal charity and, if need be, address them with friendly words. The penitent then makes the sign of the cross, saying: **In the name of the Father, and of the Son, and of the Holy Spirit. Amen.** The priest may also make the sign of the cross with the penitent. Next the priest briefly urges the penitent to have confidence in God. Penitents who are unknown to the priest are advised to inform him of their state in life, the time of their last confession, their difficulties in leading the Christian life, and anything else that may help the confessor in the exercise of his ministry.

Reading of the Word of God

17. Next, the occasion may be taken for the priest, or even the penitent, to read a text of holy Scripture, or this may be done as part of the preparation for the actual celebration of the sacrament. For through the word of God Christians receive light to recognize their sins and are called to conversion and to confidence in God's mercy.

Penitent's Confession and Acceptance of the Penance

18. Next comes the penitent's confession of sins, beginning with the general confession formulary, **I confess to almighty God**, if this is the custom. If necessary, the confessor assists the penitent to make a complete confession; he also encourages the penitent to repent sincerely for offenses against God; finally he offers practical advice for beginning a new life, and, where necessary, gives instruction on the duties of the Christian life.

A penitent who has been the cause of harm or scandal to others is to be led by the priest to resolve to make due restitution.

Next, the priest imposes an act of penance or expiation on the penitent; this should serve not only as atonement for past sins but also as an aid to a new life and an antidote for weakness. As far as possible, therefore, the penance should correspond to the seriousness and nature of their sins. This act of penance may suitably take the form of prayer, self-denial, and especially service to neighbor and works of mercy. These will underline the fact that sin and its forgiveness have a social aspect.

Penitent's Prayer and the Priest's Absolution

19. Next, through a prayer for God's pardon the penitent expresses contrition and the resolution to begin a new life. It is advantageous for this prayer to be based on the words of Scripture.

Following the penitent's prayer, the priest extends his hands, or at least his right hand, over the head of the penitent and pronounces the formulary of absolution, in which the essential words are: **I absolve you from your sins in the name of the Father and of the Son and of the Holy Spirit.** As he says the final phrase the priest makes the sign of the cross over the penitent. The form of absolution (see no. 46) indicates that the reconciliation of the penitent comes from the mercy of the Father; it shows the connection between the reconciliation of the sinner and the paschal mystery of Christ; it stresses the role of the Holy Spirit in the forgiveness of sins; finally, it underlines the ecclesial aspect of the sacrament, because reconciliation with God is asked for and given through the ministry of the Church.

Proclamation of Praise and
Dismissal of the Penitent

20. After receiving pardon for sin, the penitent praises the mercy of God and gives him thanks in a short invocation taken from Scripture. Then the priest bids the penitent to go in peace.

    The penitent continues the conversion thus begun and expresses it by a life renewed according to the Gospel and more and more steeped in the love of God, for "love covers over a multitude of sins" (1 Peter 4:8).

Shorter Rite

21. When pastoral need dictates, the priest may omit or shorten some parts of the rite but must always retain in their entirety the penitent's confession of sins and acceptance of the act of penance, the invitation to contrition (no. 44), and the formularies of absolution and dismissal. In imminent danger of death, it is sufficient for the priest to say the essential words of the form of absolution, namely: **I absolve you from your sins in the name of the Father, and of the Son, and of the Holy Spirit.**

B. RITE FOR RECONCILIATION OF SEVERAL PENITENTS WITH INDIVIDUAL CONFESSION AND ABSOLUTION

22. When a number of penitents assemble at the same time to receive sacramental reconciliation, it is fitting that they be prepared for the sacrament by a celebration of the word of God.

    Those who will receive the sacrament at another time may also take part in the service.

    Communal celebration shows more clearly the ecclesial nature of penance. The faithful listen together to the word of God, which as it proclaims his mercy invites them to conversion; at the same time they examine the conformity of their lives with that word of God and help each other through common prayer. After confessing and being absolved individually, all join in praising God together for his wonderful deeds on behalf of the people he has gained for himself through the blood of his Son.

    If necessary, several priests should be available in suitable places to hear individual confessions and to reconcile the penitents.

Introductory Rites

23. When the faithful have gathered, a suitable hymn may be sung. Then the priest greets them and, if necessary, he or another minister gives a brief introduction to the celebration and explains the order of service. Next he invites all to pray and after a period of silence completes the opening prayer.

Celebration of the Word of God

24. The sacrament of penance should begin with a hearing of God's word, because through his word God calls his people to repentance and leads them to a true conversion of heart.

One or more readings may be chosen. If more than one are read, a psalm, another suitable song, or a period of silence should be inserted between them, so that the word of God may be more deeply understood and heartfelt assent may be given to it. If there is only one reading, it is preferable that it be from a gospel.

Readings should be chosen that will:

a. let God's voice be heard, calling his people back to conversion and ever closer conformity with Christ;
b. call to mind the mystery of our reconciliation through the death and resurrection of Christ and through the gift of the Holy Spirit;
c. bring to bear on people's lives God's judgment of good and evil as a light for the examination of conscience.

25. The homily, taking as its source the scriptural text, should lead the penitents to examine their conscience and to turn away from sin and toward God. It should remind the faithful that sin works against God, against the community and one's neighbors, and against the person of the sinner. Therefore it would be good to recall:

a. the infinite mercy of God, greater than all our sins, by which again and again he calls us back to himself;
b. the need for inner repentance, by which we are genuinely prepared to make reparation for sin;
c. the social dimension of grace and sin whose effect is that in some way the actions of individuals affect the whole Body of the Church;
d. the duty of expiation for sin, which is effective because of Christ's expiation and requires especially, in addition to works of repentance, the exercise of true charity

26. After the homily a suitable period of silence should be allowed for an examination of conscience and the awakening of true contrition for sin. The priest or a deacon or other minister may help the faithful with brief considerations or a litany, adapted to their background, age, etc.

If it should seem suitable, the community's examination of conscience and awakening of contrition may take the place of the homily. But in this case the text of Scripture that has just been read should serve as the starting point.

Rite of Reconciliation

27. At the invitation of the deacon or other minister, all kneel or bow down and say a form of general confession (for example, the prayer, **I confess to almighty God**). Then they stand, if this seems useful, and join in a litany or suitable song to express confession of sins, heartfelt contrition, prayer for forgiveness, and trust in God's mercy. Finally, they say the Lord's Prayer, which is never omitted.

28. After the Lord's Prayer the priests go to the places assigned for confession. The penitents who desire to confess their sins go to the priest of their choice. After they have accepted a suitable act of penance, the priest absolves them, using the formulary for the reconciliation of an individual penitent.

29. When the confessions are over, the priests return to the sanctuary. The priest who presides invites all to make an act of thanksgiving to praise God for his mercy. This may be done in a psalm or hymn or litany. Finally, the priest concludes the celebration with one of the prayers in praise of God for this great love.

Dismissal of the People

30. After the prayer of thanksgiving the priest blesses the faithful. Then the deacon or the priest himself dismisses the congregation.

C. RITE FOR RECONCILIATION OF PENITENTS WITH GENERAL CONFESSION AND ABSOLUTION

Discipline of General Absolution

31. An individual, complete confession and the receiving of absolution constitute the sole, ordinary means for a member of the faithful who is conscious of serious sin to be reconciled with God and the Church. Physical or moral impossibility alone excuses from this kind of confession; in the case of such impossibility, reconciliation is possible in other ways.

Absolution without prior, individual confession cannot be given collectively to a number of penitents unless:

a. the danger of death is imminent and there is no time for a priest or priests to hear the confessions of the individual penitents.

b. a serious need is present, namely, given the number of penitents, not enough confessors are available to hear the individual confessions properly within a reasonable time, with the result that through no fault of their own, the faithful would be forced to be for a long time without the grace of the sacrament or without communion. The need in question is not regarded as sufficient when the nonavailability of confessors is based solely on there being a large number of penitents, such as may be the case at some great festival or pilgrimage.[46]

32. To make the judgment on whether the requisite conditions already stated in no. 31[b] are verified belongs to the diocesan bishop. After considering the criteria agreed on with the other members of the conference of bishops, he can decide which cases involve the need in question.[47]

33. For the valid reception of general sacramental absolution it is required that the faithful not only be properly disposed but at the same time have the resolution to confess in due time each of those serious sins that they cannot at the present time confess in this way.

On the occasion of the reception of general absolution, the faithful, to the extent possible, are to be instructed on the requirements just mentioned; even in the case of danger of death when time allows, the imparting of general absolution is to be preceded by an exhortation that each recipient strive to make an act of contrition.[48]

34. Unless there is a good reason preventing it, those who receive pardon for serious sins through general absolution are to go to individual confession as soon as they have the opportunity before any further reception of general absolution. And unless a moral impossibility stands in the way, they are absolutely bound to go to a confessor within one year. For the precept binding every one of the faithful binds them as well, namely, to confess individually to a priest at least once a year all those grave sins not hitherto confessed one by one.[49]

Rite of General Absolution

35. For the reconciliation of penitents by general confession and absolution in the cases provided by law, everything takes place as described already for the reconciliation of several penitents with individual confession and absolution, with the following exceptions.

a. After the homily or during it, the faithful who seek general absolution are to be instructed to dispose themselves properly, that is, to have a personal sorrow for sins committed and the resolve to avoid committing them again; the intention to repair any scandal and harm caused and likewise to confess in due time each one of the grave sins that they cannot confess at present.[50] Some expiatory penance should be proposed for all to perform; individuals may add to this penance if they wish.

b. The deacon, another minister, or the priest then calls upon the penitents who wish to receive absolution to show their intention by some sign (for example, by bowing their heads, kneeling, or giving some other sign determined by the conference of bishops). They should also say together a form of general confession (for example, the prayer, **I confess to almighty God**), which may be followed by a litany or a penitential song. Then the Lord's Prayer is sung or said by all, as indicated in no. 27.

c. Then the priest pronounces the invocation that expresses prayer for the grace of the Holy Spirit to pardon sin, proclamation of victory over sin through Christ's death and resurrection, and the sacramental absolution given to the penitents.

d. Finally, the priest invites the people to give thanks, as indicated in no. 29 and, omitting the concluding prayer, he immediately blesses and dismisses them.

V. PENITENTIAL SERVICES

Nature and Structure

36. Penitential services are gatherings of the people of God to hear God's word as an invitation to conversion and renewal of life and as the message of our liberation from sin through Christ's death and resurrection. The structure of these services is the same as that usually followed in celebrations of the word of God[51] and given in the *Rite for Reconciliation of Several Penitents*.

It is appropriate, therefore, that after the introductory rites (song, greeting, and opening prayer) one or more biblical readings be chosen with songs, psalms, or periods of silence inserted between them. In the homily these readings should be explained and applied to the congregation. Before or after the readings from Scripture, readings from the Fathers or other writers may also be selected that will help the community and each person to a true awareness of sin and heartfelt sorrow, in other words, to bring about conversion of life.

After the homily and reflection on God's word, it is desirable that the congregation, united in voice and spirit, pray together in a litany or in some other way suited to general participation. At the end the Lord's Prayer is said, asking God our Father "to forgive us our sins as we forgive those who sin against us . . . and deliver us from evil." The priest or the minister who presides concludes with a prayer and the dismissal of the people.

Benefit and Importance

37. Care must be taken to ensure that the faithful do not confuse these celebrations with the celebration of the sacrament of penance.[52] Penitential services are very helpful in promoting conversion of life and purification of heart.[53]

It is desirable to arrange them especially for these purposes:

— to foster the spirit of penance with the Christian community;
— to help the faithful to prepare for individual confession that can be made later at a convenient time;
— to help children gradually form their conscience about sin in human life and about freedom from sin through Christ;
— to help catechumens during their conversion.

Penitential services, moreover, are very useful in places where no priest is available to give sacramental absolution. They offer help in reaching that perfect contrition that comes from charity and that enables the faithful to receive God's grace through a desire for the sacrament of penance in the future.[54]

VI. ADAPTATIONS OF THE RITE TO VARIOUS REGIONS AND CIRCUMSTANCES

Adaptations by the Conferences of Bishops

38. In preparing particular rituals, the conferences of bishops have the authority to adapt the rite of penance to the needs of individual regions so that, after confirmation of the conference's decisions by the Apostolic See, the rituals may be used in the respective regions. It is the responsibility of the conferences of bishops in this matter:

a.   to establish regulations for the discipline of the sacrament of penance, particularly those affecting the ministry of priests;

b.   to determine more precisely regulations about the confessional for the ordinary celebration of the sacrament of penance (see no. 12) and about the signs of repentance to be shown by the faithful before general absolution (see no. 35);

c.   to prepare translations of texts adapted to the character and language of each people; also to compose new texts of prayer for use by the faithful and the minister, keeping the essential sacramental formulary intact.

The Competence of the Bishop

39. It is for the diocesan bishop:

a.   to regulate the discipline of penance in his diocese,[55] even to the extent of adapting the rite according to the rules proposed by the conference of bishops;

b.   to make the decision, after considering the conditions required by the law (see no. 31[b]) and the criteria agreed on with the other members of the conference of bishops, regarding the cases of need in which general absolution may be permitted.[56]

Adaptations by the Minister

40. It is for priests, and especially parish priests (pastors):

a. in celebrating reconciliation with individuals or with a community, to adapt the rite to the concrete circumstances of the penitents. They must preserve the essential structure and the entire form of absolution, but if necessary they may omit some parts of the rite for pastoral reasons or enlarge upon them, may select the texts of readings or prayers, and may choose a place more suitable for the celebration according to the regulations of the conference of bishops, so that the entire celebration may be enriching and effective;

b. to celebrate and prepare occasional penitential services during the year especially in Lent. In order that the texts chosen and the order of the celebration may be adapted to the conditions and circumstances of the community or group (for example, children, sick persons, etc.), priests may be assisted by others, including the laity.

NOTES

1   See 2 Corinthians 5:18ff.; Colossians 1:20.

2   See John 8:34-36.

3   See 1 Peter 2:9.

4   See Luke 15.

5   Luke 5:20, 27-32; 7:48.

6   See Matthew 9:2-8.

7   See Romans 4:25.

8   See Roman Missal, Eucharistic Prayer III.

9   See Matthew 26:28.

10   See John 20:19-23.

11   See Luke 24:47.

12   See Acts 3:19, 26; 17:30.

13   See Romans 6:4-10.

14   See Roman Missal, Eucharistic Prayer III.

15   See Roman Missal, Eucharistic Prayer II.

16   See Council of Trent, sess. XIV, *De sacramento Paenitentiae*, Chapter 1: Denz-Schön 1668 and 1670; can. 1: Denz-Schön 1701.

17   Ambrose, Letter 41:12; *PL* 16, 1116.

18   See Revelation 19:7.

19   See Ephesians 1:22-23; Second Vatican Council, constitution *Lumen gentium*, no. 7: AAS 57 (1965) 9-11.

20   Second Vatican Council, constitution *Lumen gentium*, no. 8: ibid., 12.

21   See 1 Peter 4:13.

22   See 1 Peter 4:8.

23   See Council of Trent, sess. XIV, *De sacramento Paenitentiae*: Denz-Schön 1638, 1740, 1743. Congregation of Rites, Instr. *Eucharisticum mysterium*, May 25, 1967, no. 35: AAS 59 (1967) 560-561; Roman Missal, *General Instruction*, nos. 29, 30, 56 a, b, g.

24   Second Vatican Council, constitution *Lumen gentium*, no. 11: AAS 57 (1965) 15-16.

25   Paul VI, Ap. Const. *Paenitemini*, February 17, 1966: AAS 58 (1966) 179. See also Second Vatican Council, constitution *Lumen gentium*, no. 11: AAS 57 (1965) 15-16.

26   See Galatians 2:20; Ephesians 5:25.

27   See Titus 3:6.

28   Paul VI, Ap. Const. *Indulgentiarum doctrina*, January 1, 1967, no. 4: AAS 59 (1967) 9. See also Pius XII, Encycl. *Mystici Corporis*, June 29, 1943: AAS 35 (1943) 213.

29   See Council of Trent, sess. XIV, *De sacramento Paenitentiae*, Chapter 3: Denz-Schön 1673-1675 [the *ed. typica* erroneously cites Chapter 1].

30   Ibid., Chapter 4: Denz-Schön 1676.

31   Paul VI, Ap. Const. *Paenitemini*, February 17, 1966: AAS 58 (1966) 179.

32   See Council of Trent, sess. XIV, *De sacramanto Paenitentiae*, Chapter 5: Denz-Schön 1679.

33   See Council of Trent, sess. XIV, *De sacramanto Paenitentiae*, Chapter 8: Denz-Schön 1690-1692; Paul VI, Ap. Const. *Indulgentiarum doctrina*, January 1, 1967, nos. 2-3: AAS 59 (1967) 6-8.

34   See Titus 3:4-5.

35   See Luke 15:7, 10, 32.

[36]   See Council of Trent, sess. XIV, *De sacramento Paenitentiae*, can. 7-8: Denz-Schön 1707-1708.

[37]   See 2 Corinthians 4:10.

[38]   See Galatians 4:31.

[39]   See Matthew 18:18; John 20:23.

[40]   See Second Vatican Council, constitution *Lumen gentium*, no. 26: AAS 57 (1965) 31-32.

[41]   See Philippians 1:9-10.

[42]   See Congregation for the Doctrine of the Faith, Pastoral Norms for General Absolution, June 16, 1972, Norm XII: AAS 64 (1972) 514.

[43]   See Second Vatican Council, constitution *Sacrosanctum Concilium*, no. 7: AAS 56 (1964) 100-101.

[44]   See CIC, can. 964.

[45]   See Congregation of Rites, Instr. *Eucharisticum mysterium*, May 25, 1967, no. 35: AAS 59 (1967) 560-561.

[46]   See CIC, can. 960 and 961 §1.

[47]   See CIC, can. 961 §2.

[48]   See CIC, can. 962 §§1 and 2.

[49]   See Congregation for the Doctrine of the Faith, Pastoral Norms on General Absolution, June 16, 1972, Norms VII and VIII: AAS 64 (1972) 512-513; CIC, can. 963, 989.

[50]   See ibid., Norm VI: AAS 64 (1972) 512.

[51]   See Congregation of Rites, Instr. *Inter Oecumenici*, September 26, 1964, nos. 37-39: AAS 56 (1964) 110-111.

[52]   See Congregation for the Doctrine of the Faith, Pastoral Norms for General Absolution, June 16, 1972, Norm X: AAS 64 (1972) 513-514.

[53]   Ibid.

[54]   See Council of Trent, sess. XIV, *De sacramento Paenitentiae*, Chapter 5: Denz-Schön 1677.

[55]   See Second Vatican Council, constitution *Lumen gentium*, no. 26: AAS 57 (1965) 31-32.

[56]   See Congregation for the Doctrine of the Faith, Pastoral Norms on General Absolution, June 16, 1972, Norm V: AAS 64 (1972) 512; CIC, can. 961 §§1 and 2.

CHAPTER I
RITE FOR RECONCILIATION OF INDIVIDUAL PENITENTS

RECEPTION OF THE PENITENT

41. When the penitent comes to confess his sins, the priest welcomes him warmly and greets him with kindness.

42. Then the penitent makes the sign of the cross which the priest may make also.

In the name of the Father, and of the Son, and of the Holy Spirit. Amen.

The priest invites the penitent to have trust in God, in these or similar words:

**May God, who has enlightened every heart,
help you to know your sins
and trust in his mercy.**

The penitent answers:

Amen.

Other forms of reception of the penitent may be chosen from nos. 67-71.

READING OF THE WORD OF GOD (OPTIONAL)

43. Then the priest may read or say from memory a text of Scripture which proclaims God's mercy and calls man to conversion.

A reading may also be chosen from those given in nos. 72-83 and 101-201 for the reconciliation of several penitents. The priest and penitent may choose other readings from scripture.

CONFESSION OF SINS AND ACCEPTANCE OF SATISFACTION

44. Where it is the custom, the penitent says a general formula for confession (for example, **I confess to almighty God**) before he confesses his sins.

If necessary, the priest helps the penitent to make an integral confession and gives him suitable counsel. He urges him to be sorry for his faults, reminding him that through the sacrament of penance the Christian dies and rises with Christ and is thus renewed in the paschal mystery. The priest proposes an act of penance which the penitent accepts to make satisfaction for sin and to amend his life.

The priest should make sure that he adapts his counsel to the penitent's circumstances.

PRAYER OF THE PENITENT AND ABSOLUTION

45. The priest then asks the penitent to express his sorrow, which the penitent may do in these or similar words:

My God,
I am sorry for my sins with all my heart.
In choosing to do wrong
and failing to do good,
I have sinned against you
whom I should love above all things.

I firmly intend, with your help,
to do penance,
to sin no more,
and to avoid whatever leads me to sin.
Our Savior Jesus Christ
suffered and died for us.
In his name, my God, have mercy.

Other prayers of the penitent may be chosen from nos. 85-92.

Or:

Lord Jesus, Son of God,
have mercy on me, a sinner.

46. Then the priest extends his hands over the penitent's head (or at least extends his right hand) and says:

**God, the Father of mercies,
through the death and resurrection of his Son
has reconciled the world to himself
and sent the Holy Spirit among us
for the forgiveness of sins;
through the ministry of the Church
may God give you pardon and peace,
and I absolve you from your sins
in the name of the Father, and of the Son, ✠
and of the Holy Spirit.**

The penitent answers:

Amen.

PROCLAMATION OF PRAISE OF GOD AND DISMISSAL

47. After the absolution, the priest continues:

Give thanks to the Lord, for he is good.

The penitent concludes:

His mercy endures for ever.

Then the priest dismisses the penitent who has been reconciled, saying:

The Lord has freed you from your sins. Go in peace.

Or [93]:

**May the Passion of our Lord Jesus Christ,
the intercession of the Blessed Virgin Mary, and of all
the saints,
whatever good you do and suffering you endure,
heal your sins,
help you to grow in holiness,
and reward you with eternal life.
Go in peace.**

Or:

**The Lord has freed you from sin.
May he bring you safely to his kingdom in heaven.
Glory to him for ever.**

R. Amen.

Or:

Blessed are those
whose sins have been forgiven,
whose evil deeds have been forgotten.
Rejoice in the Lord,
and go in peace.

Or:

Go in peace,
and proclaim to the world
the wonderful works of God
who has brought you salvation.

CHAPTER II

RITE FOR RECONCILIATION OF SEVERAL PENITENTS WITH INDIVIDUAL CONFESSION AND ABSOLUTION

INTRODUCTORY RITES

SONG

48. When the faithful have assembled, they may sing a psalm, antiphon, or other appropriate song while the priest is entering the church, for example:

Hear us, Lord,
for you are merciful and kind.
In your great compassion,
look on us with love.

Or:

Let us come with confidence before the throne of grace
to receive God's mercy,
and we shall find pardon and strength
in our time of need.

GREETING

49. After the song the priest greets the congregation:

**Grace, mercy, and peace be with you
from God the Father
and Christ Jesus our Savior.**

℟. And also with you.

Or:

**Grace and peace be with you
from God the Father
and from Jesus Christ
who loved us
and washed away our sins in his blood.**

℟. Glory to him for ever. Amen.

Or other forms of greeting may be chosen from nos. 94-96.

Then the priest or another minister speaks briefly about the importance
and purpose of the celebration and the order of the service.

OPENING PRAYER

50. The priest invites all to pray, using these or similar words:

Brothers and sisters, God calls us to conversion; let us therefore ask him for the grace of sincere repentance.

All pray in silence for a brief period. Then the priest sings or says the prayer:

Lord,
hear the prayers of those who call on you,
forgive the sins of those who confess to you,
and in your merciful love
give us your pardon and your peace.
We ask this through Christ our Lord.

R/. Amen.

Or:

Lord,
send your Spirit among us
to cleanse us in the waters of repentance.
May he make of us a living sacrifice
so that in every place,
by his life-giving power,
we may praise your glory
and proclaim your loving compassion.
We ask this through Christ our Lord.

R/. Amen.

Other forms of the opening prayer may be chosen from nos. 97-100.

CELEBRATION OF THE WORD OF GOD

51. The celebration of the word follows. If there are several readings a psalm or other appropriate song or even a period of silence should intervene between them, so that everyone may understand the word of God more deeply and give it his heartfelt assent. If there is only one reading, it is preferable that it be from the gospel.

FIRST EXAMPLE

Love is the fullness of the law.

FIRST READING

A reading from the Book of Deuteronomy
5:1-3, 6-7, 11-12, 16-21a; 6:4-6

Love the Lord your God with all your heart.

Moses summoned all Israel and said to them,
"Hear, O Israel, the statutes and decrees
which I proclaim in your hearing this day,
that you may learn them and take care to
observe them.
The LORD, our God, made a covenant with us at Horeb;
not with our fathers did he make this covenant,
but with us, all of us who are alive here this day.

He said:

"'I, the LORD, am your God,
  who brought you out of the land of Egypt,
  that place of slavery.
You shall not have other gods besides me.

"'You shall not take the name of the LORD, your God,
      in vain.
For the LORD will not leave unpunished
  him who takes his name in vain.

"'Take care to keep holy the sabbath day
  as the LORD, your God, commanded you.

"'Honor your father and your mother, as the LORD, your
      God, has commanded you,
  that you may have a long life and prosperity
  in the land which the LORD, your God, is giving you.

"'You shall not kill.

"'You shall not commit adultery.

"'You shall not steal.

"'You shall not bear dishonest witness against your
      neighbor.

"'You shall not covet your neighbor's wife.'

"Hear, O Israel!
The LORD is our God, the LORD alone!
Therefore, you shall love the LORD, your God,
  with all your heart, and with all your soul,
  and with all your strength.

Take to heart these words which I enjoin on you today."

The word of the Lord.

RESPONSORIAL PSALM   Bar 1:15-22

R̰. (3:2) Listen and have pity, Lord, because you
         are merciful.

Justice is with the LORD, our God;
    and we today are flushed with shame,
that we have sinned in the LORD's sight
    and disobeyed him.

R̰. Listen and have pity, Lord, because you are merciful.

We have neither heeded the voice of the LORD, our God,
    nor followed the precepts which the LORD set before us.
We have been disobedient to the LORD, our God,
    and only too ready to disregard his voice.

R̰. Listen and have pity, Lord, because you are merciful.

We did not heed
    the voice of the LORD, our God,
But each one of us went off after the devices of our own
         wicked hearts,
    and did evil in the sight of the LORD, our God.

R̰. Listen and have pity, Lord, because you are merciful.

SECOND READING

A reading from the Letter of Saint Paul
to the Ephesians   **5:1-14**

You were once darkness, but now you are light in the Lord.
Live as children of light.

Brothers and sisters:

Be imitators of God, as beloved children,
  and live in love,
  as Christ loved us and handed himself over for us
  as a sacrificial offering to God for a fragrant aroma.

Immorality or any impurity or greed
  must not even be mentioned among you,
  as is fitting among holy ones,
  no obscenity or silly or suggestive talk, which is out
    of place,
  but instead, thanksgiving.

Be sure of this,
  that no immoral or impure or greedy person, that is,
    an idolater,
  has any inheritance in the Kingdom of Christ and
    of God.

Let no one deceive you with empty arguments,
  for because of these things
  the wrath of God is coming upon the disobedient.

So do not be associated with them.
For you were once darkness,
    but now you are light in the Lord.
Live as children of light,
    for light produces every kind of goodness and
          righteousness and truth.
Try to learn what is pleasing to the Lord.
Take no part in the fruitless works of darkness;
    rather expose them,
    for it is shameful even to mention the things done by
          them in secret;
    but everything exposed by the light becomes visible,
    for everything that becomes visible is light.
Therefore, it says:
    "Awake, O sleeper,
    and arise from the dead,
    and Christ will give you light."

The word of the Lord.

GOSPEL ACCLAMATION　　　　　　　　　Jn 8:12

I am the light of the world, says the Lord;
    whoever follows me will have the light of life.

GOSPEL

✠ A reading from the holy Gospel
according to Matthew   **22:34-40**

*You shall love the Lord, your God, with all your heart
and your neighbor as yourself.*

When the Pharisees heard that Jesus had silenced
        the Sadducees,
    they gathered together, and one of them,
    a scholar of the law, tested him by asking,
    "Teacher, which commandment in the law is
        the greatest?"

He said to him,
    "You shall love the Lord, your God, with all your heart,
    with all your soul, and with all your mind.
This is the greatest and the first commandment.
The second is like it:
    You shall love your neighbor as yourself.
The whole law and the prophets depend on these two
        commandments."

The Gospel of the Lord.

2

✠ A reading from the holy Gospel
according to John   **13:34-35; 15:10-13**

I give you a new commandment: love one another.

Jesus said to his Apostles:
"I give you a new commandment: love one another.
As I have loved you, so you also should love one another.
This is how all will know that you are my disciples,
    if you have love for one another."

"If you keep my commandments, you will remain in
            my love,
    just as I have kept my Father's commandments
    and remain in his love.

"I have told you this so that my joy be in you
    and your joy be complete.
This is my commandment: love one another as I love you.
No one has greater love than this,
    to lay down one's life for one's friends."

The Gospel of the Lord.

SECOND EXAMPLE

Your mind must be renewed.

FIRST READING

A reading from the Book of the Prophet Isaiah   1:10-18

Wash yourselves clean; put away your misdeeds from before my eyes.

Hear the word of the LORD,
    princes of Sodom!
Listen to the instruction of our God,
    people of Gomorrah!
What care I for the number of your sacrifices?
    says the LORD.
 I have had enough of whole-burnt rams
    and fat of fatlings;
In the blood of calves, lambs and goats
    I find no pleasure.

When you come in to visit me,
    who asks these things of you?
Trample my courts no more!
    Bring no more worthless offerings;
your incense is loathsome to me.
    New moon and sabbath, calling of assemblies,
octaves with wickedness: these I cannot bear.
    Your new moons and festivals I detest;
they weigh me down, I tire of the load.

When you spread out your hands,
I close my eyes to you;
  Though you pray the more,
I will not listen.
  Your hands are full of blood!
Wash yourselves clean!
  Put away your misdeeds from before my eyes;
cease doing evil; learn to do good.
Make justice your aim: redress the wronged,
  hear the orphan's plea, defend the widow.

Come now, let us set things right,
  says the Lord:
Though your sins be like scarlet,
  they may become white as snow;

Though they be crimson red,
  they may become white as wool.

The word of the Lord.

RESPONSORIAL PSALM   Ps 51:3-4, 12-13, 18-19

℞. (19a) A humbled heart is pleasing to God.

Have mercy on me, O God, in your goodness;
  in the greatness of your compassion wipe out
      my offense.
Thoroughly wash me from my guilt
  and of my sin cleanse me.

℟. A humbled heart is pleasing to God.

A clean heart create for me, O God,
   and a steadfast spirit renew within me.
Cast me not out from your presence,
   and your Holy Spirit take not from me.

℟. A humbled heart is pleasing to God.

For you are not pleased with sacrifices;
   should I offer a burnt offering, you would not accept it.
My sacrifice, O God, is a contrite spirit;
   a heart contrite and humbled, O God, you will
         not spurn.

℟. A humbled heart is pleasing to God.

SECOND READING

A reading from the Letter of Saint Paul
to the Ephesians   **4:23-32**

   Be renewed in the spirit of your minds, and put on the new self.

Be renewed in the spirit of your minds,
   and put on the new self,
      created in God's way in righteousness and holiness
         of truth.

Therefore, putting away falsehood,
   speak the truth,

each one to his neighbor,
for we are members one of another.
Be angry but do not sin;
do not let the sun set on your anger,
and do not leave room for the Devil.
The thief must no longer steal,
but rather labor,
doing honest work with his own hands,
so that he may have something to share with one
in need.
No foul language should come out of your mouths,
but only such as is good for needed edification,
that it may impart grace to those who hear.
And do not grieve the Holy Spirit of God,
with which you were sealed for the day of redemption.
All bitterness, fury, anger, shouting, and reviling
must be removed from you,
along with all malice.
And be kind to one another, compassionate,
forgiving one another as God has forgiven you
in Christ.

The word of the Lord.

GOSPEL ACCLAMATION   Mt 11:28

Come to me, all you that labor and are burdened,
and I will give you rest, says the Lord.

GOSPEL

✠ A reading from the holy Gospel
according to Matthew   5:1-12

When Jesus saw the crowds, he went up the mountain,
and his disciples came to him.

When Jesus saw the crowds, he went up the mountain,
    and after he had sat down, his disciples came to him.
He began to teach them, saying:

    "Blessed are the poor in spirit,
        for theirs is the Kingdom of heaven.
    Blessed are they who mourn,
        for they will be comforted.
    Blessed are the meek,
        for they will inherit the land.
    Blessed are they who hunger and thirst for
          righteousness,
        for they will be satisfied.
    Blessed are the merciful,
        for they will be shown mercy.
    Blessed are the clean of heart,
        for they will see God.
    Blessed are the peacemakers,
        for they will be called children of God.
    Blessed are they who are persecuted for the sake
          of righteousness,
        for theirs is the Kingdom of heaven.

Blessed are you when they insult you and persecute you
    and utter every kind of evil against you falsely
            because of me.
Rejoice and be glad,
    for your reward will be great in heaven.
Thus they persecuted the prophets who were before you."

The Gospel of the Lord.

> Other optional texts are given in nos. 101-201.

HOMILY

52. The homily which follows is based on the texts of the readings and should lead the penitents to examine their consciences and renew their lives.

EXAMINATION OF CONSCIENCE

53. A period of time may be spent in making an examination of conscience and in arousing true sorrow for sins. The priest, deacon, or another minister may help the faithful by brief statements or a kind of litany, taking into consideration their circumstances, age, etc.

RITE OF RECONCILIATION

GENERAL CONFESSION OF SINS

54. The deacon or another minister invites all to kneel or bow, and to join in saying a general formula for confession (for example, **I confess to almighty God**). Then they stand and say a litany or sing an appropriate song. The Lord's Prayer is always added at the end.

FIRST EXAMPLE

Deacon or minister:

My brothers and sisters, confess your sins and pray for each other, that you may be healed.

All say:

I confess to almighty God,
and to you, my brothers and sisters,
that I have sinned through my own fault

They strike their breast:

in my thoughts and in my words,
in what I have done,
and in what I have failed to do;
and I ask blessed Mary, ever virgin,
all the angels and saints,
and you, my brothers and sisters,
to pray for me to the Lord our God.

Deacon or minister:

The Lord is merciful. He makes us clean of heart and leads us out into his freedom when we acknowledge our guilt. Let us ask him to forgive us and bind up the wounds inflicted by our sins.
Give us the grace of true repentance.

R⁄. We pray you, hear us.

Pardon your servants and release them
from the debt of sin.

R⁄. We pray you, hear us.

Forgive your children who confess their sins, and restore them to full communion with your Church.

R⁄. We pray you, hear us.

Renew the glory of baptism in those
who have lost it by sin.

R⁄. We pray you, hear us.

Welcome them to your altar, and
renew their spirit with the hope of eternal glory.

R⁄. We pray you, hear us.

Keep them faithful to your sacraments and
loyal in your service.

R⁄. We pray you, hear us.

**Renew your love in their hearts, and
make them bear witness to it in their daily lives.**

R̸. We pray you, hear us.

**Keep them always obedient to your commandments
and protect within them your gift of eternal life.**

R̸. We pray you, hear us.

Deacon or minister:

**Let us now pray to God our Father in the words
Christ gave us, and ask him for his forgiveness and
protection from all evil.**

All say together:

Our Father . . .

The priest concludes:

**Lord,
draw near to your servants
who in the presence of your Church
confess that they are sinners.
Through the ministry of the Church
free them from all sin
so that renewed in spirit
they may give you thankful praise.
We ask this through Christ our Lord.**

R̸. Amen.

SECOND EXAMPLE

Deacon or minister:

Brothers and sisters, let us call to mind the goodness of God our Father, and acknowledge our sins, so that we may receive his merciful forgiveness.

All say:

I confess to almighty God,
and to you, my brothers and sisters,
that I have sinned through my own fault

They strike their breast:

in my thoughts and in my words,
in what I have done,
and in what I have failed to do;
and I ask blessed Mary, ever virgin,
all the angels and saints,
and you, my brothers and sisters,
to pray for me to the Lord our God.

Deacon or minister:

**Christ our Savior is our advocate with the Father:
with humble hearts let us ask him to forgive us
our sins
and cleanse us from every stain.
You were sent with good news for the poor and
healing for the contrite.**

℟. Lord, be merciful to me, a sinner.
    Or: Lord, have mercy.

You came to call sinners, not the just.

℟. Lord, be merciful to me, a sinner.
    Or: Lord, have mercy.

**You forgave the many sins of the woman
who showed you great love.**

℟. Lord, be merciful to me, a sinner.
    Or: Lord, have mercy.

You did not shun the company of outcasts and sinners.

℟. Lord, be merciful to me, a sinner.
    Or: Lord, have mercy.

You carried back to the fold the sheep that had strayed.

℟. Lord, be merciful to me, a sinner.
    Or: Lord, have mercy.

**You did not condemn the woman taken in adultery,
but sent her away in peace.**

℟. Lord, be merciful to me, a sinner.
    Or: Lord, have mercy.

You called Zacchaeus to repentance and a new life.

℟. Lord, be merciful to me, a sinner.
    Or: Lord, have mercy.

You promised Paradise to the repentant thief.

R̸. Lord, be merciful to me, a sinner.
      Or: Lord, have mercy.

**You are always interceding for us
at the right hand of the Father.**

R̸. Lord, be merciful to me, a sinner.
      Or: Lord, have mercy.

Deacon or minister:

**Now, in obedience to Christ himself, let us join in
prayer to the Father, asking him to forgive us as we
forgive others.**

All say together:

Our Father . . .

The priest concludes:

**Father, our source of life,
you know our weakness.
May we reach out with joy to grasp your hand and
      walk more readily in your ways.
We ask this through Christ our Lord.**

R̸. Amen.

For other texts see numbers 202-205.

INDIVIDUAL CONFESSION AND ABSOLUTION

55. Then the penitents go to the priests designated for individual confession, and confess their sins. Each one receives and accepts a fitting act of satisfaction and is absolved. After hearing the confession and offering suitable counsel, the priest extends his hands over the penitent's head (or at least extends his right hand) and gives him absolution. Everything else which is customary in individual confession is omitted.

God, the Father of mercies,
through the death and resurrection of his Son
has reconciled the world to himself
and sent the Holy Spirit among us
for the forgiveness of sins;
through the ministry of the Church
may God give you pardon and peace,
and I absolve you from your sins
in the name of the Father, and of the Son, ✠
and of the Holy Spirit.

The penitent answers:

Amen.

PROCLAMATION OF PRAISE FOR GOD'S MERCY

56. When the individual confessions have been completed, the other priests stand near the one who is presiding over the celebration. The latter invites all present to offer thanks and encourages them to do good works which will proclaim the grace of repentance in the life of the entire community and each of its members. It is fitting for all to sing a psalm or hymn or to

say a litany in acknowledgment of God's power and mercy, for example, the canticle of Mary (Lk 1:46-55), or Ps 136:1-9, 13-14, 16, 25-26, or one of the psalms as given in no. 206.

Ps 136:1-9, 16, 24-26

Give thanks to the LORD, for he is good,
    for his mercy endures forever;
give thanks to the God of gods,
    for his mercy endures forever;
give thanks to the LORD of lords,
    for his mercy endures forever.

Who alone does great wonders,
    for his mercy endures forever;
who made the heavens in wisdom,
    for his mercy endures forever;
who spread out the earth upon the waters,
    for his mercy endures forever.

Who made the great lights,
    for his mercy endures forever;
the sun to rule over the day,
    for his mercy endures forever;
the moon and the stars to rule over the night,
    for his mercy endures forever.
who led his people through the wilderness,
    for his mercy endures forever.

Who freed us from our foes,
    for his mercy endures forever;

who gives food to all flesh,
for his mercy endures forever;
give thanks to the God of heaven,
for his mercy endures forever.

CONCLUDING PRAYER OF THANKSGIVING

57. After the song of praise or the litany, the priest concludes the common prayer:

Almighty and merciful God,
how wonderfully you created man
and still more wonderfully remade him.
You do not abandon the sinner
but seek him out with a father's love.
You sent your Son into the world
to destroy sin and death
by his passion,
and to restore life and joy
by his resurrection.
You sent the Holy Spirit into our hearts
to make us your children
and heirs of your kingdom.
You constantly renew our spirit
in the sacraments of your redeeming love,
freeing us from slavery to sin
and transforming us ever more closely
into the likeness of your beloved Son.
We thank you for the wonders of your mercy,

and with heart and hand and voice
we join with the whole Church
in a new song of praise:
Glory to you
through Christ
in the Holy Spirit,
now and for ever.

R̷. Amen.

Or:

All-holy Father,
you have shown us your mercy
and made us a new creation
in the likeness of your Son.
Make us living signs of your love
for the whole world to see.
We ask this through Christ our Lord.

R̷. Amen.

Other concluding prayers may be chosen from nos. 207-211.

CONCLUDING RITE

58. Then the priest blesses all present:

May the Lord guide your hearts in the way of his love
and fill you with Christ-like patience.

R̷. Amen.

**May he give you strength
to walk in newness of life
and to please him in all things.**

R̷. Amen.

**May almighty God bless you,
the Father, and the Son, ✠ and the Holy Spirit.**

R̷. Amen.

Other blessings may be selected from nos. 212-214.

59. The deacon or other minister or the priest himself dismisses the assembly:

The Lord has freed you from your sins. Go in peace.

All answer:

Thanks be to God.

Any other appropriate form may be used.

CHAPTER III
RITE FOR RECONCILIATION OF SEVERAL PENITENTS WITH GENERAL CONFESSION AND ABSOLUTION

60. For the reconciliation of several penitents with general confession and absolution, in the cases provided for in the law, everything is done as described above for the reconciliation of several penitents with individual absolution, but with the following changes only.

INSTRUCTION

After the homily or as part of the homily, the priest explains to the faithful who wish to receive general absolution that they should be properly disposed. Each one should repent of his sins and resolve to turn away from these sins, to make up for any scandal and harm he may have caused, and to confess individually at the proper time each of the serious sins which cannot now be confessed. Some form of satisfaction should be proposed to all, and each individual may add something if he desires.

GENERAL CONFESSION

61. Then the deacon or other minister or the priest himself invites the penitents who wish to receive absolution to indicate this by some kind of sign. He may say:

Will those of you who wish to receive sacramental absolution please kneel and acknowledge that you are sinners.

Or:

Will those of you who wish to receive sacramental absolution please bow your heads and acknowledge that you are sinners.

Or he may suggest a sign laid down by the episcopal conference.

The penitents say a general formula for confession (for example, **I confess to almighty God**). A litany or appropriate song may follow, as described above for the reconciliation of several penitents with individual confession and absolution (no. 54). The Lord's Prayer is always added at the end.

GENERAL ABSOLUTION

62. The priest then gives absolution, holding his hands extended over the penitents and saying:

God the Father does not wish the sinner to die
but to turn back to him and live.
He loved us first and sent his Son into the world to be
its Savior.
May he show you his merciful love and give you peace.

R⁄. Amen.

Our Lord Jesus Christ was given up to death for
our sins,
and rose again for our justification.
He sent the Holy Spirit on his apostles
and gave them power to forgive sins.
Through the ministry entrusted to me
may he deliver you from evil
and fill you with his Holy Spirit.

R⁄. Amen.

The Spirit, the Comforter, was given to us for the
forgiveness of sins.
In him we approach the Father.
May he cleanse your hearts and clothe you in his glory,
so that you may proclaim the mighty acts of God
who has called you out of darkness into the splendor
of his light.

R⁄. Amen.

**And I absolve you from your sins
in the name of the Father, and of the Son, ✠
and of the Holy Spirit.**

R̸. Amen.

Or:

**God, the Father of mercies,
through the death and resurrection of his Son
has reconciled the world to himself
and sent the Holy Spirit among us
for the forgiveness of sins;
through the ministry of the Church
may God give you pardon and peace,
and I absolve you from your sins
in the name of the Father, and of the Son, ✠
and of the Holy Spirit.**

R̸. Amen.

PROCLAMATION OF PRAISE
AND CONCLUSION

63. The priest invites all to thank God and to acknowledge his mercy. After a suitable song or hymn, he blesses the people and dismisses them, as described above, nos. 58-59, but without the concluding prayer (no. 57).

SHORT RITE

64. In case of necessity, the rite for reconciling several penitents with general confession and absolution may be shortened. If possible, there is a brief reading from scripture. After giving the usual instruction (no. 60) and indicating the act of penance, the priest invites the penitents to make a general confession (for example, **I confess to almighty God**), and gives the absolution with the form which is indicated in no. 62.

65. In imminent danger of death, it is enough for the priest to use the form of absolution itself. In this case it may be shortened to the following:

I absolve you from your sins in the name of the Father, and of the Son, ✠ and of the Holy Spirit.

℟. Amen.

66. A person who receives general absolution from grave sins is bound to confess each grave sin at his next individual confession.

CHAPTER IV

Various Texts Used in the Celebration of Reconciliation

I. FOR THE RECONCILIATION OF ONE PENITENT

Invitation to Trust in God

67. Ez 33:11

The Lord does not wish the sinner to die
but to turn back to him and live.
Come before him with trust in his mercy.

68. Lk 5:32

May the Lord Jesus welcome you.
He came to call sinners, not the just.
Have confidence in him.

69.

May the grace of the Holy Spirit
fill your heart with light,
that you may confess your sins with loving trust
and come to know that God is merciful.

70.

May the Lord be in your heart
and help you to confess your sins with true sorrow.

71. 1 Jn 2:1-2

If you have sinned, do not lose heart.
We have Jesus Christ to plead for us with the Father:
he is the Holy One,
the atonement for our sins
and for the sins of the whole world.

Short Readings from Scripture

72.
Let us look on Jesus
who suffered to save us
and rose again for our justification.

Is 53:4-6

Yet it was our infirmities that he bore,
    our sufferings that he endured,
While we thought of him as stricken,
    as one smitten by God and afflicted.
But he was pierced for our offenses,
    crushed for our sins;
Upon him was the chastisement that makes us whole,
    by his stripes we were healed.

We had all gone astray like sheep,
   each following his own way;
But the Lord laid upon him
   the guilt of us all.

73. Ez 11:19-20

Listen to what the Lord says to us:

I will give them a new heart
   and put a new spirit within them;
   I will remove the stony heart from their bodies,
   and replace it with a natural heart,
   so that they will live according to my statutes,
   and observe and carry out my ordinances;
   thus they shall be my people and I will be their God.

74. Mt 6:14-15

Listen to what the Lord says to us:

"If you forgive men their transgressions,
   your heavenly Father will forgive you.
But if you do not forgive men,
   neither will your Father forgive your transgressions."

75. Mk 1:14-15

After John had been arrested,
Jesus came to Galilee proclaiming the Gospel of God:
   "This is the time of fulfillment.
The Kingdom of God is at hand.
Repent, and believe in the Gospel."

76. Lk 6:31-38

Listen to what the Lord says to us:
"Do to others as you would have them do to you.
For if you love those who love you,
    what credit is that to you?
Even sinners love those who love them.
And if you do good to those who do good to you,
    what credit is that to you?
Even sinners do the same.
If you lend money to those from whom you
          expect repayment,
    what credit is that to you?
Even sinners lend to sinners,
    and get back the same amount.
But rather, love your enemies and do good to them,
    and lend expecting nothing back;
    then your reward will be great
    and you will be children of the Most High,
    for he himself is kind to the ungrateful and the wicked.
Be merciful, just as also your Father is merciful.

"Stop judging and you will not be judged.
Stop condemning and you will not be condemned.
Forgive and you will be forgiven.
Give and gifts will be given to you;
    a good measure, packed together, shaken down,
        and overflowing,
    will be poured into your lap.
For the measure with which you measure
    will in return be measured out to you."

77. Lk 15:1-7

The tax collectors and sinners were all drawing near to
        listen to Jesus,
    but the Pharisees and scribes began to complain, saying,
    "This man welcomes sinners and eats with them."
So Jesus addressed this parable to them.
"What man among you having a hundred sheep and
        losing one of them
    would not leave the ninety-nine in the desert
    and go after the lost one until he finds it?
And when he does find it,
    he sets it on his shoulders with great joy
    and, upon his arrival home,
    he calls together his friends and neighbors and says
        to them,
    'Rejoice with me because I have found my lost sheep.'
I tell you, in just the same way
    there will be more joy in heaven over one sinner
        who repents
    than over ninety-nine righteous people
    who have no need of repentance."

78. Jn 20:19-23

On the evening of that first day of the week,
    when the doors were locked, where the disciples were,
    for fear of the Jews,
    Jesus came and stood in their midst
    and said to them, "Peace be with you."
When he had said this, he showed them his hands and
        his side.

The disciples rejoiced when they saw the Lord.
Jesus said to them again, "Peace be with you.
As the Father has sent me, so I send you."
And when he had said this, he breathed on them and said
   to them,
 "Receive the Holy Spirit.
Whose sins you forgive are forgiven them,
 and whose sins you retain are retained."

79. Rom 5:8-9

God proves his love for us
 in that while we were still sinners Christ died for us.
How much more then, since we are now justified by
   his blood,
 will we be saved through him from the wrath.

80. Eph 5:1-2

So be imitators of God, as beloved children, and live
   in love,
 as Christ loved us and handed himself over for us
 as a sacrificial offering to God for a fragrant aroma.

81. Col 1:12-14

Let us give thanks to the Father,
 who has made you fit to share
 in the inheritance of the holy ones in light.
He delivered us from the power of darkness
 and transferred us to the Kingdom of his beloved Son,
 in whom we have redemption, the forgiveness of sins.

82. Col 3:8 and 5, 9-10, 12-17

Now you must put them all away:
>   anger, fury, malice, slander,
>   and obscene language out of your mouths.
Put to death, then, the parts of you that are earthly:
>   immorality, impurity, passion, evil desire,
>   and the greed that is idolatry.
Stop lying to one another,
>   since you have taken off the old self with its practices
>   and have put on the new self,
>   which is being renewed, for knowledge,
>   in the image of its creator.

Put on, as God's chosen ones, holy and beloved,
>   heartfelt compassion, kindness, humility, gentleness,
>   and patience,
>   bearing with one another and forgiving one another,
>   if one has a grievance against another;
>   as the Lord has forgiven you, so must you also do.
And over all these put on love,
>   that is, the bond of perfection.
And let the peace of Christ control your hearts,
>   the peace into which you were also called in one Body.
And be thankful.
Let the word of Christ dwell in you richly,
>   as in all wisdom you teach and admonish one another,
>   singing psalms, hymns, and spiritual songs
>   with gratitude in your hearts to God.

And whatever you do, in word or in deed,
    do everything in the name of the Lord Jesus,
    giving thanks to God the Father through him.

83. 1 Jn 1:6-7, 9

If we say, "We have fellowship with him,"
    while we continue to walk in darkness,
    we lie and do not act in truth.
But if we walk in the light as he is in the light,
    then we have fellowship with one another,
    and the Blood of his Son Jesus cleanses us from all sin.
If we acknowledge our sins, he is faithful and just
    and will forgive our sins and cleanse us from
        every wrongdoing.

84. A reading may also be chosen from those given in nos. 101-201 for the reconciliation of several penitents. The priest and penitent may choose other readings from scripture.

Prayer of the Penitent

85. Ps 25:6-7

Remember that your compassion, O Lord,
    and your love are from of old.

In your kindness remember me,
    because of your goodness, O Lord.

86. Ps 51:4-5

Thoroughly wash me from my guilt
  and of my sin cleanse me.
For I acknowledge my offense,
  and my sin is before me always.

87. Lk 15:18; 18:13

Father, I have sinned [. . .] against you.
I no longer deserve to be called your son.
  Be merciful to me, a sinner.

88.

Father of mercy,
like the prodigal son
I return to you and say:
"I have sinned against you
and am no longer worthy to be called your son."
Christ Jesus, Savior of the world,
I pray with the repentant thief
to whom you promised paradise:
"Lord, remember me in your kingdom."
Holy Spirit, fountain of love,
I call on you with trust:
"Purify my heart,
and help me to walk as a child of the light."

89.

Lord Jesus,
you opened the eyes of the blind,

healed the sick,
forgave the sinful woman,
and after Peter's denial confirmed him in your love.
Listen to my prayer:
forgive all my sins,
renew your love in my heart,
help me to live in perfect unity with my fellow Christians
that I may proclaim your saving power to all the world.

90.

Lord Jesus,
you chose to be called the friend of sinners.
By your saving death and resurrection
free me from my sins.
May your peace take root in my heart
and bring forth a harvest
of love, holiness, and truth.

91.

Lord Jesus Christ,
you are the Lamb of God;
you take away the sins of the world.
Through the grace of the Holy Spirit
restore me to friendship with your Father,
cleanse me from every stain of sin
in the blood you shed for me,
and raise me to new life
for the glory of your name.

92.

Lord God,
in your goodness have mercy on me:
do not look on my sins,
but take away all my guilt.
Create in me a clean heart
and renew within me an upright spirit.

Or:

Lord Jesus, Son of God,
have mercy on me, a sinner.

AFTER THE ABSOLUTION

93. In place of the proclamation of God's praise and the dismissal, the priest
may say:

**May the Passion of our Lord Jesus Christ,
the intercession of the Blessed Virgin Mary and of all
 the saints,
whatever good you do and suffering you endure,
heal your sins,
help you grow in holiness,
and reward you with eternal life.
Go in peace.**

Or:

The Lord has freed you from sin.
May he bring you safely to his kingdom in heaven.
Glory to him for ever.

℞. Amen.

Or:

Blessed are those
whose sins have been forgiven,
whose evil deeds have been forgotten.
Rejoice in the Lord,
and go in peace.

Or:

Go in peace,
and proclaim to the world
the wonderful works of God,
who has brought you salvation.

II. FOR THE RECONCILIATION
OF SEVERAL PENITENTS

GREETING

94.
Grace, mercy, and peace
from God the Father and Jesus Christ his Son
be with you in truth and love.

℞. Amen.

95.

**May God open your hearts to his law
and give you peace;
may he answer your prayers
and restore you to his friendship.**

R̷. Amen.

96.

**Grace and peace be with you
from God our Father
and from the Lord Jesus Christ
who laid down his life for our sins.**

R̷. Glory to him for ever. Amen.

The greetings from the introductory rites of Mass may also be used.

OPENING PRAYERS

97.

**Lord,
turn to us in mercy
and forgive us all our sins
that we may serve you in true freedom.
We ask this through Christ our Lord.**

R̷. Amen.

98.
**Lord our God,
you are patient with sinners
and accept our desire to make amends.
We acknowledge our sins
and are resolved to change our lives.
Help us to celebrate this sacrament of your mercy
so that we may reform our lives
and receive from you the gift of everlasting joy.
We ask this through Christ our Lord.**

℟. Amen.

99.
**Almighty and merciful God,
you have brought us together in the name of your Son
to receive your mercy and grace in our time of need.
Open our eyes to see the evil we have done.
Touch our hearts and convert us to yourself.**

**Where sin has divided and scattered,
may your love make one again;
where sin has brought weakness,
may your power heal and strengthen;
where sin has brought death,
may your Spirit raise to new life.**

**Give us a new heart to love you,
so that our lives may reflect the image of your Son.**

**May the world see the glory of Christ
revealed in your Church,
and come to know
that he is the one whom you have sent,
Jesus Christ, your Son, our Lord.**

R̷. Amen.

100.
**Father of mercies
and God of all consolation,
you do not wish the sinner to die
but to be converted and live.
Come to the aid of your people,
that they may turn from their sins
and live for you alone.
May we be attentive to your word,
confess our sins, receive your forgiveness,
and be always grateful for your loving kindness.
Help us to live the truth in love
and grow into the fullness of Christ, your Son,
who lives and reigns for ever and ever.**

R̷. Amen.

Biblical Readings

The following readings are proposed as a help for pastors and others involved in the selection of readings. For diversity, and according to the nature of the group, other readings may be selected.

Readings from the Old Testament

101.

A reading from the Book of Genesis   3:1-8

She took some of its fruit and ate it.

Now the serpent was the most cunning of all the animals
    that the Lord God had made.
The serpent asked the woman,
    "Did God really tell you not to eat
    from any of the trees in the garden?"
The woman answered the serpent:
    "We may eat of the fruit of the trees in the garden;
    it is only about the fruit of the tree
    in the middle of the garden that God said,
    'You shall not eat it or even touch it, lest you die.'"
But the serpent said to the woman:
    "You certainly will not die!
No, God knows well that the moment you eat of it
    your eyes will be opened and you will be like gods
    who know what is good and what is evil."
The woman saw that the tree was good for food,
    pleasing to the eyes, and desirable for gaining wisdom.

So she took some of its fruit and ate it;
  and she also gave some to her husband, who was
      with her,
  and he ate it.
Then the eyes of both of them were opened,
  and they realized that they were naked;
  so they sewed fig leaves together
  and made loincloths for themselves.

When they heard the sound of the Lord God moving about
      in the garden
  at the breezy time of the day,
  the man and his wife hid themselves from the Lord God
  among the trees of the garden.
The Lord God called to Adam and asked him, "Where
      are you?"
He answered, "I heard you in the garden;
  but I was afraid, because I was naked,
  so I hid myself."
Then he asked, "Who told you that you were naked?
You have eaten, then,
  from the tree of which I had forbidden you to eat!"
The man replied, "The woman whom you put here
      with me—
  she gave me fruit from the tree, and so I ate it."
The Lord God then asked the woman,
  "Why did you do such a thing?"
The woman answered, "The serpent tricked me into it, so
      I ate it."

Then the Lord God said to the serpent:

"Because you have done this, you shall be banned
    from all the animals
    and from all the wild creatures;
On your belly shall you crawl,
    and dirt shall you eat
    all the days of your life.
I will put enmity between you and the woman,
    and between your offspring and hers;
He will strike at your head,
    while you strike at his heel."

To the woman he said:

"I will intensify the pangs of your childbearing;
    in pain shall you bring forth children.
Yet your urge shall be for your husband,
    and he shall be your master."

To the man he said: "Because you listened to your wife
    and ate from the tree of which I had forbidden you to eat,

"Cursed be the ground because of you!
    In toil shall you eat its yield
    all the days of your life.
Thorns and thistles shall it bring forth to you,
    as you eat of the plants of the field.
By the sweat of your face
    shall you get bread to eat,

Until you return to the ground,
   from which you were taken;
For you are dirt,
   and to dirt you shall return."

The word of the Lord.

102.
A reading from the Book of Genesis   4:1-15

Cain attacked his brother Abel and killed him.

The man had relations with his wife Eve,
   and she conceived and bore Cain, saying,
     "I have produced a man with the help of the Lord."
Next she bore his brother Abel.
Abel became a keeper of flocks, and Cain a tiller of
       the soil.
In the course of time Cain brought an offering to the Lord
   from the fruit of the soil,
   while Abel, for his part,
   brought one of the best firstlings of his flock.
The Lord looked with favor on Abel and his offering,
   but on Cain and his offering he did not.
Cain greatly resented this and was crestfallen.
So the Lord said to Cain:
   "Why are you so resentful and crestfallen.
If you do well, you can hold up your head;
   but if not, sin is a demon lurking at the door:
   his urge is toward you, yet you can be his master."

Cain said to his brother Abel, "Let us go out in the field."
When they were in the field,
    Cain attacked his brother Abel and killed him.
Then the Lord asked Cain, "Where is your brother Abel?"
He answered, "I do not know.
Am I my brother's keeper?"
The Lord then said: "What have you done!
Listen: your brother's blood cries out to me from the soil!
Therefore you shall be banned from the soil
    that opened its mouth to receive
    your brother's blood from your hand.
If you till the soil, it shall no longer give you its produce.
You shall become a restless wanderer on the earth."
Cain said to the Lord: "My punishment is too great to bear.
Since you have now banished me from the soil,
    and I must avoid your presence
    and become a restless wanderer on the earth,
    anyone may kill me at sight."
"Not so!" the Lord said to him.
"If anyone kills Cain, Cain shall be avenged sevenfold."
So the Lord put a mark on Cain, lest anyone should kill
        him at sight.

The word of the Lord.

103.

A reading from the Book of Genesis   **18:17-33**

For the sake of those ten, I will not destroy it.

The LORD reflected: "Shall I hide from Abraham what I am
        about to do,
    now that he is to become a great and populous nation,
    and all the nations of the earth are to find blessing
        in him?
Indeed, I have singled him out
    that he may direct his children and his household
        after him
    to keep the way of the LORD
    by doing what is right and just,
    so that the LORD may carry into effect for Abraham
    the promises he made about him."
Then the LORD said:
    "The outcry against Sodom and Gomorrah is so great,
    and their sin so grave,
    that I must go down and see whether or not their actions
    fully correspond to the cry against them that comes to me.
    I mean to find out."

While the two men walked on farther toward Sodom,
    the LORD remained standing before Abraham.
Then Abraham drew nearer to him and said:
    "Will you sweep away the innocent with the guilty?
Suppose there were fifty innocent people in the city;
    would you wipe out the place, rather than spare it
    for the sake of the fifty innocent people within it?

Far be it from you to do such a thing,
to make the innocent die with the guilty,
so that the innocent and the guilty would be
treated alike!
Should not the judge of all the world act with justice?"
The Lord replied,
"If I find fifty innocent people in the city of Sodom,
I will spare the whole place for their sake."
Abraham spoke up again:
"See how I am presuming to speak to my Lord,
though I am but dust and ashes!
What if there are five less than fifty innocent people?
Will you destroy the whole city because of those five?"
He answered, "I will not destroy it if I find forty-five there."
But Abraham persisted, saying, "What if only forty are
found there?"
He replied, "I will forbear doing it for the sake of forty."
Then Abraham said, "Let not my Lord grow impatient if I
go on.
What if only thirty are found there?"
He replied, "I will forbear doing it if I can find but thirty
there."
Still Abraham went on,
"Since I have thus dared to speak to my Lord,
what if there are no more than twenty?"
He answered, "I will not destroy it for the sake of
the twenty."
But he still persisted:
"Please, let not my Lord grow angry if I speak up
this last time.

What if there are at least ten there?"
He replied, "For the sake of those ten, I will not
        destroy it."

The Lord departed as soon as he had finished speaking
        with Abraham,
  and Abraham returned home.

The word of the Lord.

104.
A reading from the Book of Exodus   17:1-7

They tested the Lord, saying, "Is the Lord in our midst or not?"

From the desert of Sin the whole congregation of the
        children of Israel
  journeyed by stages, as the Lord directed,
  and encamped at Rephidim.

There was no water for the people to drink.
They quarreled, therefore, with Moses and said,
    "Give us water to drink."
Moses replied, "Why do you quarrel with me?
Why do you put the Lord to a test?"
[. . .] Then, in their thirst for water,
    the people grumbled against Moses,
    saying, "Why did you ever make us leave Egypt?
Was it just to have us die here of thirst
    with our children and our livestock?"

So Moses cried out to the LORD,
   "What shall I do with this people?
A little more and they will stone me!"
The LORD answered Moses,
     "Go over there in front of the people,
     along with some of the elders of Israel,
     holding in your hand, as you go,
     the staff with which you struck the river.
I will be standing there in front of you on the rock
          in Horeb.
Strike the rock, and the water will flow from it
     for the people to drink."
This Moses did, in the presence of the elders of Israel.
The place was called Massah and Meribah,
     because the children of Israel quarreled there
     and tested the LORD, saying,
     "Is the LORD in our midst or not?"

The word of the Lord.

105.

A reading from the Book of Exodus   20:1-21

   I, the LORD, am your God. You shall not have other gods.

God delivered all these commandments:

"I, the LORD, am your God,
     who brought you out of the land of Egypt, that place
          of slavery.

You shall not have other gods besides me.
You shall not carve idols for yourselves
    in the shape of anything in the sky above
    or on the earth below or in the waters beneath
        the earth;
    you shall not bow down before them or worship them.
For I, the Lord, your God, am a jealous God,
    inflicting punishment for their fathers' wickedness
    on the children of those who hate me,
    down to the third and fourth generation;
    but bestowing mercy down to the thousandth generation
    on the children of those who love me and keep my
        commandments.

"You shall not take the name of the Lord, your God,
        in vain.
For the Lord will not leave unpunished
    him who takes his name in vain.

"Remember to keep holy the sabbath day.
Six days you may labor and do all your work,
    but the seventh day is the sabbath of the Lord,
        your God.
No work may be done then either by you, or your son
        or daughter,
    or your male or female slave, or your beast,
    or by the alien who lives with you.
In six days the Lord made the heavens and the earth,
    the sea and all that is in them;
    but on the seventh day he rested.

That is why the Lord has blessed the sabbath day and
     made it holy.

"Honor your father and your mother,
    that you may have a long life in the land
    which the Lord, your God, is giving you.

"You shall not kill.

"You shall not commit adultery.

"You shall not steal.

"You shall not bear false witness against your neighbor.

"You shall not covet your neighbor's house.
You shall not covet your neighbor's wife,
    nor his male or female slave, nor his ox or as
    nor anything else that belongs to him."

When the people witnessed the thunder and lightning,
    the trumpet blast and the mountain smoking,
    they all feared and trembled.
So they took up a position much farther away
    and said to Moses,
    "You speak to us, and we will listen;
    but let not God speak to us, or we shall die."
Moses answered the people,
    "Do not be afraid,

for God has come to you only to test you and put his
     fear upon you,
lest you should sin."
Still the people remained at a distance,
    while Moses approached the cloud where God was.

The word of the Lord.

106.
A reading from the Book of Deuteronomy   6:4-9

Love the LORD, your God, with all your heart.

In those days
Moses said to the people:
"Hear, O Israel! The LORD is our God, the LORD alone!
Therefore, you shall love the LORD, your God,
    with all your heart,
    and with all your soul,
    and with all your strength.
Take to heart these words which I enjoin on you today.
Drill them into your children.
Speak of them at home and abroad, whether you are busy
      or at rest.
Bind them at your wrist as a sign
    and let them be as a pendant on your forehead.
Write them on the doorposts of your houses and on
     your gates."

The word of the Lord.

107.

A reading from the Book of Deuteronomy   9:7-19

Your people have become depraved; they have already
turned aside from the way I pointed out to them

In those days,
    Moses said to the people:
    "Bear in mind and do not forget
    how you angered the Lord, your God, in the desert.
From the day you left the land of Egypt
    until you arrived in this place,
    you have been rebellious toward the Lord.
At Horeb you so provoked the Lord
    that he was angry enough to destroy you,
    when I had gone up the mountain to receive
    the stone tablets of the covenant
    which the Lord made with you.
Meanwhile I stayed on the mountain forty days and
       forty nights
    without eating or drinking,
    till the Lord gave me the two tablets of stone
    inscribed, by God's own finger, with a copy of all
       the words
    that the Lord spoke to you on the mountain
    from the midst of the fire on the day of the assembly.
Then, at the end of the forty days and forty nights,
    when the Lord had given me the two stone tablets of
       the covenant, he said to me,

'Go down from here now, quickly,
for your people whom you have brought out of Egypt
have become depraved;
they have already turned aside from the way I pointed
out to them
and have made for themselves a molten idol.
I have seen now how stiff-necked this people is,' the LORD
said to me.
'Let me be, that I may destroy them
and blot out their name from under the heavens.
I will then make of you a nation mightier and greater
than they.'

"When I had come down again from the blazing,
fiery mountain,
with the two tablets of the covenant in both my hands,
I saw how you had sinned against the LORD, your God:
you had already turned aside from the way
which the LORD had pointed out to you
by making for yourselves a molten calf!
Raising the two tablets with both hands
I threw them from me and broke them before your eyes.
Then, as before, I lay prostrate before the LORD
for forty days and forty nights without eating or drinking,
because of all the sin you had committed in the sight
of the LORD
and the evil you had done to provoke him.

For I dreaded the fierce anger of the LORD against you:
  his wrath would destroy you.
Yet once again the LORD listened to me."

The word of the Lord.

108.

A reading from the Book of Deuteronomy   30:15-20

Today I have set before you life and prosperity, death and doom.

Moses said to the people:
  "Today I have set before you
  life and prosperity, death and doom.
If you obey the commandments of the LORD, your God,
    which I enjoin on you today,
    loving him, and walking in his ways,
    and keeping his commandments, statutes and decrees,
    you will live and grow numerous,
    and the LORD, your God,
    will bless you in the land you are entering to occupy.
If, however, you turn away your hearts and will not listen,
    but are led astray and adore and serve other gods,
    I tell you now that you will certainly perish;
    you will not have a long life
    on the land that you are crossing the Jordan to enter
        and occupy.
I call heaven and earth today to witness against you:
    I have set before you life and death,
    the blessing and the curse.

Choose life, then,
> that you and your descendants may live, by loving the
>> LORD, your God,
> heeding his voice, and holding fast to him.
For that will mean life for you,
> a long life for you to live on the land that the
>> LORD swore
> he would give to your fathers Abraham, Isaac
>> and Jacob."

The word of the Lord.

109.

A reading from the second Book of Samuel   **12:1-9, 13**

> *David said to Nathan, "I have sinned against the LORD."*
> *Nathan answered David: "The LORD on his part*
> *has forgiven your sin: you shall not die."*

In those days, the LORD sent Nathan to David, and when
> he came to him,
> he said: "Judge this case for me!
In a certain town there were two men, one rich, the
> other poor.
The rich man had flocks and herds in great numbers.
But the poor man had nothing at all
> except one little ewe lamb that he had bought.
He nourished her, and she grew up with him and
> his children.

She shared the little food he had
    and drank from his cup and slept in his bosom.
She was like a daughter to him.
Now, the rich man received a visitor,
    but he would not take from his own flocks and herds
    to prepare a meal for the wayfarer who had come
        to him.
Instead he took the poor man's ewe lamb
    and made a meal of it for his visitor."
David grew very angry with that man and said to Nathan:
    "As the Lord lives, the man who has done this
        merits death!
He shall restore the ewe lamb fourfold
    because he has done this and has had no pity."
Then Nathan said to David: "You are the man!
Thus says the Lord God of Israel:
    'I anointed you king of Israel.
    I rescued you from the hand of Saul.
I gave you your lord's house and your lord's wives for
        your own.
I gave you the house of Israel and of Judah.
And if this were not enough,
    I could count up for you still more.
Why have you spurned the Lord
    and done evil in his sight?
You have cut down Uriah the Hittite with the sword;
    you took his wife as your own,
    and him you killed with the sword of the Ammonites.

Then David said to Nathan, "I have sinned against
   the Lord."
Nathan answered David:
   "The Lord on his part has forgiven your sin: you shall
      not die."

The word of the Lord.

110.
A reading from the Book of Nehemiah   9:1-20

The children of Israel gathered together fasting and confessed their sins.

On the twenty-fourth day of this month,
   the children of Israel gathered together fasting and
      in sackcloth,
   their heads covered with dust.
Those descended from the children of Israel separated
      themselves
   from all who were of foreign extraction,
   then stood forward and confessed their sins
   and the guilty deeds of their fathers.
When they had taken their places,
   they read from the book of the law of the Lord
      their God,
   for a fourth part of the day,
   and during another fourth part they made their confession
   and prostrated themselves before the Lord their God.

Standing on the platform of the Levites
    were Jeshua, Binnui, Kadmiel, Shebaniah, Bunni,
        Sherebiah, Bani, and Chenani,
    who cried out to the Lord their God, with a loud voice.
The Levites Jeshua, Kadmiel, Bani, Hashabneiah,
        Sherebiah, Hodiah,
    Shebaniah, and Pethahiah said,

"Arise, bless the Lord, your God,
    from eternity to eternity!"

The children of Israel answered with the blessing,

    "Blessed is your glorious name,
        and exalted above all blessing and praise."

Then Ezra said: "It is you, O Lord,
    you are the only one;
    you made the heavens, the highest heavens and all
        their host,
    the earth and all that is upon it,
    the seas and all that is in them.
To all of them you give life,
    and the heavenly hosts bow down before you.

"You, O Lord, are the God who chose Abram,
    who brought him out from Ur of the Chaldees,
    and named him Abraham.

When you had found his heart faithful in your sight,
    you made the covenant with him to give to him and
        his posterity
    the land of the Canaanites, Hittites, Amorites,
        Perizzites, Jebusites, and Girgashites.
These promises of yours you fulfilled, for you are just.

    "You saw the affliction of our fathers in Egypt,
    you heard their cry by the Red Sea;
You worked signs and wonders against Pharaoh,
    against all his servants and the people of his land,
Because you knew of their insolence toward them;
    thus you made for yourself a name even to this day.
The sea you divided before them,
    on dry ground they passed through the midst of
        the sea;
Their pursuers you hurled into the depths,
    like a stone into the mighty waters.
With a column of cloud you led them by day,
    and by night with a column of fire,
To light the way of their journey,
    the way in which they must travel.
On Mount Sinai you came down,
    you spoke with them from heaven;
You gave them just ordinances, firm laws,
    good statutes, and commandments;
Your holy sabbath you made known to them,
        commandments, statutes, and law you prescribed
        for them,
    by the hand of Moses your servant.

Food from heaven you gave them in their hunger,
    water from a rock you sent them in their thirst.
You bade them enter and occupy the land
    which you had sworn with upraised hand to give them.

"But they, our fathers, proved to be insolent;
    they held their necks stiff
    and would not obey your commandments.
They refused to obey and no longer remembered
    the miracles you had worked for them.
They stiffened their necks and turned their heads
    to return to their slavery in Egypt.
But you are a God of pardons,
    gracious and compassionate, slow to anger and rich
        in mercy;
    you did not forsake them.
Though they made for themselves a molten calf, and
        proclaimed,
    'Here is your God who brought you up out of Egypt,'
    and were guilty of great effronteries,
    yet in your great mercy you did not forsake them in
        the desert.
The column of cloud did not cease to lead them by day on
        their journey,
    nor did the column of fire by night cease to light for them
    the way by which they were to travel.

"Your good spirit you bestowed on them,
    to give them understanding;

your manna you did not withhold from their mouths,
and you gave them water in their thirst."

The word of the Lord.

111.
A reading from the Book of Wisdom   1:1-16

Love justice because into a soul that plots evil wisdom enters not,
nor dwells she in a body under debt of sin.

Love justice, you who judge the earth;
　　think of the LORD in goodness,
　　and seek him in integrity of heart;
Because he is found by those who test him not,
　　and he manifests himself to those who do not
　　　　disbelieve him.
For perverse counsels separate a man from God,
　　and his power, put to the proof, rebukes the foolhardy;
Because into a soul that plots evil wisdom enters not,
　　nor dwells she in a body under debt of sin.
For the holy spirit of discipline flees deceit
　　and withdraws from senseless counsels;
　　and when injustice occurs it is rebuked.
For wisdom is a kindly spirit,
　　yet she acquits not the blasphemer of his guilty lips;
Because God is the witness of his inmost self
　　and the sure observer of his heart
　　and the listener to his tongue.

For the spirit of the LORD fills the world,
    is all-embracing, and knows what man says.
Therefore no one who utters wicked things can go unnoticed,
    nor will chastising condemnation pass him by.
For the devices of the wicked man shall be scrutinized,
    and the sound of his words shall reach the LORD,
    for the chastisement of his transgressions;
Because a jealous ear hearkens to everything,
    and discordant grumblings are no secret.
Therefore guard against profitless grumbling,
    and from calumny withhold your tongues;
For a stealthy utterance does not go unpunished,
    and a lying mouth slays the soul.
Court not death by your erring way of life,
    nor draw to yourselves destruction by the works of
        your hands.
Because God did not make death,
    nor does he rejoice in the destruction of the living.
For he fashioned all things that they might have being;
    and the creatures of the world are wholesome,
And there is not a destructive drug among them
    nor any domain of the nether world on earth,
For justice is undying.

It was the wicked who with hands and words invited death,
    considered it a friend, and pined for it,
    and made a covenant with it,
Because they deserve to be in its possession.

The word of the Lord.

112.

A reading from the Book of Wisdom   5:1-16

The hope of the wicked is like thistledown borne
on the wind. But the just live forever.

Then shall the just one with great assurance confront
    his oppressors who set at nought his labors.
Seeing this, they shall be shaken with dreadful fear,
    and amazed at the unlooked-for salvation.
They shall say among themselves, rueful
    and groaning through anguish of spirit:
"This is he whom once we held as a laughingstock
    and as a type for mockery, fools that we were!
His life we accounted madness,
    and his death dishonored.
See how he is accounted among the sons of God;
    how his lot is with the saints!
We, then, have strayed from the way of truth,
    and the light of justice did not shine for us, and the sun
        did not rise for us.
We had our fill of the ways of mischief and of ruin;
    we journeyed through impassable deserts,
    but the way of the Lord we knew not.
What did our pride avail us?
    What have wealth and its boastfulness afforded us?
All of them passed like a shadow
    and like a fleeting rumor;

Like a ship traversing the heaving water,
    of which, when it has passed, no trace can be found,
    no path of its keel in the waves.
Or like a bird flying through the air;
    no evidence of its course is to be found—
But the fluid air, lashed by the beat of pinions,
    and cleft by the rushing force
Of speeding wings, is traversed:
    and afterward no mark of passage can be found in it.
Or as, when an arrow has been shot at a mark,
    the parted air straightway flows together again
    so that none discerns the way it went through—
Even so we, once born, abruptly came to nought
    and held no sign of virtue to display,
    but were consumed in our wickedness."
Yes, the hope of the wicked is like thistledown borne on
            the wind,
    and like fine, tempest-driven foam;
Like smoke scattered by the wind,
    and like the passing memory of the nomad camping for
        a single day.
But the just live forever,
    and in the LORD is their recompense,
    and the thought of them is with the Most High.
Therefore shall they receive the splendid crown,
    the beauteous diadem, from the hand of the LORD—
For he shall shelter them with his right hand,
    and protect them with his arm.

The word of the Lord.

113.

A reading from the Book of Sirach   28:1-7

*Forgive your neighbor's injustice; then
when you pray, your own sins will be forgiven.*

The vengeful will suffer the LORD's vengeance,
　　for he remembers their sins in detail.
Forgive your neighbor's injustice;
　　then when you pray, your own sins will be forgiven.
Should a man nourish anger against his fellows
　　and expect healing from the LORD?
Should a man refuse mercy to his fellows,
　　yet seek pardon for his own sins?
If he who is but flesh cherishes wrath,
　　who will forgive his sins?
Remember your last days, set enmity aside;
　　remember death and decay, and cease from sin!
Think of the commandments, hate not your neighbor;
　　of the Most High's covenant, and overlook faults.

The word of the Lord.

114.

A reading from the Book of the Prophet Isaiah **1:2-6, 15-18**

Sons have I raised and reared, but they have disowned me!

Hear, O heavens, and listen, O earth,
　　for the LORD speaks:

Sons have I raised and reared,
    but they have disowned me!
An ox knows its owner,
    and an ass, its master's manger;
But Israel does not know,
    my people has not understood.
Ah! sinful nation, people laden with wickedness,
    evil race, corrupt children!
They have forsaken the LORD,
    spurned the Holy One of Israel,
    apostatized.
Where would you yet be struck,
    you that rebel again and again?
The whole head is sick,
    the whole heart faint.
From the sole of the foot to the head
    there is no sound spot:
Wound and welt and gaping gash,
    not drained, or bandaged,
    or eased with salve.

When you spread out your hands,
    I close my eyes to you;
Though you pray the more,
    I will not listen.
Your hands are full of blood!
    Wash yourselves clean!
Put away your misdeeds from before my eyes;
    cease doing evil; learn to do good.

Make justice your aim: redress the wronged,
    hear the orphan's plea, defend the widow.

Come now, let us set things right,
    says the LORD:
Though your sins be like scarlet,
    they may become white as snow;
Though they be crimson red,
    they may become white as wool.

The word of the Lord.

115.
A reading from the Book of the Prophet Isaiah   5:1-7

*My friend had a vineyard. He looked for the crop
of grapes, but what it yielded was wild grapes.*

Let me now sing of my friend,
    my friend's song concerning his vineyard.
My friend had a vineyard
    on a fertile hillside;
He spaded it, cleared it of stones,
    and planted the choicest vines;
Within it he built a watchtower,
    and hewed out a wine press.
Then he looked for the crop of grapes,
    but what it yielded was wild grapes.

Now, inhabitants of Jerusalem and people of Judah,
    judge between me and my vineyard:

What more was there to do for my vineyard
    that I had not done?
Why, when I looked for the crop of grapes,
    did it bring forth wild grapes?
Now, I will let you know
    what I mean to do with my vineyard:
Take away its hedge, give it to grazing,
    break through its wall, let it be trampled!
Yes, I will make it a ruin:
    it shall not be pruned or hoed,
    but overgrown with thorns and briers;
I will command the clouds
    not to send rain upon it.
The vineyard of the LORD of hosts is the house of Israel,
    and the people of Judah are his cherished plant;
He looked for judgment, but see, bloodshed!
    for justice, but hark, the outcry!

The word of the Lord.

116.
A reading from the Book of the Prophet Isaiah   **43:22-28**

It is I, I, who wipe out, for my own sake, your offenses.

Thus says the Lord:
Yet you did not call upon me, O Jacob,
    for you grew weary of me, O Israel.
You did not bring me sheep for your burnt offerings,
    nor honor me with your sacrifices.

I did not exact from you the service of offerings,
    nor weary you for frankincense.
You did not buy me sweet cane for money,
    nor fill me with the fat of your sacrifices;
Instead, you burdened me with your sins,
    and wearied me with your crimes.
It is I, I, who wipe out,
    for my own sake, your offenses;
    your sins I remember no more.
Would you have me remember, have us come to trial?
    Speak up, prove your innocence!
Your first father sinned;
    your spokesmen rebelled against me
Till I repudiated the holy gates,
    put Jacob under the ban,
    and exposed Israel to scorn.

The word of the Lord.

117.
A reading from the Book of the Prophet Isaiah   **53:1-12**

The LORD laid upon him the guilt of us all.

Who would believe what we have heard?
    To whom has the arm of the LORD been revealed?
He grew up like a sapling before him,
    like a shoot from the parched earth;
There was in him no stately bearing to make us look at him,
    nor appearance that would attract us to him.

He was spurned and avoided by people,
    a man of suffering, accustomed to infirmity,
One of those from whom people hide their faces,
    spurned, and we held him in no esteem.

Yet it was our infirmities that he bore,
    our sufferings that he endured,
While we thought of him as stricken,
    as one smitten by God and afflicted.
But he was pierced for our offenses,
    crushed for our sins;
Upon him was the chastisement that makes us whole,
    by his stripes we were healed.
We had all gone astray like sheep,
    each following his own way;
But the LORD laid upon him
the guilt of us all.

Though he was harshly treated, he submitted
    and opened not his mouth;
Like a lamb led to the slaughter
    or a sheep before the shearers,
    he was silent and opened not his mouth.

Oppressed and condemned, he was taken away,
    and who would have thought any more of his destiny?
When he was cut off from the land of the living,
    and smitten for the sin of his people,
A grave was assigned him among the wicked
    and a burial place with evildoers,

Though he had done no wrong
   nor spoken any falsehood.
But the Lord was pleased
   to crush him in infirmity.

If he gives his life as an offering for sin,
   he shall see his descendants in a long life,
   and the will of the Lord shall be accomplished
      through him.

Because of his affliction
   he shall see the light in fullness of days;
Through his suffering, my servant shall justify many,
   and their guilt he shall bear.
Therefore I will give him his portion among the great,
   and he shall divide the spoils with the mighty,
Because he surrendered himself to death
   and was counted among the wicked;
And he shall take away the sins of many,
   and win pardon for their offenses.

The word of the Lord.

118.

A reading from the Book of the Prophet Isaiah   **55:1-11**

Let the scoundrel forsake his way, and the wicked man his thoughts;
let him turn to the LORD for mercy; to our God, who is generous in forgiving.

All you who are thirsty,
   come to the water!
You who have no money,
   come, receive grain and eat;
Come, without paying and without cost,
   drink wine and milk!
Why spend your money for what is not bread,
   your wages for what fails to satisfy?
Heed me, and you shall eat well,
   you shall delight in rich fare.
Come to me heedfully,
   listen, that you may have life.
I will renew with you the everlasting covenant,
   the benefits assured to David.
As I made him a witness to the peoples,
   a leader and commander of nations,
So shall you summon a nation you knew not,
   and nations that knew you not shall run to you,
Because of the LORD, your God,
   the Holy One of Israel, who has glorified you.

Seek the LORD while he may be found,
    call him while he is near.
Let the scoundrel forsake his way,
    and the wicked man his thoughts;
Let him turn to the LORD for mercy;
    to our God, who is generous in forgiving.
For my thoughts are not your thoughts,
    nor are your ways my ways, says the LORD.
As high as the heavens are above the earth,
    so high are my ways above your ways
    and my thoughts above your thoughts.

For just as from the heavens
    the rain and snow come down
And do not return there
    till they have watered the earth,
    making it fertile and fruitful,
Giving seed to the one who sows
    and bread to the one who eats,
So shall my word be
    that goes forth from my mouth;
My word shall not return to me void,
    but shall do my will,
    achieving the end for which I sent it.

The word of the Lord.

119.

A reading from the Book of the Prophet Isaiah   58:1-11

Then light shall rise for you in the darkness,
and the gloom shall become for you like midday.

Thus says the Lord:
Cry out full-throated and unsparingly,
    lift up your voice like a trumpet blast;
Tell my people their wickedness,
    and the house of Jacob their sins.
They seek me day after day,
    and desire to know my ways,
Like a nation that has done what is just
    and not abandoned the law of their God;
They ask me to declare what is due them,
    pleased to gain access to God.
"Why do we fast, and you do not see it?
    afflict ourselves, and you take no note of it?"

Lo, on your fast day you carry out your own pursuits,
    and drive all your laborers.
Yes, your fast ends in quarreling and fighting,
    striking with wicked claw.
Would that today you might fast
    so as to make your voice heard on high!
Is this the manner of fasting I wish,
    of keeping a day of penance:
That a man bow his head like a reed
    and lie in sackcloth and ashes?

Do you call this a fast,
    a day acceptable to the Lord?
This, rather, is the fasting that I wish:
    releasing those bound unjustly,
    untying the thongs of the yoke;
Setting free the oppressed,
    breaking every yoke;
Sharing your bread with the hungry,
    sheltering the oppressed and the homeless;
Clothing the naked when you see them,
    and not turning your back on your own.
Then your light shall break forth like the dawn,
    and your wound shall quickly be healed;
Your vindication shall go before you,
    and the glory of the Lord shall be your rear guard.
Then you shall call, and the Lord will answer,
    you shall cry for help, and he will say: Here I am!
If you remove from your midst oppression,
    false accusation and malicious speech;
If you bestow your bread on the hungry
    and satisfy the afflicted;
Then light shall rise for you in the darkness,
    and the gloom shall become for you like midday;
Then the Lord will guide you always
    and give you plenty even on the parched land.

He will renew your strength,
   and you shall be like a watered garden,
   like a spring whose water never fails,
   for the mouth of the LORD has spoken.

The word of the Lord.

120.
A reading from the Book of the Prophet Isaiah   59:1-4, 9-15

It is your crimes that separate you from your God.

Lo, the hand of the LORD is not too short to save,
   nor his ear too dull to hear.
Rather, it is your crimes
   that separate you from your God,
It is your sins that make him hide his face
   so that he will not hear you.
For your hands are stained with blood,
   your fingers with guilt;
Your lips speak falsehood,
   and your tongue utters deceit.
No one brings suit justly,
   no one pleads truthfully;
They trust in emptiness and tell lies;
   they conceive mischief and bring forth malice.

That is why right is far from us
    and justice does not reach us.
We look for light, and lo, darkness;
    for brightness, but we walk in gloom!
Like blind men we grope along the wall,
    like people without eyes we feel our way.
We stumble at midday as at dusk,
    in Stygian darkness, like the dead.
We all growl like bears,
    like doves we moan without ceasing.
We look for right, but it is not there;
    for salvation, and it is far from us.
For our offenses before you are many,
    our sins bear witness against us.
Yes, our offenses are present to us,
    and our crimes we know:
Transgressing, and denying the LORD,
    turning back from following our God,
Threatening outrage, and apostasy,
    uttering words of falsehood the heart has conceived.
Right is repelled,
    and justice stands far off;
For truth stumbles in the public square,
    uprightness cannot enter.
Honesty is lacking,
    and the man who turns from evil is despoiled.
    The LORD saw this, and was aggrieved
    that right did not exist.

The word of the Lord.

121.

A reading from the Book of the Prophet Jeremiah 2:1-13

Two evils have my people done: they have forsaken me, the source of living waters;
They have dug themselves cisterns, broken cisterns, that hold no water.

This word of the LORD came to me:
Go, cry out this message for Jerusalem to hear!

I remember the devotion of your youth,
 how you loved me as a bride,
Following me in the desert,
 in a land unsown.
Sacred to the LORD was Israel,
 the first fruits of his harvest;
Should anyone presume to partake of them,
 evil would befall him, says the LORD.

Listen to the word of the LORD, O house of Jacob!
 All you clans of the house of Israel,
 thus says the LORD:
What fault did your fathers find in me
 that they withdrew from me,
Went after empty idols,
 and became empty themselves?
They did not ask, "Where is the LORD
 who brought us up from the land of Egypt,
Who led us through the desert,
 through a land of wastes and gullies,

Through a land of drought and darkness,
   through a land which no one crosses,
   where no man dwells?"

When I brought you into the garden land
   to eat its goodly fruits,
You entered and defiled my land,
   you made my heritage loathsome.
The priests asked not,
   "Where is the LORD?"
Those who dealt with the law knew me not:
   the shepherds rebelled against me.
The prophets prophesied by Baal,
   and went after useless idols.
Therefore will I yet accuse you, says the LORD,
   and even your children's children I will accuse.
Pass over to the coast of the Kittim and see,
   send to Kedar and carefully inquire:
   Where has the like of this been done?
Does any other nation change its gods?—
   yet they are not gods at all!
But my people have changed their glory
   for useless things.
Be amazed at this, O heavens,
   and shudder with sheer horror, says the LORD.
Two evils have my people done:
   they have forsaken me, the source of living waters;
They have dug themselves cisterns,
   broken cisterns, that hold no water.

The word of the Lord.

122.

A reading from the Book of the Prophet Jeremiah   **7:21-26**

Listen to my voice; then I will be your God and you shall be my people.

Thus says the LORD of hosts, the God of Israel:
   Heap your burnt offerings upon your sacrifices;
   eat up the flesh!
In speaking to your fathers
   on the day I brought them out of the land of Egypt,
   I gave them no command concerning burnt offering
      or sacrifice.
This rather is what I commanded them:
   Listen to my voice;
   then I will be your God
   and you shall be my people.
Walk in all the ways that I command you,
   so that you may prosper.

But they obeyed not,
   nor did they pay heed.
They walked in the hardness of their evil hearts
   and turned their backs, not their faces, to me.
From the day that your fathers left the land of Egypt even
      to this day,
   I have sent you untiringly all my servants the prophets.
Yet they have not obeyed me nor paid heed;
   they have stiffened their necks and done worse than
      their fathers.

The word of the Lord.

123.

A reading from the Book of the Prophet Ezekiel   11:14-21

I will remove the stony heart from their bodies, and replace it with
a natural heart, so that they will live according to my statutes.

Thus the word of the LORD came to me:
　　Son of man, it is about your kinsmen,
　　your fellow exiles, and the whole house of Israel
　　that the inhabitants of Jerusalem say,
　　"They are far away from the LORD;
　　to us the land of Israel has been given as our possession."
Therefore say: Thus says the Lord GOD:
　　Though I have removed them far among the nations
　　and scattered them over foreign countries—
　　and was for a while their only sanctuary
　　in the countries to which they had gone—
　　I will gather you from the nations
　　and assemble you from the countries over which you
　　　　have been scattered,
　　and I will restore to you the land of Israel.
They shall return to it and remove from it all its
　　　　detestable abominations.
I will give them a new heart and put a new spirit
　　　　within them;
　　I will remove the stony heart from their bodies,
　　and replace it with a natural heart,
　　so that they will live according to my statutes,
　　and observe and carry out my ordinances;
　　thus they shall be my people and I will be their God.

But as for those whose hearts are devoted to their
        detestable abominations,
   I will bring down their conduct upon their heads, says
        the Lord God.

The word of the Lord.

124.
A reading from the Book of the Prophet Ezekiel   **18:20-32**

> *If the wicked man turns away from all the sins*
> *he committed, he shall surely live, he shall not die.*

The word of the Lord came to me thus:
Only the one who sins shall die.
The son shall not be charged with the guilt of his father,
   nor shall the father be charged with the guilt of his son.
The virtuous man's virtue shall be his own,
   as the wicked man's wickedness shall be his own.
But if the wicked man turns away from all the sins
        he committed,
   if he keeps all my statutes and does what is right
        and just,
   he shall surely live, he shall not die.
None of the crimes he committed shall be remembered
        against him;
   he shall live because of the virtue he has practiced.
Do I indeed derive any pleasure from the death of
        the wicked?
   says the Lord God.

Do I not rather rejoice
    when he turns from his evil way that he may live?
And if the virtuous man turns from the path of virtue
        to do evil,
    the same kind of abominable things that the wicked
        man does,
    can he do this and still live?
None of his virtuous deeds shall be remembered,
    because he has broken faith and committed sin;
    because of this, he shall die.
You say, "The LORD's way is not fair!"
Hear now, house of Israel:
    Is it my way that is unfair,
    or rather, are not your ways unfair?
When a virtuous man turns away from virtue to commit
        iniquity, and dies,
    it is because of the iniquity he committed that he
        must die.
But if a wicked man, turning from the wickedness he
        has committed,
    does what is right and just,
    he shall preserve his life;
    since he has turned away from all the sins which
        he committed,
    he shall surely live, he shall not die.
And yet the house of Israel says,
    "The LORD's way is not fair!"
Is it my way that is not fair, house of Israel,
    or rather, is it not that your ways are not fair?

Therefore I will judge you, house of Israel,
   each one according to his ways, says the Lord GOD.
Turn and be converted from all your crimes,
   that they may be no cause of guilt for you.
Cast away from you all the crimes you have committed,
   and make for yourselves a new heart and a new spirit.
Why should you die, O house of Israel?
For I have no pleasure in the death of anyone who dies,
         says the Lord GOD.
Return and live!

The word of the Lord.

125.

A reading from the Book of the Prophet Ezekiel   **36:23-28**

> *I will sprinkle clean water upon you and place a new spirit*
> *within you and make you live by my statutes.*

Thus says the LORD:
I will prove the holiness of my great name,
   profaned among the nations,
   in whose midst you have profaned it.
Thus the nations shall know that I am the LORD, says the
         Lord GOD,
   when in their sight I prove my holiness through you.
For I will take you away from among the nations,
   gather you from all the foreign lands,
   and bring you back to your own land.

I will sprinkle clean water upon you
    to cleanse you from all your impurities,
    and from all your idols I will cleanse you.
I will give you a new heart and place a new spirit
        within you,
    taking from your bodies your stony hearts
    and giving you natural hearts.
I will put my spirit within you and make you live by
        my statutes,
    careful to observe my decrees.
You shall live in the land I gave your fathers;
    you shall be my people, and I will be your God.

The word of the Lord.

126.

A reading from the Book of the Prophet Hosea   2:16-25

I will make a covenant for them on that day.

Thus says the LORD:
I will allure her;
    I will lead her into the desert
    and speak to her heart.
From there I will give her the vineyards she had,
    and the valley of Achor as a door of hope.
She shall respond there as in the days of her youth,
    when she came up from the land of Egypt.
    On that day, says the LORD,

She shall call me "My husband,"
  and never again "My baal."
Then will I remove from her mouth the names of
        the Baals,
  so that they shall no longer be invoked.
I will make a covenant for them on that day,
  with the beasts of the field,
With the birds of the air,
  and with the things that crawl on the ground.
Bow and sword and war
  I will destroy from the land,
  and I will let them take their rest in security.
I will espouse you to me forever:
  I will espouse you in right and in justice,
  in love and in mercy;
I will espouse you in fidelity,
  and you shall know the LORD.
On that day I will respond, says the LORD;
  I will respond to the heavens,
  and they shall respond to the earth;
The earth shall respond to the grain, and wine, and oil,
  and these shall respond to Jezreel.
I will sow him for myself in the land,
  and I will have pity on Lo-ruhama.
I will say to Lo-ammi, "You are my people,"
  and he shall say, "My God!"

The word of the Lord.

127.

A reading from the Book of the Prophet Hosea   **11:1-11**

I took them in my arms; I drew them with human cords.

Thus says the Lord;
When Israel was a child I loved him,
   out of Egypt I called my son.
The more I called them,
   the farther they went from me,
Sacrificing to the Baals
   and burning incense to idols.
Yet it was I who taught Ephraim to walk,
   who took them in my arms;
I drew them with human cords,
   with bands of love;
I fostered them like one
   who raises an infant to his cheeks;
Yet, though I stooped to feed my child,
   they did not know that I was their healer.

He shall return to the land of Egypt,
   and Assyria shall be his king;
The sword shall begin with his cities
   and end by consuming his solitudes.
Because they refused to repent,
   their own counsels shall devour them.
His people are in suspense about returning to him;
   and God, though in unison they cry out to him,
   shall not raise them up.

How could I give you up, O Ephraim,
　　or deliver you up, O Israel?
How could I treat you as Admah,
　　or make you like Zeboiim?
My heart is overwhelmed,
　　my pity is stirred.
I will not give vent to my blazing anger,
　　I will not destroy Ephraim again;
For I am God and not man,
　　the Holy One present among you;
　　I will not let the flames consume you.

They shall follow the LORD,
　　who roars like a lion;
When he roars,
　　his sons shall come frightened from the west,
Out of Egypt they shall come trembling, like sparrows,
　　from the land of Assyria, like doves;
And I will resettle them in their homes, says the LORD.

The word of the Lord.

128.

A reading from the Book of the Prophet Hosea　　**14:2-10**

Return, O Israel, to the LORD, your God.

Thus says the LORD:
Return, O Israel, to the LORD, your God;
　　you have collapsed through your guilt.

Take with you words,
    and return to the Lord;
Say to him, "Forgive all iniquity,
    and receive what is good, that we may render
    as offerings the bullocks from our stalls.
Assyria will not save us,
    nor shall we have horses to mount;
We shall say no more, 'Our god,'
    to the work of our hands;
    for in you the orphan finds compassion."

I will heal their defection, says the Lord,
    I will love them freely;
    for my wrath is turned away from them.
I will be like the dew for Israel:
    he shall blossom like the lily;
He shall strike root like the Lebanon cedar,
    and put forth his shoots.
His splendor shall be like the olive tree
    and his fragrance like the Lebanon cedar.
Again they shall dwell in his shade
    and raise grain;
They shall blossom like the vine,
    and his fame shall be like the wine of Lebanon.

Ephraim! What more has he to do with idols?
    I have humbled him, but I will prosper him.
"I am like a verdant cypress tree"—
    Because of me you bear fruit!

Let him who is wise understand these things;
  let him who is prudent know them.
Straight are the paths of the Lord,
   in them the just walk,
   but sinners stumble in them.

The word of the Lord.

129.

A reading from the Book of the Prophet Joel   2:12-19

Return to me with your whole heart.

Even now, says the Lord,
   return to me with your whole heart,
   with fasting, and weeping, and mourning;
Rend your hearts, not your garments,
   and return to the Lord, your God.
For gracious and merciful is he,
   slow to anger, rich in kindness,
   and relenting in punishment.
Perhaps he will again relent
   and leave behind him a blessing,
Offerings and libations
   for the Lord, your God.

Blow the trumpet in Zion!
   proclaim a fast,
   call an assembly;

Gather the people,
   notify the congregation;
Assemble the elders,
   gather the children
   and the infants at the breast;
Let the bridegroom quit his room
   and the bride her chamber.
Between the porch and the altar
   let the priests, the ministers of the Lord, weep,
And say, "Spare, O Lord, your people,
   and make not your heritage a reproach,
   with the nations ruling over them!
Why should they say among the peoples,
   'Where is their God?'"

Then the Lord was stirred to concern for his land
   and took pity on his people.
The Lord answered and said to his people:
See, I will send you
   grain, and wine, and oil,
   and you shall be filled with them;
No more will I make you
   a reproach among the nations.

The word of the Lord.

130.

A reading from the Book of the Prophet Micah   6:1-15

Do the right and love goodness, and walk humbly with your God.

Hear, then, what the LORD says:
Arise, present your plea before the mountains,
   and let the hills hear your voice!
Hear, O mountains, the plea of the LORD,
   pay attention, O foundations of the earth!
For the LORD has a plea against his people,
   and he enters into trial with Israel.

O my people, what have I done to you,
   or how have I wearied you? Answer me!
For I brought you up from the land of Egypt,
   from the place of slavery I released you;
And I sent before you Moses,
   Aaron, and Miriam.
My people, remember what Moab's King Balak planned,
   and how Balaam, the son of Beor, answered him
   . . . from Shittim to Gilgal,
   that you may know the just deeds of the LORD.
With what shall I come before the LORD,
   and bow before God most high?
Shall I come before him with burnt offerings,
   with calves a year old?
Will the LORD be pleased with thousands of rams,
   with myriad streams of oil?

Shall I give my first-born for my crime,
    the fruit of my body for the sin of my soul?
You have been told, O man, what is good,
    and what the LORD requires of you:
Only to do the right and to love goodness,
    and to walk humbly with your God.

Hark! the LORD cries to the city.
    (It is wisdom to fear your name!)
    Hear, O tribe and city council,
You whose rich men are full of violence,
    whose inhabitants speak falsehood
    with deceitful tongues in their heads!
Am I to bear any longer criminal hoarding
    and the meager ephah that is accursed?
Shall I acquit criminal balances,
    bags of false weights?

Rather I will begin to strike you
    with devastation because of your sins.
You shall sow, yet not reap,
    tread out the olive, yet pour no oil,
    and the grapes, yet drink no wine.

The word of the Lord.

131.

A reading from the Book of the Prophet Micah   7:2-7, 18-20

*The Lord will again have compassion on us and
cast into the depths of the sea all our sins.*

The faithful are gone from the earth,
   among men the upright are no more!
They all lie in wait to shed blood,
   each one ensnares the other.
Their hands succeed at evil;
   the prince makes demands,
The judge is had for a price,
   the great man speaks as he pleases,
The best of them is like a brier,
   the most upright like a thorn hedge.
The day announced by your watchmen!
   your punishment has come;
   now is the time of your confusion.
Put no trust in a friend,
   have no confidence in a companion;
Against her who lies in your bosom
   guard the portals of your mouth.
For the son dishonors his father,
   the daughter rises up against her mother,
The daughter-in-law against her mother-in-law,
   and a man's enemies are those of his household.
But as for me, I will look to the LORD,
   I will put my trust in God my savior;
   my God will hear me!

Who is there like you, the God who removes guilt
    and pardons sin for the remnant of his inheritance;
Who does not persist in anger forever,
    but delights rather in clemency,
And will again have compassion on us,
    treading underfoot our guilt?
You will cast into the depths of the sea
    all our sins;
You will show faithfulness to Jacob,
    and grace to Abraham,
As you have sworn to our fathers
    from days of old.

The word of the Lord.

132.

A reading from the Book of the Prophet Zechariah   1:1-6

Return to me and I will return to you.

In the second year of Darius,
    in the eighth month,
    the word of the Lord came to the prophet Zechariah,
    son of Berechiah, son of Iddo:
The Lord was indeed angry with your fathers . . .
    and say to them:
        Thus says the Lord of hosts:
    Return to me, says the Lord of hosts,
    and I will return to you, says the Lord of hosts.

Be not like your fathers whom the former prophets warned:
 Thus says the LORD of hosts:
 Turn from your evil ways and from your wicked deeds.
But they would not listen or pay attention to me, says
   the LORD.
Your fathers, where are they?
And the prophets, can they live forever?
But my words and my decrees,
 which I entrusted to my servants the prophets,
 did not these overtake your fathers?
Then they repented and admitted:
 "The LORD of hosts has treated us
 according to our ways and deeds,
 just as he had determined he would."

The word of the Lord.

133.

Ps 13:2-3, 4-5, 6

℟. (6a) My hope, O Lord, is in your mercy.

How long, O LORD? Will you utterly forget me?
 How long will you hide your face from me?
How long shall I harbor sorrow in my soul,
 Grief in my heart day after day?
How long will my enemy triumph over me?

℟. My hope, O Lord, is in your mercy.

Look, answer me, O LORD, my God!
Give light to my eyes that I may not sleep in death
 lest my enemy say, "I have overcome him";
 lest my foes rejoice at my downfall.

R̷. My hope, O Lord, is in your mercy.

Though I trusted in your mercy,
 Let my heart rejoice in your salvation;
 let me sing of the LORD, "He has been good to me."

R̷. My hope, O Lord, is in your mercy.

134.

       **Ps 25:4-5ab, 6 and 7bc,
       8-9, 10 and 14, 15-16**

R̷. (16a) Turn to me, Lord, and have mercy.

Your ways, O LORD, make known to me;
 teach me your paths,
Guide me in your truth and teach me,
 for you are God my savior.

R̷. Turn to me, Lord, and have mercy.

Remember that your compassion, O LORD,
 and your kindness are from of old.
In your kindness remember me,
 because of your goodness, O LORD.

R̷. Turn to me, Lord, and have mercy.

Good and upright is the LORD;
   thus he shows sinners the way.
He guides the humble to justice,
   he teaches the humble his way.

R̸. Turn to me, Lord, and have mercy.

All the paths of the LORD are kindness and constancy
   toward those who keep his covenant and his decrees.
The friendship of the LORD is with those who fear him,
   and his covenant, for their instruction.

R̸. Turn to me, Lord, and have mercy.

My eyes are ever toward the LORD,
   for he will free my feet from the snare.
Look toward me, and have pity on me,
   for I am alone and afflicted.

R̸. Turn to me, Lord, and have mercy.

135.

Ps 31:2-3a, 3b-4, 6

R̸. (6a) You have redeemed us, Lord, God of truth.

In you, O LORD, I take refuge;
   let me never be put to shame.
In your justice rescue me,
   incline your ear to me,
   make haste to deliver me!

R̷. You have redeemed us, Lord, God of truth.

Be my rock of refuge,
　　a stronghold to give me safety.
You are my rock and my fortress;
　　for your name's sake you will lead and guide me.

R̷. You have redeemed us, Lord, God of truth.

Into your hands I commend my spirit;
　　you will redeem me, O LORD, O faithful God.

R̷. You have redeemed us, Lord, God of truth.

136.
Ps 32:1-2, 5, 6, 7, 11

R̷. (5c) Lord, forgive the wrong I have done.

Blessed is he whose fault is taken away,
　　whose sin is covered.
Blessed the man to whom the LORD imputes not guilt,
　　in whose spirit there is no guile.

R̷. Lord, forgive the wrong I have done.

Then I acknowledged my sin to you,
　　my guilt I covered not.
I said, "I confess my faults to the LORD,"
　　and you took away the guilt of my sin.

℟. Lord, forgive the wrong I have done.

For this shall every faithful man pray to you
in time of stress.
Though deep waters overflow,
they shall not reach him.

℟. Lord, forgive the wrong I have done.

You are my shelter; from distress you will preserve me;
with glad cries of freedom you will ring me round.

℟. Lord, forgive the wrong I have done.

Be glad in the LORD and rejoice, you just;
exult all you upright of heart.

℟. Lord, forgive the wrong I have done.

137.

Ps 36:6-7ab, 8-9, 10-11

℟. (8) How precious is your mercy, Lord.

O LORD, your mercy reaches to heaven;
your faithfulness, to the clouds.
Our justice is like the mountain of God:
your judgments like the mighty deep.

℟. How precious is your mercy, Lord.

How precious is your mercy, O God!
    the children of men take shadow in the refuge of
        your wings.
They have their fill of the prime gifts of your house;
    from your delightful stream you give them to drink.

R̶/. How precious is your mercy, Lord.

For with you is the fountain of life,
    and in your light we see light.
Keep up your mercy toward your friends,
    your just defense of the upright of heart.

R̶/. How precious is your mercy, Lord.

138.

**Ps 50:7-8, 14-15, 16-17,
18-19, 20-21, 22-23**

R̶/. (23b) To the upright I will show the saving power of God.

"Hear, my people, and I will speak;
    Israel, I will testify against you;
        God, your God, am I.
Not for your sacrifices do I rebuke you,
    for your burnt offerings are before me always."

R̶/. To the upright I will show the saving power of God.

"Offer to God praise as your sacrifice
    and fulfill your vows to the Most High;
Then call upon me in times of distress;
    I will rescue you, and you shall glorify me."

R⁄. To the upright I will show the saving power of God.

But to the wicked man God says:
    "Why do you recite my statutes,
    and profess my covenant with your mouth,
Though you hate discipline
    and cast my words behind you?"

R⁄. To the upright I will show the saving power of God.

"When you see a thief, you keep pace with him,
    and with adulterers you throw in your lot.
To your mouth you give free rein for evil,
    you harness your tongue to deceit."

R⁄. To the upright I will show the saving power of God.

"You sit speaking against your brother,
    against your mother's son you spread rumors.
When you do these things, shall I be deaf to it?
    Or do you think that I am like yourself?
    I will correct you by drawing them up before your eyes."

R⁄. To the upright I will show the saving power of God.

"Consider this, you who forget God,
    lest I rend you and there be no one to rescue you.
He that offers praise as a sacrifice glorifies me;
    and to him that goes the right way I will show the
        salvation of God."

R̷. To the upright I will show the saving power of God.

139.

**Ps 51:3-4, 5-6ab, 7-8, 9-11,
12-13, 14 and 17, 19**

R̷. (see 14a) Give me back the joy of your salvation.

Have mercy on me, O God, in your goodness;
    in the greatness of your compassion wipe out my offense.
Thoroughly wash me from my guilt
    and of my sin cleanse me.

R̷. Give me back the joy of your salvation.

For I acknowledge my offense,
    and my sin is before me always:
"Against you only have I sinned,
    and done what is evil in your sight."

R̷. Give me back the joy of your salvation.

Indeed, in guilt was I born,
    and in sin my mother conceived me;
Behold, you are pleased with sincerity of heart,
    and in my inmost being you teach me wisdom.

℞. Give me back the joy of your salvation.

Cleanse me of sin with hyssop, that I may be purified;
    Wash me, and I shall be whiter than snow.
Let me hear the sounds of joy and gladness;
    the bones you have crushed shall rejoice.
Turn away your face from my sins,
    and blot out all my guilt.

℞. Give me back the joy of your salvation.

A clean heart create for me, O God,
    and a steadfast spirit renew within me.
Cast me not out from your presence,
    and your Holy Spirit take not from me.

℞. Give me back the joy of your salvation.

Give me back the joy of your salvation,
    and a willing spirit sustain in me.
O Lord, open my lips,
    and my mouth shall proclaim your praise.

℞. Give me back the joy of your salvation.

My sacrifice, O God, is a contrite spirit;
    a heart contrite and humbled, O God, you will not spurn.

℞. Give me back the joy of your salvation.

140.

Ps 73:1-2, 21-22a,
23-24, 26 and 28ab

R̸. (28a) It is good for me to be with the Lord.

How good God is to the upright;
    the LORD to those who are clean of heart!
But, as for me, I almost lost my balance;
    my feet all but slipped.

R̸. It is good for me to be with the Lord.

Because my heart was embittered
    and my soul was pierced,
I was stupid and understood not.

R̸. It is good for me to be with the Lord.

Yet with you I shall always be;
    you have hold of my right hand;
With your counsel you guide me,
    and in the end you will receive me in glory.

R̸. It is good for me to be with the Lord.

Though my flesh and my heart waste away,
    God is the rock of my heart and my portion forever.
But for me, to be near God is my good;
    to make the Lord GOD my refuge.

R̸. It is good for me to be with the Lord.

141.

Ps 90:3-5a, 12-13, 14 and 17

℟. (14) Fill us with your love, O Lord, and we will sing
  for joy!

You turn man back to dust,
 saying, "Return, O children of men."
For a thousand years in your sight
 are as yesterday, now that it is past,
 or as a watch of the night.

℟. Fill us with your love, O Lord, and we will sing for joy!

Teach us to number our days aright,
 that we may gain wisdom of heart.
Return, O LORD! How long?
 Have pity on your servants!

℟. Fill us with your love, O Lord, and we will sing for joy!

Fill us at daybreak with your kindness,
 that we may shout for joy and gladness all our days.
And may the gracious care of the LORD our God be ours;
 prosper the work of our hands for us!
 Prosper the work of our hands!

℟. Fill us with your love, O Lord, and we will sing for joy!

142.

Ps 95:1-2, 6-7c, 8-9, 10-11

℟. (8a) If today you hear his voice, harden not your hearts.

Come, let us sing joyfully to the LORD;
  let us acclaim the Rock of our salvation.
Let us come into his presence with thanksgiving;
  let us joyfully sing psalms to him.

℟. If today you hear his voice, harden not your hearts.

Come, let us bow down in worship;
  let us kneel before the LORD who made us.
For he is our God,
    and we are the people he shepherds, the flock
      he guides.

℟. If today you hear his voice, harden not your hearts.

Oh, that today you would hear his voice:
    "Harden not your hearts as at Meribah,
    as in the day of Massah in the desert,
Where your fathers tempted me;
    they tested me though they had seen my works."

℟. If today you hear his voice, harden not your hearts.

Forty years I was wearied of that generation;
    I said: "This people's heart goes astray,
    they do not know my ways."

Therefore I swore in my anger:
   "They shall never enter my rest."

℞. If today you hear his voice, harden not your hearts.

143.

Ps 119:1, 10-11, 12-13, 15-16

℞. (1) Blessed are they who follow the law of the Lord!

Blessed are they whose way is blameless,
   who walk in the way of the LORD.

℞. Blessed are they who follow the law of the Lord!

With all my heart I seek you;
   let me not stray from your commands.
Within my heart I treasure your promise.
   that I may not sin against you.

℞. Blessed are they who follow the law of the Lord!

Blessed are you, O LORD;
   teach me your statutes.
With my lips I declare
   all the ordinances of your mouth.

℞. Blessed are they who follow the law of the Lord!

I will meditate on your precepts
   and consider your ways,

In your statutes I will delight;
    I will not forget your words.

R℟. Blessed are they who follow the law of the Lord!

144.

Ps 123:1-2a, 2bc, 3-4

R℟. (2c) Our eyes are fixed on the Lord.

To you I lift up my eyes
    who are enthroned in heaven—
As the eyes of servants
    are on the hands of their masters.

R℟. Our eyes are fixed on the Lord.

As the eyes of a maid
    are on the hands of her mistress,
So are our eyes on the LORD, our God,
    till he have pity on us.

R℟. Our eyes are fixed on the Lord.

Have pity on us, O LORD, have pity on us,
    for we are more than sated with contempt;
Our souls are more than sated
    with the mockery of the arrogant,
    with the contempt of the proud.

R℟. Our eyes are fixed on the Lord.

145.

Ps 130:1-2, 3-4, 5-6, 7-8.

℟. (7bc) With the Lord there is mercy and fullness
     of redemption.

Out of the depths I cry to you, O LORD;
    LORD, hear my voice!
Let your ears be attentive
    to my voice in supplication.

℟. With the Lord there is mercy and fullness
     of redemption.

If you, O LORD, mark iniquities,
    LORD, who can stand?
But with you is forgiveness,
    that you may be revered.

℟. With the Lord there is mercy and fullness
     of redemption.

I trust in the LORD;
    my soul trusts in his word.
More than sentinels wait for the dawn,
    let Israel wait for the LORD.

℟. With the Lord there is mercy and fullness
     of redemption.

For with the LORD is kindness
    and with him is plenteous redemption;
And he will redeem Israel
    from all their iniquities.

R̷. With the Lord there is mercy and fullness
       of redemption.

146.

**Ps 139:1-3, 4-6, 7-8,
9-10, 11-12, 13-14ab,
14c-15, 16, 17-18, 23-24**

R̷. (23a) You have searched me, and you know me, Lord.

O LORD, you have probed me and you know me;
    you know when I sit and when I stand;
    you understand my thoughts from afar.
My journeys and my rest you scrutinize,
    with all my ways you are familiar.

R̷. You have searched me, and you know me, Lord.

Even before a word is on my tongue,
    behold, O LORD, you know the whole of it.
Behind me and before, you hem me in
    and rest your hand upon me.
Such knowledge is too wonderful for me;
    too lofty for me to attain.

℟. You have searched me, and you know me, Lord.

Where can I go from your spirit?
    from your presence where can I flee?
If I go up to the heavens, you are there;
    if I sink to the nether world, you are present there.

℟. You have searched me, and you know me, Lord.

If I take the wings of the dawn;
    if I settle at the farthest limits of the sea
Even there your hand shall guide me,
    and your right hand hold me fast.

℟. You have searched me, and you know me, Lord.

If I say, "Surely the darkness shall hide me,
    and night shall be my light"—
For you darkness itself is not dark,
    and night shines as the day.
    darkness and light are the same.

℟. You have searched me, and you know me, Lord.

Truly you have formed my inmost being;
    you knit me in my mother's womb.
I give you thanks that I am fearfully, wonderfully made;
    wonderful are your works.

R̥. You have searched me, and you know me, Lord.

My soul also you knew full well;
    nor was my frame unknown to you
When I was made in secret,
    when I was fashioned in the depths of the earth.

R̥. You have searched me, and you know me, Lord.

Your eyes have seen my actions;
    in your book they are all written;
    my days were limited before one of them existed.

R̥. You have searched me, and you know me, Lord.

How weighty are your designs, O God,
    how vast the sum of them.
Were I to recount them, they would outnumber the sands;
    did I reach the end of them, I should still be with you.

R̥. You have searched me, and you know me, Lord.

Probe me, O God, and know my heart,
    try me, and know my thoughts;
See if my way is crooked,
    and lead me in the way of old.

R̥. You have searched me, and you know me, Lord.

147.

Ps 143:1-2, 3-4, 5-6,
7-8a, 8b-9, 10, 11

℟. (10a) Teach me to do your will, my God.

O LORD, hear my prayer;
  hearken to my pleading in your faithfulness;
  in your justice answer me.
And enter not into judgment with your servant,
  for before you no living man is just.

℟. Teach me to do your will, my God.

For the enemy pursues me;
  he has crushed my life to the ground;
He has left me dwelling in the dark
  like those long dead.
And my spirit is faint within me,
  my heart within me is appalled.

℟. Teach me to do your will, my God.

I remember the days of old;
  I meditate on all your doings;
  the works of your hands I ponder.
I stretch out my hands to you;
  my soul thirsts for you like parched land.

℟. Teach me to do your will, my God.

Hasten to answer me, O LORD;
    for my spirit fails me.
Hide not your face from me
    lest I become like those who go down into the pit.
At dawn let me hear of your mercy,
    for in you I trust.

℟. Teach me to do your will, my God.

Show me the way in which I should walk,
    for to you I lift up my soul.
Rescue me from my enemies, O LORD,
    for in you I hope.

℟. Teach me to do your will, my God.

Teach me to do your will,
    for you are my God.
May your good spirit guide me
    on level ground.

℟. Teach me to do your will, my God.

For your name's sake, O LORD, preserve me;
    in your justice free me from distress.

℟. Teach me to do your will, my God.

Readings from the New Testament

148.

A reading from the Letter of Saint Paul
to the Romans   3:22-26

They are justified freely by his grace through the redemption in Christ Jesus.

Brothers and sisters:
The righteousness of God through faith in Jesus Christ is
   for all who believe.
For there is no distinction;
   all have sinned and are deprived of the glory of God.
They are justified freely by his grace
   through the redemption in Christ Jesus,
   whom God set forth as an expiation,
   through faith, by his Blood, to prove his righteousness
   because of the forgiveness of sins previously committed,
   through the forbearance of God—
   to prove his righteousness in the present time,
   that he might be righteous
   and justify the one who has faith in Jesus.

The word of the Lord.

149.

A reading from the Letter of Saint Paul
to the Romans   5:6-11

We boast of God through our Lord Jesus Christ,
through whom we have now received reconciliation.

Brothers and sisters:
Christ, while we were still helpless,
    yet died at the appointed time for the ungodly.
Indeed, only with difficulty does one die for a just person,
    though perhaps for a good person
    one might even find courage to die.
But God proves his love for us
    in that while we were still sinners Christ died for us.
How much more then, since we are now justified by
        his Blood,
    will we be saved through him from the wrath.
Indeed, if, while we were enemies,
    we were reconciled to God through the death of
        his Son,
    how much more, once reconciled,
    will we be saved by his life.
Not only that,
    but we also boast of God through our Lord
        Jesus Christ,
    through whom we have now received reconciliation.

The word of the Lord.

150.
A reading from the Letter of Saint Paul
to the Romans   6:2-11

*You must think of yourselves as being dead to sin
and living for God in Christ Jesus.*

Brothers and sisters:
How can we who died to sin yet live in it?
Are you unaware that we who were baptized into
        Christ Jesus
    were baptized into his death?
We were indeed buried with him through baptism
        into death,
    so that, just as Christ was raised from the dead
    by the glory of the Father,
    we too might live in newness of life.

For if we have grown into union with him through a
        death like his,
    we shall also be united with him in the resurrection.
We know that our old self was crucified with him,
    so that our sinful body might be done away with,
    that we might no longer be in slavery to sin.
For a dead person has been absolved from sin.
If, then, we have died with Christ,
    we believe that we shall also live with him.
We know that Christ, raised from the dead, dies no more;
    death no longer has power over him.

As to his death, he died to sin once and for all;
    as to his life, he lives for God.
Consequently, you too must think of yourselves as being
        dead to sin
    and living for God in Christ Jesus.

The word of the Lord.

151.
A reading from the Letter of Saint Paul
to the Romans   6:12-23

For the wages of sin is death, but the gift of God
is eternal life in Christ Jesus our Lord.

Brothers and sisters:
Sin must not reign over your mortal bodies
    so that you obey their desires.
And do not present the parts of your bodies to sin
    as weapons for wickedness,
      but present yourselves to God as raised from the dead
        to life
    and the parts of your bodies to God
    as weapons for righteousness.
For sin is not to have any power over you,
    since you are not under the law but under grace.

What then? Shall we sin because we are not under the law
    but under grace?
Of course not!

Do you not know that if you present yourselves
    to someone as obedient slaves,
    you are slaves of the one you obey,
    either of sin, which leads to death,
    or of obedience, which leads to righteousness?
But thanks be to God that, although you were once slaves
        of sin,
    you have become obedient from the heart
    to the pattern of teaching to which you were entrusted.
Freed from sin, you have become slaves of righteousness.
I am speaking in human terms because of the weakness of
        your nature.
For just as you presented the parts of your bodies as slaves
        to impurity
    and to lawlessness for lawlessness,
    so now present them as slaves to righteousness
        for sanctification.
For when you were slaves of sin, you were free
        from righteousness.
But what profit did you get then
    from the things of which you are now ashamed?
For the end of those things is death.
But now that you have been freed from sin and have
        become slaves of God,
    the benefit that you have leads to sanctification,
    and its end is eternal life.
For the wages of sin is death,
    but the gift of God is eternal life in Christ Jesus our Lord.

The word of the Lord.

152.

A reading from the Letter of Saint Paul
to the Romans   7:14-25a

Miserable one that I am! Who will deliver me from this mortal body?
Thanks be to God through Jesus Christ our Lord.

Brothers and sisters:
We know that the law is spiritual;
    but I am carnal, sold into slavery to sin.
What I do, I do not understand.
For I do not do what I want,
    but I do what I hate.
Now if I do what I do not want,
    I concur that the law is good.
So now it is no longer I who do it,
    but sin that dwells in me.
I know that good does not dwell in me, that is, in my flesh.
The willing is ready at hand, but doing the good is not.
For I do not do the good I want,
    but I do the evil I do not want.
Now if I do what I do not want, it is no longer I who do it,
    but sin that dwells in me.
So, then, I discover the principle
    that when I want to do right, evil is at hand.
For I take delight in the law of God, in my inner self,
    but I see in my members another principle
    at war with the law of my mind,
    taking me captive to the law of sin that dwells in
        my members.

Miserable one that I am!
Who will deliver me from this mortal body?
Thanks be to God through Jesus Christ our Lord.

The word of the Lord.

153.
A reading from the Letter of Saint Paul
to the Romans   12:1-2, 9-18

Be transformed by the renewal of your mind.

I urge you, brothers and sisters, by the mercies of God,
    to offer your bodies as a living sacrifice,
    holy and pleasing to God, your spiritual worship.
Do not conform yourselves to this age
    but be transformed by the renewal of your mind,
    that you may discern what is the will of God,
    what is good and pleasing and perfect.

Let love be sincere;
    hate what is evil,
    hold on to what is good;
    love one another with mutual affection;
    anticipate one another in showing honor.
Do not grow slack in zeal,
    be fervent in spirit,
    serve the Lord.
Rejoice in hope,
    endure in affliction,
    persevere in prayer.

Contribute to the needs of the holy ones,
    exercise hospitality.
Bless those who persecute you,
    bless and do not curse them.
Rejoice with those who rejoice,
    weep with those who weep.
Have the same regard for one another;
    do not be haughty but associate with the lowly;
    do not be wise in your own estimation.
Do not repay anyone evil for evil;
    be concerned for what is noble in the sight of all.
If possible, on your part, live at peace with all.
Beloved, do not look for revenge
    but leave room for the wrath;
    for it is written,
    Vengeance is mine, I will repay, says the Lord.

The word of the Lord.

154.
A reading from the Letter of Saint Paul
to the Romans   **13:8-14**

Throw off the works of darkness and put on the armor of light.

Brothers and sisters:
Owe nothing to anyone, except to love one another;
    for the one who loves another has fulfilled the law.
The commandments, *You shall not commit adultery;*
    you shall not kill; you shall not steal; you shall
        not covet,

and whatever other commandment there may be,
   are summed up in this saying, namely,
   You shall love your neighbor as yourself.
Love does no evil to the neighbor;
   hence, love is the fulfillment of the law.
And do this because you know the time;
   it is the hour now for you to awake from sleep.
For our salvation is nearer now than when we first believed;
   the night is advanced, the day is at hand.
Let us then throw off the works of darkness
   and put on the armor of light;
   let us conduct ourselves properly as in the day,
   not in orgies and drunkenness,
   not in promiscuity and lust,
   not in rivalry and jealousy.
But put on the Lord Jesus Christ,
   and make no provision for the desires of the flesh.

The word of the Lord.

155.
A reading from the second Letter of Saint Paul
to the Corinthians   **5:17-21**

God was reconciling the world to himself in Christ.

Brothers and sisters:
Whoever is in Christ is a new creation:
   the old things have passed away;
   behold, new things have come.

And all this is from God,
  who has reconciled us to himself through Christ
  and given us the ministry of reconciliation,
  namely, God was reconciling the world to himself
      in Christ,
  not counting their trespasses against them
  and entrusting to us the message of reconciliation.
So we are ambassadors for Christ,
  as if God were appealing through us.
We implore you on behalf of Christ,
  be reconciled to God.
For our sake he made him to be sin who did not know sin,
  so that we might become the righteousness of God
      in him.

The word of the Lord.

156.
A reading from the Letter of Saint Paul
to the Galatians   5:16-24

Those who belong to Christ Jesus have crucified
their flesh with its passions and desires.

Brothers and sisters, live by the Spirit
  and you will certainly not gratify the desire of the flesh.
For the flesh has desires against the Spirit,
  and the Spirit against the flesh;

these are opposed to each other,
so that you may not do what you want.
But if you are guided by the Spirit, you are not under
    the law.
Now the works of the flesh are obvious:
    immorality, impurity, lust, idolatry,
    sorcery, hatreds, rivalry, jealousy,
    outbursts of fury, acts of selfishness,
    dissensions, factions, occasions of envy,
    drinking bouts, orgies, and the like.
I warn you, as I warned you before,
    that those who do such things will not inherit the
        Kingdom of God.
In contrast, the fruit of the Spirit is love, joy, peace,
    patience, kindness, generosity,
    faithfulness, gentleness, self-control.
Against such there is no law.
Now those who belong to Christ Jesus have crucified
        their flesh
    with its passions and desires.

The word of the Lord.

157.

A reading from the Letter of Saint Paul to the Ephesians

2:1-10

God, because of the great love he had for us, even when we were
dead in our transgressions, brought us to life with Christ

Brothers and sisters:
You were dead in your transgressions and sins
in which you once lived following the age of this world,
following the ruler of the power of the air,
the spirit that is now at work in the disobedient.
All of us once lived among them in the desires of
our flesh,
following the wishes of the flesh and the impulses,
and we were by nature children of wrath, like the rest.
But God, who is rich in mercy,
because of the great love he had for us,
even when we were dead in our transgressions,
brought us to life with Christ (by grace you have
been saved),
raised us up with him,
and seated us with him in the heavens in Christ Jesus,
that in the ages to come
he might show the immeasurable riches of his grace
in his kindness to us in Christ Jesus.
For by grace you have been saved through faith,
and this is not from you; it is the gift of God;
it is not from works, so no one may boast.

For we are his handiwork, created in Christ Jesus for
    good works
  that God has prepared in advance,
  that we should live in them.

The word of the Lord.

158.
A reading from the Letter of Saint Paul
to the Ephesians   4:1-3, 17-32

Be renewed in the spirit of your minds, and put on the new self.

I, then, a prisoner for the Lord,
  urge you to live in a manner
  worthy of the call you have received,
  with all humility and gentleness,
  with patience,
  bearing with one another through love,
  striving to preserve the unity of the spirit
  through the bond of peace:

So I declare and testify in the Lord
  that you must no longer live as the Gentiles do,
  in the futility of their minds;
  darkened in understanding,
  alienated from the life of God because of their ignorance,
  because of their hardness of heart,
  they have become callous
  and have handed themselves over to licentiousness
  for the practice of every kind of impurity to excess.

That is not how you learned Christ,
 assuming that you have·heard of him
 and were taught in him,
 as truth is in Jesus,
 that you should put away the old self of your former
   way of life,
 corrupted through deceitful desires,
 and be renewed in the spirit of your minds,
 and put on the new self,
 created in God's way in righteousness and holiness
   of truth.

Therefore, putting away falsehood,
 speak the truth,
 each one to his neighbor,
 for we are members one of another.
Be angry but do not sin;
 do not let the sun set on your anger,
 and do not leave room for the Devil.
The thief must no longer steal,
 but rather labor,
 doing honest work with his own hands,
 so that he may have something to share with one
   in need.
No foul language should come out of your mouths,
 but only such as is good for needed edification,
 that it may impart grace to those who hear.
And do not grieve the Holy Spirit of God,
 with which you were sealed for the day of redemption.

All bitterness, fury, anger, shouting, and reviling
   must be removed from you,
   along with all malice.
And be kind to one another, compassionate,
   forgiving one another as God has forgiven you
      in Christ.

The word of the Lord.

159.
A reading from the Letter of Saint Paul
to the Ephesians   5:1-14

> *You were once darkness, but now you are*
> *light in the Lord. Live as children of light.*

Brothers and sisters:
Be imitators of God, as beloved children,
   and live in love,
   as Christ loved us and handed himself over for us
   as a sacrificial offering to God for a fragrant aroma.
Immorality or any impurity or greed
   must not even be mentioned among you,
   as is fitting among holy ones,
   no obscenity or silly or suggestive talk, which is out
      of place,
   but instead, thanksgiving.
Be sure of this,
   that no immoral or impure or greedy person, that is,
      an idolater,
   has any inheritance in the Kingdom of Christ and of God.

Let no one deceive you with empty arguments,
  for because of these things
  the wrath of God is coming upon the disobedient.
So do not be associated with them.
For you were once darkness,
  but now you are light in the Lord.
Live as children of light,
  for light produces every kind of goodness and
    righteousness and truth.
Try to learn what is pleasing to the Lord.
Take no part in the fruitless works of darkness;
  rather expose them,
  for it is shameful even to mention the things done by
    them in secret;
  but everything exposed by the light becomes visible,
  for everything that becomes visible is light.
Therefore, it says:
  "Awake, O sleeper,
  and arise from the dead,
  and Christ will give you light."

The word of the Lord.

160.
A reading from the Letter of Saint Paul
to the Ephesians 6:10-18

Put on the armor of God, that you may be able to resist on the evil day.

Brothers and sisters:
Draw your strength from the Lord and from his
     mighty power.
Put on the armor of God so that you may be able to
     stand firm
  against the tactics of the Devil.
For our struggle is not with flesh and blood
  but with the principalities, with the powers,
  with the world rulers of this present darkness,
  with the evil spirits in the heavens.
Therefore, put on the armor of God,
  that you may be able to resist on the evil day
  and, having done everything, to hold your ground.
So stand fast with your loins girded in truth,
  clothed with righteousness as a breastplate,
  and your feet shod in readiness for the Gospel of peace.
In all circumstances, hold faith as a shield,
  to quench all the flaming arrows of the Evil One.
And take the helmet of salvation and the sword of the Spirit,
  which is the word of God.

With all prayer and supplication,
    pray at every opportunity in the Spirit.
To that end, be watchful with all perseverance
            and supplication
    for all the holy ones.

The word of the Lord.

161.
A reading from the Letter of Saint Paul
to the Colossians   3:1-10, 12-17

If you were raised with Christ, seek what is above.
Put to death, then, the parts of you that are earthly.

Brothers and sisters:
If you were raised with Christ, seek what is above,
    where Christ is seated at the right hand of God.
Think of what is above, not of what is on earth.
For you have died, and your life is hidden with Christ
            in God.
When Christ your life appears,
    then you too will appear with him in glory.

Put to death, then, the parts of you that are earthly:
    immorality, impurity, passion, evil desire,
    and the greed that is idolatry.
Because of these the wrath of God is coming upon
            the disobedient.
By these you too once conducted yourselves, when you
            lived in that way.

But now you must put them all away:
  anger, fury, malice, slander,
  and obscene language out of your mouths.
Stop lying to one another,
  since you have taken off the old self with its practices
  and have put on the new self,
  which is being renewed, for knowledge,
  in the image of its creator.

Put on, as God's chosen ones, holy and beloved,
  heartfelt compassion, kindness, humility, gentleness,
      and patience,
  bearing with one another and forgiving one another,
  if one has a grievance against another;
  as the Lord has forgiven you, so must you also do.
And over all these put on love,
  that is, the bond of perfection.
And let the peace of Christ control your hearts,
  the peace into which you were also called in one Body.
And be thankful.
Let the word of Christ dwell in you richly,
  as in all wisdom you teach and admonish one another,
  singing psalms, hymns, and spiritual songs
  with gratitude in your hearts to God.
And whatever you do, in word or in deed,
  do everything in the name of the Lord Jesus,
  giving thanks to God the Father through him.

The word of the Lord.

162.

A reading from the Letter to the Hebrews 12:1-5

*In your struggle against sin you have not
yet resisted to the point of shedding blood.*

Brothers and sisters:
Since we are surrounded by so great a cloud of witnesses,
   let us rid ourselves of every burden and sin that clings
        to us
   and persevere in running the race that lies before us
   while keeping our eyes fixed on Jesus,
   the leader and perfecter of faith.
For the sake of the joy that lay before him
   Jesus endured the cross, despising its shame,
   and has taken his seat at the right of the throne of God.
Consider how he endured such opposition from sinners,
   in order that you may not grow weary and lose heart.
In your struggle against sin
   you have not yet resisted to the point of
        shedding blood.
You have also forgotten the exhortation addressed to you
        as sons:
My son, do not disdain the discipline of the Lord
or lose heart when reproved by him.

The word of the Lord.

163.

A reading from the Letter of Saint James   1:22-27

Be doers of the word and not hearers only.

.

Beloved:
Be doers of the word and not hearers only,
        deluding yourselves.
For if anyone is a hearer of the word and not a doer,
    he is like a man who looks at his own face in a mirror.
He sees himself, then goes off and promptly forgets
    what he looked like.
But the one who peers into the perfect law of freedom
        and perseveres,
    and is not a hearer who forgets but a doer who acts;
    such a one shall be blessed in what he does.

If anyone thinks he is religious and does not bridle
        his tongue
    but deceives his heart, his religion is vain.
Religion that is pure and undefiled before God and
        the Father is this:
    to care for orphans and widows in their affliction
    and to keep oneself unstained by the world.

The word of the Lord.

164.

A reading from the Letter of Saint James   2:14-26

What good is it if someone says he has faith but does not have works?

What good is it, my brothers and sisters,
    if someone says he has faith but does not have works?
Can that faith save him?
If a brother or sister has nothing to wear
    and has no food for the day,
    and one of you says to them,
    "Go in peace, keep warm, and eat well,"
    but you do not give them the necessities of the body,
    what good is it?
So also faith of itself,
    if it does not have works, is dead.

Indeed someone might say,
    "You have faith and I have works."
Demonstrate your faith to me without works,
    and I will demonstrate my faith to you from my works.
You believe that God is one.
You do well.
Even the demons believe that and tremble.
Do you want proof, you ignoramus,
    that faith without works is useless?
Was not Abraham our father justified by works
    when he offered his son Isaac upon the altar?
You see that faith was active along with his works,
    and faith was completed by the works.

Thus the Scripture was fulfilled that says,
  Abraham believed God,
  and it was credited to him as righteousness,
  and he was called *the friend of God.*
See how a person is justified by works and not by
      faith alone.
And in the same way, was not Rahab the harlot also
      justified by works
  when she welcomed the messengers
  and sent them out by a different route?
For just as a body without a spirit is dead,
  so also faith without works is dead.

The word of the Lord.

165.

A reading from the Letter of Saint James   **3:1-12**

  If anyone does not fall short in speech, he is a perfect man.

Not many of you should become teachers, my brothers
      and sisters,
  for you realize that we will be judged more strictly,
  for we all fall short in many respects.
If anyone does not fall short in speech, he is a
      perfect man,
  able to bridle the whole body also.
If we put bits into the mouths of horses to make them
      obey us,
  we also guide their whole bodies.

It is the same with ships:
 even though they are so large and driven by
   fierce winds,
 they are steered by a very small rudder
 wherever the pilot's inclination wishes.
In the same way the tongue is a small member
 and yet has great pretensions.

Consider how small a fire can set a huge forest ablaze.
The tongue is also a fire.
It exists among our members as a world of malice,
 defiling the whole body
 and setting the entire course of our lives on fire,
 itself set on fire by Gehenna.
For every kind of beast and bird, of reptile and
   sea creature,
 can be tamed and has been tamed by the
   human species,
 but no man can tame the tongue.
It is a restless evil, full of deadly poison.
With it we bless the Lord and Father,
 and with it we curse men
 who are made in the likeness of God.
 From the same mouth come blessing and cursing.

My brothers and sisters, this need not be so.
Does a spring gush forth from the same opening
 both pure and brackish water?

Can a fig tree, my brothers and sisters, produce olives,
   or a grapevine figs?
Neither can salt water yield fresh.

The word of the Lord.

166.

A reading from the first Letter of Saint Peter   1:13-23

You were ransomed not with perishable things like silver or gold
but with the precious Blood of Christ as of a spotless unblemished Lamb.

Beloved:
Gird up the loins of your mind, live soberly,
   and set your hopes completely on the grace to be
         brought to you
   at the revelation of Jesus Christ.
Like obedient children,
   do not act in compliance with the desires of your
         former ignorance
   but, as he who called you is holy,
   be holy yourselves in every aspect of your conduct,
   for it is written, *Be holy because I am holy.*
Realize that you were ransomed from your futile conduct,
   handed on by your ancestors,
   not with perishable things like silver or gold
   but with the precious Blood of Christ
   as of a spotless unblemished Lamb.
He was known before the foundation of the world
   but revealed in the final time for you,

who through him believe in God
who raised him from the dead and gave him glory,
so that your faith and hope are in God.

Since you have purified yourselves
by obedience to the truth for sincere brotherly love,
love one another intensely from a pure heart.
You have been born anew,
not from perishable but from imperishable seed,
through the living and abiding word of God.

The word of the Lord.

167.
A reading from the second Letter of Saint Peter   1:3-11

Be all the more eager to make your call and election firm.

Beloved:
His divine power has bestowed on us
everything that makes for life and devotion,
through the knowledge of him
who called us by his own glory and power.
Through these, he has bestowed on us
the precious and very great promises,
so that through them you may come to share in the
divine nature,
after escaping from the corruption that is in the world
because of evil desire.
For this very reason,
make every effort to supplement your faith with virtue,

virtue with knowledge, knowledge with self-control,
self-control with endurance, endurance with devotion,
devotion with mutual affection, mutual affection
      with love.
If these are yours and increase in abundance,
    they will keep you from being idle or unfruitful
    in the knowledge of our Lord Jesus Christ.
Anyone who lacks them is blind and shortsighted,
    forgetful of the cleansing of his past sins.
Therefore, brothers and sisters, be all the more eager
    to make your call and election firm,
    for, in doing so, you will never stumble.
For, in this way, entry into the eternal Kingdom
    of our Lord and savior Jesus Christ
    will be richly provided for you.

The word of the Lord.

168.
A reading from the first Letter of Saint John   1:5–2:2

If we acknowledge our sins, he is faithful and just
and will forgive our sins and cleanse us from every wrongdoing.

Beloved:
This is the message that we have heard from Jesus Christ
    and proclaim to you: God is light,
    and in him there is no darkness at all.
If we say, "We have fellowship with God,"
    while we continue to walk in darkness,
    we lie and do not act in truth.

But if we walk in the light as he is in the light,
    then we have fellowship with one another,
    and the Blood of his Son Jesus cleanses us from all sin.
If we say, "We are without sin," we deceive ourselves,
    and the truth is not in us.
If we acknowledge our sins, he is faithful and just
    and will forgive our sins and cleanse us from every
        wrongdoing.
If we say, "We have not sinned," we make him a liar,
    and his word is not in us.

My children, I am writing this to you so that you may not
        commit sin.
But if anyone does sin, we have an Advocate with
        the Father,
    Jesus Christ the righteous one.
He is expiation for our sins,
    and not for our sins only but for those of the whole world.

The word of the Lord.

169.
A reading from the first Letter of Saint John   **2:3-11**

Whoever hates his brother, is still in the darkness.

Beloved:
The way we may be sure that we know Jesus
    is to keep his commandments.

Whoever says, "I know him," but does not keep
     his commandments
  is a liar, and the truth is not in him.
But whoever keeps his word,
  the love of God is truly perfected in him.
This is the way we may know that we are in union
     with him:
  whoever claims to abide in him ought to walk just as
     he walked.

Beloved, I am writing no new commandment to you
  but an old commandment that you had from
     the beginning.
The old commandment is the word that you have heard.
And yet I do write a new commandment to you,
  which holds true in him and among you,
  for the darkness is passing away,
  and the true light is already shining.
Whoever says he is in the light,
  yet hates his brother, is still in the darkness.
Whoever loves his brother remains in the light,
  and there is nothing in him to cause a fall.
Whoever hates his brother is in darkness;
  he walks in darkness
  and does not know where he is going
  because the darkness has blinded his eyes.

The word of the Lord.

170.

A reading from the first Letter of Saint John   3:1-24

We know that we have passed from death to life because we love our brothers.

See what love the Father has bestowed on us
    that we may be called the children of God.
Yet so we are.
The reason the world does not know us
    is that it did not know him.
Beloved, we are God's children now;
    what we shall be has not yet been revealed.
We do know that when it is revealed
    we shall be like him,
        for we shall see him as he is.
Everyone who has this hope based on him makes
           himself pure,
    as he is pure.

Everyone who commits sin commits lawlessness,
    for sin is lawlessness.
You know that he was revealed to take away sins,
    and in him there is no sin.
No one who remains in him sins;
    no one who sins has seen him or known him.
Children, let no one deceive you.
The person who acts in righteousness is righteous,
    just as he is righteous.
Whoever sins belongs to the Devil,
    because the Devil has sinned from the beginning.

Indeed, the Son of God was revealed to destroy the works
        of the Devil.
No one who is begotten by God commits sin,
    because God's seed remains in him;
    he cannot sin because he is begotten by God.
In this way, the children of God and the children of the
        Devil are made plain;
    no one who fails to act in righteousness belongs to God,
    nor anyone who does not love his brother.

For this is the message you have heard from
        the beginning:
    we should love one another,
    unlike Cain who belonged to the Evil One and
        slaughtered his brother.
Why did he slaughter him?
Because his own works were evil,
    and those of his brother righteous.
Do not be amazed, then, brothers and sisters,
    if the world hates you.
We know that we have passed from death to life
    because we love our brothers.
Whoever does not love remains in death.
Everyone who hates his brother is a murderer,
    and you know that no murderer has eternal life
        remaining in him.
The way we came to know love
    was that he laid down his life for us;
    so we ought to lay down our lives for our brothers.

If someone who has worldly means sees a brother in need
    and refuses him compassion, how can the love of God
        remain in him?
Children, let us love not in word or speech but in deed
        and truth.
Now this is how we shall know that we belong to
        the truth
    and reassure our hearts before him in whatever our
        hearts condemn,
    for God is greater than our hearts and knows
        everything.
Beloved, if our hearts do not condemn us,
    we have confidence in God
    and receive from him whatever we ask,
    because we keep his commandments and do what
        pleases him.
And his commandment is this:
    we should believe in the name of his Son, Jesus Christ,
    and love one another just as he commanded us.
Those who keep his commandments remain in him, and
        he in them,
    and the way we know that he remains in us
    is from the Spirit that he gave us.

The word of the Lord.

171.

A reading from the first Letter of Saint John   4:16-21

God is love, and whoever remains in love remains in God and God in him.

Beloved:
We have come to know and to believe in the love God has
        for us.

God is love, and whoever remains in love remains in God
        and God in him.
In this is love brought to perfection among us,
    that we have confidence on the day of judgment
    because as he is, so are we in this world.
There is no fear in love,
    but perfect love drives out fear
    because fear has to do with punishment,
    and so one who fears is not yet perfect in love.
Beloved, we love God because
    he first loved us.
If anyone says, "I love God,"
    but hates his brother, he is a liar;
    for whoever does not love a brother whom he has seen
    cannot love God whom he has not seen.
This is the commandment we have from him:
Whoever loves God must also love his brother.

The word of the Lord.

172.

A reading from the Book of Revelation   2:1-5

Repent, and do the works you did at first.

To the angel of the Church in Ephesus, write this:
  "'The one who holds the seven stars in his right hand
  and walks in the midst of the seven gold lampstands
        says this:
  "I know your works, your labor, and your endurance,
  and that you cannot tolerate the wicked;
  you have tested those who call themselves apostles but
        are not,
  and discovered that they are impostors.
Moreover, you have endurance and have suffered for
        my name,
  and you have not grown weary.
Yet I hold this against you:
  you have lost the love you had at first.
Realize how far you have fallen.
Repent, and do the works you did at first.
Otherwise, I will come to you and remove your lampstand
        from its place,
  unless you repent."'"

The word of the Lord.

173.

A reading from the Book of Revelation 3:14-22

Because you are lukewarm, neither hot nor cold, I will spit you out of my mouth.

"To the angel of the Church in Laodicea, write this:

"'The Amen, the faithful and true witness,
    the source of God's creation, says this:
    "I know your works;
    I know that you are neither cold nor hot.
I wish you were either cold or hot.
So, because you are lukewarm, neither hot nor cold,
    I will spit you out of my mouth.
For you say, 'I am rich and affluent and have no need
            of anything,'
    and yet do not realize that you are wretched,
    pitiable, poor, blind, and naked.
I advise you to buy from me gold refined by fire so that
            you may be rich,
    and white garments to put on
    so that your shameful nakedness may not be exposed,
    and buy ointment to smear on your eyes so that you
            may see.
Those whom I love, I reprove and chastise.
Be earnest, therefore, and repent.

""Behold, I stand at the door and knock.
If anyone hears my voice and opens the door,
    then I will enter his house and dine with him,
    and he with me.

I will give the victor the right to sit with me on my throne,
   as I myself first won the victory
   and sit with my Father on his throne.

""""Whoever has ears ought to hear
   what the Spirit says to the churches.""""

The word of the Lord.

174.
A reading from the Book of Revelation   20:11-15

All the dead were judged according to their deeds.

Next I saw a large white throne and the one who was
         sitting on it.
The earth and the sky fled from his presence
   and there was no place for them.
I saw the dead, the great and the lowly, standing before
         the throne,
   and scrolls were opened.
Then another scroll was opened, the book of life.
The dead were judged according to their deeds,
   by what was written in the scrolls.
The sea gave up its dead;
   then Death and Hades gave up their dead.
All the dead were judged according to their deeds.
Then Death and Hades were thrown into the pool of fire.
(This pool of fire is the second death.)

Anyone whose name was not found written in the book
      of life
  was thrown into the pool of fire.

The word of the Lord.

175.

A reading from the Book of Revelation   **21:1-8**

The victor will inherit these gifts, and I shall be his God, and he will be my son.

I, John, saw a new heaven and a new earth.
The former heaven and the former earth had passed away,
   and the sea was no more.
I also saw the holy city, a new Jerusalem,
   coming down out of heaven from God,
   prepared as a bride adorned for her husband.
I heard a loud voice from the throne saying,
   "Behold, God's dwelling is with the human race.
He will dwell with them and they will be his people
   and God himself will always be with them as their God.
He will wipe every tear from their eyes,
   and there shall be no more death or mourning, wailing
      or pain,
   for the old order has passed away."

The one who sat on the throne said,
   "Behold, I make all things new."
Then he said, "Write these words down,
   for they are trustworthy and true."

He said to me, "They are accomplished.
I am the Alpha and the Omega,
   the beginning and the end.
To the thirsty I will give a gift
   from the spring of life-giving water.
The victor will inherit these gifts,
   and I shall be his God,
   and he will be my son.
But as for cowards, the unfaithful, the depraved,
   murderers, the unchaste, sorcerers, idol-worshipers,
   and deceivers of every sort,
   their lot is in the burning pool of fire and sulfur,
   which is the second death."

The word of the Lord.

READINGS FROM THE GOSPELS

176.
✠ A reading from the holy Gospel
according to Matthew   3:1-12

Repent, for the Kingdom of heaven is at hand!

John the Baptist appeared, preaching in the desert
            of Judea
      and saying, "Repent, for the Kingdom of heaven is
            at hand!"
It was of him that the prophet Isaiah had spoken when
            he said:

A voice of one crying out in the desert,
Prepare the way of the Lord,
   make straight his paths.
John wore clothing made of camel's hair
  and had a leather belt around his waist.
His food was locusts and wild honey.
At that time Jerusalem, all Judea,
   and the whole region around the Jordan
   were going out to him
   and were being baptized by him in the Jordan River
   as they acknowledged their sins.

When he saw many of the Pharisees and Sadducees
   coming to his baptism, he said to them, "You brood
      of vipers!
Who warned you to flee from the coming wrath?
Produce good fruit as evidence of your repentance.
And do not presume to say to yourselves,
  'We have Abraham as our father.'
For I tell you,
   God can raise up children to Abraham from
      these stones.
Even now the ax lies at the root of the trees.
Therefore every tree that does not bear good fruit
  will be cut down and thrown into the fire.
I am baptizing you with water, for repentance,
  but the one who is coming after me is mightier than I.
I am not worthy to carry his sandals.
He will baptize you with the Holy Spirit and fire.
His winnowing fan is in his hand.

He will clear his threshing floor
    and gather his wheat into his barn,
    but the chaff he will burn with unquenchable fire."

The Gospel of the Lord.

177.
✠ A reading from the holy Gospel
according to Matthew   4:12-17

Repent, for the Kingdom of heaven is at hand.

When Jesus heard that John had been arrested,
    he withdrew to Galilee.
He left Nazareth and went to live in Capernaum by the sea,
    in the region of Zebulun and Naphtali,
    that what had been said through Isaiah the prophet
    might be fulfilled:

Land of Zebulun and land of Naphtali,
    the way to the sea, beyond the Jordan,
    Galilee of the Gentiles,
the people who sit in darkness
    have seen a great light,
on those dwelling in a land overshadowed by death
    light has arisen.

From that time on, Jesus began to preach and say,
    "Repent, for the Kingdom of heaven is at hand."

The Gospel of the Lord.

178.

✠ A reading from the holy Gospel
according to Matthew   5:1-12

*When Jesus saw the crowds, he went up
the mountain, and his disciples came to him.*

When Jesus saw the crowds, he went up the mountain,
   and after he had sat down, his disciples came to him.
He began to teach them, saying:

   "Blessed are the poor in spirit,
      for theirs is the Kingdom of heaven.
   Blessed are they who mourn,
      for they will be comforted.
   Blessed are the meek,
      for they will inherit the land.
   Blessed are they who hunger and thirst for
         righteousness,
      for they will be satisfied.
   Blessed are the merciful,
      for they will be shown mercy.
   Blessed are the clean of heart,
      for they will see God.
   Blessed are the peacemakers,
      for they will be called children of God.
   Blessed are they who are persecuted for the sake
         of righteousness,
      for theirs is the Kingdom of heaven.

Blessed are you when they insult you and persecute you
   and utter every kind of evil against you falsely because
      of me.
Rejoice and be glad,
   for your reward will be great in heaven.
Thus they persecuted the prophets who were before you."

The Gospel of the Lord.

179.
✠ A reading from the holy Gospel
according to Matthew   5:13-16

Your light must shine before others.

Jesus said to his disciples:
"You are the salt of the earth.
But if salt loses its taste, with what can it be seasoned?
It is no longer good for anything
   but to be thrown out and trampled underfoot.
You are the light of the world.
A city set on a mountain cannot be hidden.
Nor do they light a lamp and then put it under a
         bushel basket;
   it is set on a lampstand,
   where it gives light to all in the house.
Just so, your light must shine before others,
   that they may see your good deeds
   and glorify your heavenly Father."

The Gospel of the Lord.

180.
✠ A reading from the holy Gospel
according to Matthew   5:17-47

But I say to you.

Jesus said to his disciples:
"Do not think that I have come to abolish the law or
     the prophets.
I have come not to abolish but to fulfill.
Amen, I say to you, until heaven and earth pass away,
   not the smallest letter or the smallest part of a letter
   will pass from the law,
   until all things have taken place.
Therefore, whoever breaks one of the least of these
     commandments
   and teaches others to do so
   will be called least in the Kingdom of heaven.
But whoever obeys and teaches these commandments
   will be called greatest in the Kingdom of heaven.
I tell you, unless your righteousness surpasses
   that of the scribes and Pharisees,
   you will not enter the Kingdom of heaven.

"You have heard that it was said to your ancestors,
   *You shall not kill; and whoever kills will be liable
        to judgment.*
But I say to you,
   whoever is angry with brother
   will be liable to judgment;

171

and whoever says to brother, *Raqa,*
    will be answerable to the Sanhedrin;
    and whoever says, 'You fool,'
    will be liable to fiery Gehenna.
Therefore, if you bring your gift to the altar,
    and there recall that your brother
    has anything against you,
    leave your gift there at the altar,
    go first and be reconciled with your brother,
    and then come and offer your gift.
Settle with your opponent quickly while on the way
        to court.
Otherwise your opponent will hand you over to the judge,
    and the judge will hand you over to the guard,
    and you will be thrown into prison.
Amen, I say to you,
    you will not be released until you have paid the
        last penny.

"You have heard that it was said,
    You shall not commit adultery.
But I say to you,
    everyone who looks at a woman with lust
    has already committed adultery with her in his heart.
If your right eye causes you to sin,
    tear it out and throw it away.
It is better for you to lose one of your members
    than to have your whole body thrown into Gehenna.

And if your right hand causes you to sin,
  cut it off and throw it away.
It is better for you to lose one of your members
  than to have your whole body go into Gehenna.

"It was also said,
  Whoever divorces his wife must give her a bill of divorce.
But I say to you,
  whoever divorces his wife—unless the marriage
      is unlawful—
  causes her to commit adultery,
  and whoever marries a divorced woman commits adultery.

"Again you have heard that it was said to your ancestors,
  Do not take a false oath,
  but make good to the Lord all that you vow.
But I say to you, do not swear at all;
  not by heaven, for it is God's throne;
  nor by the earth, for it is his footstool;
  nor by Jerusalem, for it is the city of the great King.
Do not swear by your head,
  for you cannot make a single hair white or black.
Let your 'Yes' mean 'Yes,' and your 'No' mean 'No.'
  Anything more is from the Evil One.

"You have heard that it was said,
  An eye for an eye and a tooth for a tooth.
But I say to you, offer no resistance to one who is evil.
When someone strikes you on your right cheek,
  turn the other one as well.

If anyone wants to go to law with you over your tunic,
 hand over your cloak as well.
Should anyone press you into service for one mile,
 go for two miles.
Give to the one who asks of you,
 and do not turn your back on one who wants to borrow.

"You have heard that it was said,
 You shall love your neighbor and hate your enemy.
But I say to you, love your enemies
 and pray for those who persecute you,
 that you may be children of your heavenly Father,
 for he makes his sun rise on the bad and the good,
 and causes rain to fall on the just and the unjust.
For if you love those who love you, what recompense will
 you have?
Do not the tax collectors do the same?
And if you greet your brothers only,
 what is unusual about that?
Do not the pagans do the same?"

The Gospel of the Lord.

181.
✠ A reading from the holy Gospel
according to Matthew   9:1-8

Courage, child, your sins are forgiven.

After entering a boat, Jesus made the crossing, and came
 into his own town.

And there people brought to him a paralytic lying on
       a stretcher.
When Jesus saw their faith, he said to the paralytic,
   "Courage, child, your sins are forgiven."
At that, some of the scribes said to themselves,
   "This man is blaspheming."
Jesus knew what they were thinking, and said,
   "Why do you harbor evil thoughts?
Which is easier, to say, 'Your sins are forgiven,'
   or to say, 'Rise and walk'?
But that you may know that the Son of Man
   has authority on earth to forgive sins"—
   he then said to the paralytic,
   "Rise, pick up your stretcher, and go home."
He rose and went home.
   When the crowds saw this they were struck with awe
   and glorified God who had given such authority
      to men.

The Gospel of the Lord.

182.
✠ A reading from the holy Gospel
according to Matthew   **9:9-13**

I did not come to call the righteous but sinners.

As Jesus passed on from there,
   he saw a man named Matthew sitting at the
      customs post.

He said to him, "Follow me."
And he got up and followed him.
While he was at table in his house,
     many tax collectors and sinners came
     and sat with Jesus and his disciples.
The Pharisees saw this and said to his disciples,
     "Why does your teacher eat with tax collectors and
          sinners?"
He heard this and said,
     "Those who are well do not need a physician, but the
          sick do.
Go and learn the meaning of the words,
     I desire mercy, not sacrifice.
I did not come to call the righteous but sinners."

The Gospel of the Lord.

183.
✠ A reading from the holy Gospel
according to Matthew   18:15-20

You have won over your brother.

Jesus said to his disciples:
"If your brother sins against you,
     go and tell him his fault between you and him alone.
If he listens to you, you have won over your brother.
If he does not listen,
     take one or two others along with you,
     so that every fact may be established
     on the testimony of two or three witnesses.

If he refuses to listen to them, tell the Church.
If he refuses to listen even to the Church,
    then treat him as you would a Gentile or a tax collector.
Amen, I say to you,
    whatever you bind on earth shall be bound in heaven,
    and whatever you loose on earth shall be loosed
            in heaven.
Again, amen, I say to you, if two of you agree on earth
    about anything for which they are to pray,
    it shall be granted to them by my heavenly Father.
For where two or three are gathered together in my name,
    there am I in the midst of them."

The Gospel of the Lord.

184.
✠ A reading from the holy Gospel
according to Matthew   18:21-35

> *So will my heavenly Father do to you, unless*
> *each of you forgives your brother from your heart.*

Peter approached Jesus and asked him,
    "Lord, if my brother sins against me,
    how often must I forgive him?
As many as seven times?"
Jesus answered, "I say to you, not seven times but
            seventy-seven times.
That is why the Kingdom of heaven may be likened to
            a king
    who decided to settle accounts with his servants.

When he began the accounting,
    a debtor was brought before him who owed him a
        huge amount.
Since he had no way of paying it back,
    his master ordered him to be sold,
    along with his wife, his children, and all his property,
    in payment of the debt.
At that, the servant fell down, did him homage, and said,
    'Be patient with me, and I will pay you back in full.'
Moved with compassion the master of that servant
    let him go and forgave him the loan.
When that servant had left, he found one of his
        fellow servants
    who owed him a much smaller amount.
He seized him and started to choke him, demanding,
    'Pay back what you owe.'
Falling to his knees, his fellow servant begged him,
    'Be patient with me, and I will pay you back.'
But he refused.
Instead, he had him put in prison
    until he paid back the debt.
Now when his fellow servants saw what had happened,
    they were deeply disturbed, and went to their master
    and reported the whole affair.
His master summoned him and said to him, 'You
        wicked servant!
I forgave you your entire debt because you begged me to.
Should you not have had pity on your fellow servant,
    as I had pity on you?'

Then in anger his master handed him over to the torturers
    until he should pay back the whole debt.
So will my heavenly Father do to you,
    unless each of you forgives your brother from
         your heart."

The Gospel of the Lord.

185.

✠ A reading from the holy Gospel
according to Matthew   **25:31-46**

Whatever you did for one of these least brothers of mine, you did for me.

Jesus said to his disciples:
    "When the Son of Man comes in his glory,
    and all the angels with him,
    he will sit upon his glorious throne,
    and all the nations will be assembled before him.
And he will separate them one from another,
    as a shepherd separates the sheep from the goats.
He will place the sheep on his right and the goats on
        his left.
Then the king will say to those on his right,
    'Come, you who are blessed by my Father.
Inherit the kingdom prepared for you from the foundation
        of the world.
For I was hungry and you gave me food,
    I was thirsty and you gave me drink,
    a stranger and you welcomed me,

naked and you clothed me,
    ill and you cared for me,
    in prison and you visited me.'
Then the righteous will answer him and say,
    'Lord, when did we see you hungry and feed you,
    or thirsty and give you drink?
When did we see you a stranger and welcome you,
    or naked and clothe you?
When did we see you ill or in prison, and visit you?'
And the king will say to them in reply,
    'Amen, I say to you, whatever you did
    for one of these least brothers of mine, you did for me.'
Then he will say to those on his left,
    'Depart from me, you accursed,
    into the eternal fire prepared for the Devil and his angels.
For I was hungry and you gave me no food,
    I was thirsty and you gave me no drink,
    a stranger and you gave me no welcome,
    naked and you gave me no clothing,
    ill and in prison, and you did not care for me.'
Then they will answer and say,
    'Lord, when did we see you hungry or thirsty
    or a stranger or naked or ill or in prison,
    and not minister to your needs?'
He will answer them, 'Amen, I say to you,
    what you did not do for one of these least ones,
    you did not do for me.'

And these will go off to eternal punishment,
   but the righteous to eternal life."

The Gospel of the Lord.

186.
✠ A reading from the holy Gospel
according to Matthew   26:69-75

He went out and began to weep bitterly.

Now Peter was sitting outside in the courtyard.
One of the maids came over to him and said,
   "You too were with Jesus the Galilean."
But he denied it in front of everyone, saying,
   "I do not know what you are talking about!"
As he went out to the gate, another girl saw him
   and said to those who were there,
   "This man was with Jesus the Nazorean."
Again he denied it with an oath,
   "I do not know the man!"
A little later the bystanders came over and said to Peter,
   "Surely you too are one of them;
   even your speech gives you away."
At that he began to curse and to swear,
   "I do not know the man."
And immediately a cock crowed.

Then Peter remembered the word that Jesus had spoken:
   "Before the cock crows you will deny me three times."
   He went out and began to weep bitterly.

The Gospel of the Lord.

187.
✠ A reading from the holy Gospel according to Mark **12:28-34**

The first of all the commandments.

One of the scribes came to Jesus and asked him,
   "Which is the first of all the commandments?"
Jesus replied, "The first is this:
   Hear, O Israel!
   The Lord our God is Lord alone!
You shall love the Lord your God with all your heart,
   with all your soul,
   with all your mind,
   and with all your strength.
The second is this:
   You shall love your neighbor as yourself.
There is no other commandment greater than these."
The scribe said to him, "Well said, teacher.
You are right in saying,
   He is One and there is no other than he.
And *to love him with all your heart,*
   with all your understanding,
   with all your strength,
   and to love your neighbor as yourself
   is worth more than all burnt offerings and sacrifices."

And when Jesus saw that he answered with understanding,
  he said to him,
  "You are not far from the Kingdom of God."
  And no one dared to ask him any more questions.

The Gospel of the Lord.

188.
✠ A reading from the holy Gospel according to Luke   7:36-50

But the one to whom little is forgiven, loves little.

A certain Pharisee invited Jesus to dine with him,
  and he entered the Pharisee's house and reclined
      at table.
Now there was a sinful woman in the city
  who learned that he was at table in the house of
      the Pharisee.
Bringing an alabaster flask of ointment,
  she stood behind him at his feet weeping
  and began to bathe his feet with her tears.
Then she wiped them with her hair,
  kissed them, and anointed them with the ointment.
When the Pharisee who had invited him saw this he said
      to himself,
  "If this man were a prophet,
  he would know who and what sort of woman this is
      who is touching him,
  that she is a sinner."
Jesus said to him in reply,
  "Simon, I have something to say to you."

"Tell me, teacher," he said.
"Two people were in debt to a certain creditor;
    one owed five hundred days' wages and the other
        owed fifty.
Since they were unable to repay the debt, he forgave it
        for both.
Which of them will love him more?"
Simon said in reply,
    "The one, I suppose, whose larger debt was forgiven."
He said to him, "You have judged rightly."
Then he turned to the woman and said to Simon,
    "Do you see this woman?
When I entered your house, you did not give me water for
        my feet,
    but she has bathed them with her tears
    and wiped them with her hair.
You did not give me a kiss,
    but she has not ceased kissing my feet since the time
        I entered.
You did not anoint my head with oil,
    but she anointed my feet with ointment.
So I tell you, her many sins have been forgiven;
    hence, she has shown great love.
But the one to whom little is forgiven, loves little."
He said to her, "Your sins are forgiven."
The others at table said to themselves,
    "Who is this who even forgives sins?"

But he said to the woman,
   "Your faith has saved you; go in peace."

The Gospel of the Lord.

189.

✠ A reading from the holy Gospel according to Luke   **13:1-5**

If you do not repent, you will all perish as they did!

Some people told Jesus about the Galileans
   whose blood Pilate had mingled with the blood of
         their sacrifices.
He said to them in reply,
   "Do you think that because these Galileans suffered in
         this way
   they were greater sinners than all other Galileans?
By no means!
But I tell you, if you do not repent,
   you will all perish as they did!
Or those eighteen people who were killed
   when the tower at Siloam fell on them—
   do you think they were more guilty
   than everyone else who lived in Jerusalem?
By no means!
But I tell you, if you do not repent,
   you will all perish as they did!"

The Gospel of the Lord.

190.

✠ A reading from the holy Gospel according to Luke **15:1-10**

There will be more joy in heaven over one sinner who repents.

The tax collectors and sinners were all drawing near to
        listen to Jesus,
    but the Pharisees and scribes began to complain, saying,
    "This man welcomes sinners and eats with them."
So Jesus addressed this parable to them.
"What man among you having a hundred sheep and
        losing one of them
    would not leave the ninety-nine in the desert
    and go after the lost one until he finds it?
And when he does find it,
    he sets it on his shoulders with great joy
    and, upon his arrival home,
    he calls together his friends and neighbors and says
        to them,
    'Rejoice with me because I have found my lost sheep.'
I tell you, in just the same way
    there will be more joy in heaven over one sinner
        who repents
    than over ninety-nine righteous people
    who have no need of repentance.

"Or what woman having ten coins and losing one
    would not light a lamp and sweep the house,
    searching carefully until she finds it?

And when she does find it,
   she calls together her friends and neighbors
   and says to them,
     'Rejoice with me because I have found the coin that
         I lost.'
In just the same way, I tell you,
   there will be rejoicing among the angels of God
   over one sinner who repents."

The Gospel of the Lord.

191.
✠ A reading from the holy Gospel
according to Luke   **15:1-3, 11-32**

While he was still a long way off, his father
caught sight of him, and was filled with compassion.

Jesus addressed this parable to them.
"A man had two sons, and the younger son said to
        his father,
   'Father, give me the share of your estate that should
        come to me.'
So the father divided the property between them.
After a few days, the younger son collected all his belongings
   and set off to a distant country
   where he squandered his inheritance on a life
        of dissipation.
When he had freely spent everything,
   a severe famine struck that country,
   and he found himself in dire need.

So he hired himself out to one of the local citizens
    who sent him to his farm to tend the swine.
And he longed to eat his fill of the pods on which the
        swine fed,
    but nobody gave him any.
Coming to his senses he thought,
    'How many of my father's hired workers
    have more than enough food to eat,
    but here am I, dying from hunger.
I shall get up and go to my father and I shall say to him,
    "Father, I have sinned against heaven and against you.
I no longer deserve to be called your son;
    treat me as you would treat one of your hired workers."'
So he got up and went back to his father.
While he was still a long way off,
    his father caught sight of him, and was filled
        with compassion.
He ran to his son, embraced him and kissed him.
His son said to him,
    'Father, I have sinned against heaven and against you;
    I no longer deserve to be called your son.'
But his father ordered his servants,
    'Quickly, bring the finest robe and put it on him;
    put a ring on his finger and sandals on his feet.
Take the fattened calf and slaughter it.
Then let us celebrate with a feast,
    because this son of mine was dead, and has come to
        life again;
    he was lost, and has been found.'

Then the celebration began.
Now the older son had been out in the field
    and, on his way back, as he neared the house,
    he heard the sound of music and dancing.
He called one of the servants and asked what this might mean.
The servant said to him,
    'Your brother has returned
    and your father has slaughtered the fattened calf
    because he has him back safe and sound.'
He became angry,
    and when he refused to enter the house,
    his father came out and pleaded with him.
He said to his father in reply,
    'Look, all these years I served you
and not once did I disobey your orders;
    yet you never gave me even a young goat to feast on
            with my friends.
But when your son returns
    who swallowed up your property with prostitutes,
    for him you slaughter the fattened calf.'
He said to him,
    'My son, you are here with me always;
    everything I have is yours.
But now we must celebrate and rejoice,
    because your brother was dead and has come to life again;
    he was lost and has been found.'"

The Gospel of the Lord.

192.

✠ A reading from the holy Gospel according to Luke   **17:1-4**

If your brother wrongs you seven times in one day
and returns to you seven times saying, "I am sorry,"
you should forgive him.

Jesus said to his disciples,
　"Things that cause sin will inevitably occur,
　but woe to the one through whom they occur.
It would be better for him if a millstone were put around
　　　his neck
　and he be thrown into the sea
　than for him to cause one of these little ones to sin.
Be on your guard!
If your brother sins, rebuke him;
　and if he repents, forgive him.
And if he wrongs you seven times in one day
　and returns to you seven times saying, 'I am sorry,'
　you should forgive him."

The Gospel of the Lord.

193.

✠ A reading from the holy Gospel according to Luke **18:9-14**

O God, be merciful to me a sinner.

Jesus addressed this parable
　to those who were convinced of their own righteousness
　and despised everyone else.

"Two people went up to the temple area to pray;
    one was a Pharisee and the other was a tax collector.
The Pharisee took up his position and spoke this prayer to
        himself,
    'O God, I thank you that I am not like the rest
        of humanity—
    greedy, dishonest, adulterous—or even like this
        tax collector.
I fast twice a week,
    and I pay tithes on my whole income.'
But the tax collector stood off at a distance
    and would not even raise his eyes to heaven
    but beat his breast and prayed,
    'O God, be merciful to me, a sinner.'
I tell you, the latter went home justified, not the former;
    for everyone who exalts himself will be humbled,
    and the one who humbles himself will be exalted."

The Gospel of the Lord.

194.

✠ A reading from the holy Gospel according to Luke   **19:1-10**

The Son of Man has come to seek and to save what was lost.

At that time Jesus came to Jericho and intended to pass
        through the town.
Now a man there named Zacchaeus,
    who was a chief tax collector and also a wealthy man,
    was seeking to see who Jesus was;

but he could not see him because of the crowd,
for he was short in stature.
So he ran ahead and climbed a sycamore tree in order to
see Jesus,
who was about to pass that way.
When he reached the place, Jesus looked up and said,
"Zacchaeus, come down quickly,
for today I must stay at your house."
And he came down quickly and received him with joy.
When they saw this, they began to grumble, saying,
"He has gone to stay at the house of a sinner."
But Zacchaeus stood there and said to the Lord,
"Behold, half of my possessions, Lord, I shall give to
the poor,
and if I have extorted anything from anyone
I shall repay it four times over."
And Jesus said to him,
"Today salvation has come to this house
because this man too is a descendant of Abraham.
For the Son of Man has come to seek
and to save what was lost."

The Gospel of the Lord.

195.

✠ A reading from the holy Gospel according to Luke **23:39-43**

Today you will be with me in Paradise.

One of the criminals hanging in crucifixion
    reviled Jesus, saying,
    "Are you not the Christ?
    Save yourself and us."
The other man however, rebuking him, said in reply,
    "Have you no fear of God,
    for you are subject to the same condemnation?
And indeed, we have been condemned justly,
    for the sentence we received corresponds to our crimes,
    but he has done nothing criminal."
Then he said,
    "Jesus, remember me when you come into your
        Kingdom."
He replied to him,
    "Amen, I say to you,
    today you will be with me in Paradise."

The Gospel of the Lord.

196.

✠ A reading from the holy Gospel according to John   8:1-11

Go, and from now on do not sin any more.

Jesus went to the Mount of Olives.
But early in the morning he arrived again in the
        temple area,
  and all the people started coming to him,
  and he sat down and taught them.
Then the scribes and the Pharisees brought a woman
  who had been caught in adultery
  and made her stand in the middle.
They said to him,
  "Teacher, this woman was caught
  in the very act of committing adultery.
Now in the law, Moses commanded us to stone such women.
So what do you say?"
They said this to test him,
  so that they could have some charge to bring against him.
Jesus bent down and began to write on the ground with
        his finger.
But when they continued asking him,
  he straightened up and said to them,
  "Let the one among you who is without sin
  be the first to throw a stone at her."
Again he bent down and wrote on the ground.
And in response, they went away one by one,
  beginning with the elders.
So he was left alone with the woman before him.

Then Jesus straightened up and said to her,
    "Woman, where are they?
Has no one condemned you?"
She replied, "No one, sir."
Then Jesus said, "Neither do I condemn you.
Go, and from now on do not sin any more."

The Gospel of the Lord.

197.
✠ A reading from the holy Gospel according to John **8:31-36**

> *Everyone who commits sin is a slave of sin.*

Jesus said to those Jews who believed in him,
    "If you remain in my word, you will truly be
        my disciples,
    and you will know the truth, and the truth will set
        you free."
They answered him, "We are descendants of Abraham
    and have never been enslaved to anyone.
How can you say, 'You will become free'?"
Jesus answered them, "Amen, amen, I say to you,
    everyone who commits sin is a slave of sin.
A slave does not remain in a household forever,
    but a son always remains.
So if the Son frees you, then you will truly be free."

The Gospel of the Lord.

198.

✠ A reading from the holy Gospel according to John   15:1-8

He takes away every branch in me that does not bear fruit,
and everyone that does he prunes so that it bears more fruit.

Jesus said to his disciples:
"I am the true vine, and my Father is the vine grower.
He takes away every branch in me that does not bear fruit,
    and everyone that does he prunes so that it bears
            more fruit.
You are already pruned because of the word that I spoke
            to you.
Remain in me, as I remain in you.
Just as a branch cannot bear fruit on its own
    unless it remains on the vine,
    so neither can you unless you remain in me.
I am the vine, you are the branches.
Whoever remains in me and I in him will bear much fruit,
    because without me you can do nothing.
Anyone who does not remain in me
    will be thrown out like a branch and wither;
    people will gather them and throw them into a fire
    and they will be burned.
If you remain in me and my words remain in you,
    ask for whatever you want and it will be done for you.
By this is my Father glorified,
    that you bear much fruit and become my disciples."

The Gospel of the Lord.

199.

✠ A reading from the holy Gospel according to John **15:9-14**

You are my friends if you do what I command you.

Jesus said to his disciples:
"As the Father loves me, so I also love you.
Remain in my love.
If you keep my commandments, you will remain in
      my love,
  just as I have kept my Father's commandments
  and remain in his love.

"I have told you this so that my joy might be in you
  and your joy might be complete.
This is my commandment: love one another as I love you.
No one has greater love than this,
  to lay down one's life for one's friends.
You are my friends if you do what I command you."

The Gospel of the Lord.

200.

✠ A reading from the holy Gospel according to John **19:13-37**

They will look upon him whom they have pierced.

When Pilate heard these words he brought Jesus out
  and seated him on the judge's bench
  in the place called Stone Pavement, in Hebrew,
      Gabbatha.

It was preparation day for Passover, and it was about noon.
And he said to the Jews,
    "Behold, your king!"
They cried out,
    "Take him away, take him away! Crucify him!"
Pilate said to them,
    "Shall I crucify your king?"
The chief priests answered,
    "We have no king but Caesar."
Then he handed him over to them to be crucified.

So they took Jesus, and, carrying the cross himself,
        he went out to what is called the Place of the Skull,
        in Hebrew, Golgotha.
There they crucified him, and with him two others,
        one on either side, with Jesus in the middle.
Pilate also had an inscription written and put on the cross.
It read,
    "Jesus the Nazorean, the King of the Jews."
Now many of the Jews read this inscription,
        because the place where Jesus was crucified was near
            the city;
        and it was written in Hebrew, Latin, and Greek.
So the chief priests of the Jews said to Pilate,
    "Do not write 'The King of the Jews,'
    but that he said, 'I am the King of the Jews.'"
Pilate answered,
    "What I have written, I have written."

When the soldiers had crucified Jesus,
    they took his clothes and divided them into four shares,
    a share for each soldier.
They also took his tunic, but the tunic was seamless,
    woven in one piece from the top down.
So they said to one another,
    "Let's not tear it, but cast lots for it to see whose it
        will be,"
    in order that the passage of Scripture might be fulfilled
        that says:
        They divided my garments among them,
            and for my vesture they cast lots.
This is what the soldiers did.
Standing by the cross of Jesus were his mother
    and his mother's sister, Mary the wife of Clopas,
    and Mary Magdalene.
When Jesus saw his mother and the disciple there whom
        he loved
    he said to his mother, "Woman, behold, your son."
Then he said to the disciple,
    "Behold, your mother."
And from that hour the disciple took her into his home.

After this, aware that everything was now finished,
    in order that the Scripture might be fulfilled,
    Jesus said, "I thirst."
There was a vessel filled with common wine.
So they put a sponge soaked in wine on a sprig of hyssop
    and put it up to his mouth.

When Jesus had taken the wine, he said,
    "It is finished."
And bowing his head, he handed over the spirit.

Now since it was preparation day,
    in order that the bodies might not remain on the cross
        on the sabbath,
    for the sabbath day of that week was a solemn one,
    the Jews asked Pilate that their legs be broken
    and that they be taken down.
So the soldiers came and broke the legs of the first
    and then of the other one who was crucified with Jesus.
But when they came to Jesus and saw that he was
        already dead,
    they did not break his legs,
    but one soldier thrust his lance into his side,
    and immediately Blood and water flowed out.
An eyewitness has testified, and his testimony is true;
    he knows that he is speaking the truth,
    so that you also may come to believe.
For this happened so that the Scripture passage might
        be fulfilled:
    Not a bone of it will be broken.
And again another passage says:
    They will look upon him whom they have pierced.

The Gospel of the Lord.

201.

✠ A reading from the holy Gospel according to John **20:19-23**

Receive the Holy Spirit. Whose sins you forgive are forgiven them.

On the evening of that first day of the week,
    when the doors were locked, where the disciples were,
    for fear of the Jews,
    Jesus came and stood in their midst
    and said to them, "Peace be with you."
When he had said this, he showed them his hands and
        his side.
The disciples rejoiced when they saw the Lord.
Jesus said to them again, "Peace be with you.
As the Father has sent me, so I send you."
And when he had said this, he breathed on them and said
        to them,
    "Receive the Holy Spirit.
Whose sins you forgive are forgiven them,
    and whose sins you retain are retained."

The Gospel of the Lord.

INVITATION OF THE MINISTER FOR THE GENERAL CONFESSION OF SINS

202. If the prayer is directed to the Father:

I

Dear friends in Christ, our merciful Father does not desire the death of the sinner but rather that he should turn back to him and have life. Let us pray that we who are sorry for our past sins may fear no future evil and sin no more.

℟. Spare us, Lord; spare your people.

2

God who is infintely merciful pardons all who are repentant and takes away their guilt. Confident in his goodness, let us ask him to forgive all our sins as we confess them with sincerity of heart.

℟. Lord, hear our prayer.

3

God gave us his Son for our sins and raised him up to make us holy. Let us humbly pray to the Father.

℟. Lord, have mercy on your people.

4

God our Father waits for the return of those who are lost and welcomes them back as his children. Let us pray that we may turn back to him and be received with kindness into his house.

℟. Lord, do not hold our sins against us.

Or:

Father, we have sinned in your sight; we are unworthy to
      be called your children.

5

Our God seeks out what is lost, leads home the abandoned, binds up what is broken and gives strength to the weak; let us ask him to help us.

℟. Lord, heal our weakness.

203. If the prayer is directed to Christ:

I

Jesus Christ is the victor over sin and death: in his mercy may he pardon our offenses against God and reconcile us with the Church we have wounded by our sins.

℟. Lord Jesus, be our salvation.

2

In his great love Christ willingly suffered and died for our sins and for the sins of all mankind. Let us come before him with faith and hope to pray for the salvation of the world.

℟. Christ, graciously hear us.

3

Let us pray with confidence to Christ, the Good Shepherd, who seeks out the lost sheep and carries it back with joy.

℟. Lord, seek us out and bring us home.

4

Christ our Lord bore our sins upon the cross and by his suffering has brought us healing, so that we live for God and are dead to sin. Let us pray with humility and trust.

℟. Lord, to whom shall we go? You have the words of eternal life. We have come to believe and to know that you are the Christ, the Son of God.

Or:

Have pity on us, and help us.

5

Christ our Lord was given up to death for our sins and rose again for our justification. Let us pray to him with confidence in his goodness.

R̷. You are our Savior.

Or:

Jesus Christ, Son of the living God, have pity on us.

PENITENTIAL INTERCESSIONS

(At least one of the intercessions should always be a petition for a true conversion of heart.)

204. If the prayer is addressed to the Father:

I

—By human weakness we have disfigured the holiness of the Church: pardon all our sins and restore us to full communion with our brethren.

R̷. Lord, hear our prayer. Or: Lord, hear us.

Or another suitable response may be used.

—Your mercy is our hope: welcome us to the sacrament of reconciliation. R̷.

—Give us the will to change our lives, and the lives of others, by charity, good example and prayer. ℞.

—As we make our confession, rescue us from slavery to sin and lead us to the freedom enjoyed by your children. ℞.

—Make us a living sign of your love for all to see: people reconciled with you and with each other. ℞.

—Through the sacrament of reconciliation may we grow in your peace and seek to spread it throughout the world. ℞.

—In this sign of your love you forgive us our sins: may it teach us to love others and to forgive their sins against us. ℞.

—In your mercy clothe us in the wedding garment of grace and welcome us to your table. ℞.

—Forgive us our sins, lead us in the ways of goodness and love, and bring us to the reward of everlasting peace. ℞.

—Give light to our darkness and lead us by your truth. ℞.

—In justice you punish us: in your mercy set us free for the glory of your name. ℞.

—May your power keep safe from all danger those whom your love sets free from the chains of sin. ℞.

—Look on our weakness: do not be angry and condemn, but in your love cleanse, guide and save us. ℟.

—In your mercy free us from the past and enable us to begin a new life of holiness. ℟.

—When we stray from you, guide us back into the way of holiness, love and peace. ℟.

—By your redeeming love overcome our sinfulness and the harm it has brought us. ℟.

—Blot out the sins of the past and fit us for the life that is to come. ℟.

2

The following intercessions may be used with a variable response or with an invariable response as in the *Liturgy of the Hours*.

In your goodness, forgive our sins against the unity of
         your family,
—make us one in heart, one in spirit.

We have sinned, Lord, we have sinned,
—take away our sins by your saving grace.

Give us pardon for our sins,
—and reconciliation with your Church.

Touch our hearts and change our lives, make us grow
       always in your friendship,
—help us to make up for our sins against your wisdom
       and goodness.

Cleanse and renew your Church, Lord,
—may it grow in strength as a witness to you.

Touch the hearts of those who have abandoned you
       through sin and scandal,
—call them back to you and keep them faithful in your love.

May we show forth in our lives the sufferings of your Son,
—you raised us up to life when you raised him from
       the dead.

Have mercy on us, Lord, as we praise and thank you,
—with your pardon give us also your peace.

Lord, our sins are many, but we trust in your mercy,
—call us, and we shall turn to you.

Receive us as we come before you with humble and
       contrite hearts,
—those who trust in you shall never trust in vain.

We have turned away from you and fallen into sin,
—we have followed evil ways and rejected your
       commandments.

Turn to us, Lord, and show us your mercy; blot out our sins,
—cast them into the depths of the sea.

Restore us, Lord, to your favor, and give us joy in
      your presence,
—may our glory be to serve you with all our hearts.

205. If the prayer is addressed to Christ:

I

Rom 5:10
—By your death you reconciled us with the Father and
      brought us salvation.
R/. Lord, have mercy. Or: Christ, hear us.

Or another suitable response may be used.

Rom 8:34
—You died and rose again, and sit at the right hand of the
      Father, to make intercession for us. R/.

1 Cor 1:30
—You came from God as our wisdom and justice, our
      sanctification and redemption. R/.

1 Cor 6:11
—You washed mankind in the Spirit of our God; you made
      us holy and righteous. R/.

1 Cor 8:12
—You warned us that if we sin against each other we sin
      against you. R/.

2 Cor 8:9

—Though you were rich you became poor for our sake, so
that by your poverty we might become rich. R∕.

Gal 1:4

—You gave yourself up for our sins to save us from this
evil world. R∕.

1 Thes 1:10

—You rose from the dead to save us from the anger that
was to come. R∕.

1 Tm 1:15

—You came into the world to save sinners. R∕.

1 Tm 2:6

—You gave yourself up to bring redemption to all. R∕.

2 Tm 1:10

—You destroyed death and gave light to life. R∕.

2 Tm 4:1

—You will come to judge the living and the dead. R∕.

Ti 2:14

—You gave yourself up for us to redeem us from all sin
and to prepare for yourself a holy people, marked
as your own, devoted to good works. R∕.

Heb 2:17

—You showed us your mercy, and as a faithful high priest
in the things of God you made atonement for the
sins of the people. R∕.

Heb 5:9

—You became the source of salvation for all who obey you. ℟.

Heb 9:15

—Through the Holy Spirit you offered yourself to God as a spotless victim, cleansing our consciences from lifeless works. ℟.

Heb 9:28

—You were offered in sacrifice to undo the sins of the many. ℟.

1 Pt 3:18

—Once and for all you died for our sins, the innocent one for the guilty. ℟.

1 Jn 2:2

—You are the atonement for our sins and for the sins of the world. ℟.

Jn 3:16, 35

—You died that those who believe in you may not perish but have eternal life. ℟.

Mt 18:11

—You came into the world to seek and save what was lost. ℟.

Jn 3:17

—You were sent by the Father, not to judge the world but to save it. ℟.

Mk 2:10

—You have power on earth to forgive sins. ℟.

Mt 11:28

—You invite all who labor and are burdened to come to
  you to be refreshed. ℟.

Mt 16:19, 18:18

—You gave your apostles the keys to the kingdom of
  heaven, the power to bind and to loose. ℟.

Mt 22:38-40

—You told us that the whole law depends on love of God
  and of our neighbor. ℟.

Jn 10:10

—Jesus, life of all mankind, you came into the world to
  give us life, life in its fullness. ℟.

Jn 10:11

—Jesus, Good Shepherd, you gave your life for your
  sheep. ℟.

Jn 14:6; 8:32, 36

—Jesus, eternal truth, you give us true freedom. ℟.

Jn 14:6

—Jesus, you are the way to the Father. ℟.

Jn 11:25

—Jesus, you are the resurrection and life; those who
  believe in you, even if they are dead, will live. ℟.

Jn 15:1-2

—Jesus, true vine, the Father prunes your branches to
  make them bear even greater fruit. ℟.

2

The following intercessions may be used with a variable response or with an invariable response as in the *Liturgy of the Hours*.

Healer of the body and soul, bind up the wounds of
      our hearts,
—that our lives may grow strong through grace.

Help us to strip ourselves of sin,
—and put on the new life of grace.

Redeemer of the world, give us the spirit of penance and a
      deeper devotion to your passion,
—so that we may have a fuller share in your risen glory.

May your Mother, the refuge of sinners, intercede for us,
—and ask you in your goodness to pardon our sins.

You forgave the woman who repented,
—show us also your mercy.

You brought back the lost sheep on your shoulders,
—pity us and lead us home.

You promised paradise to the good thief,
—take us with you into your Kingdom.

You died for us and rose again,
—make us share in your death and resurrection.

PROCLAMATION OF PRAISE

206.

I

Ps 32:1-2, 3-4, 5, 6, 7, 10-11

℟. Let the just exult and rejoice in the Lord.

Blessed is he whose fault is taken away,
    whose sin is covered.
Blessed the man to whom the LORD imputes not guilt,
    in whose spirit there is no guile.

℟. Let the just exult and rejoice in the Lord.

As long as I would not speak, my bones wasted away
    with my groaning all the day,
For day and night your hand was heavy upon me;
    my strength was dried up as by the heat of summer.

℟. Let the just exult and rejoice in the Lord.

Then I acknowledged my sin to you,
    my guilt I covered not.
I said, "I confess my faults to the LORD,"
    and you took away the guilt of my sin.

℟. Let the just exult and rejoice in the Lord.

For this shall every faithful man pray to you
    in time of stress.
Though deep waters overflow,
    they shall not reach him.

R̸. Let the just exult and rejoice in the Lord.

You are my shelter; from distress you will preserve me;
    with glad cries of freedom you will ring me round.

R̸. Let the just exult and rejoice in the Lord.

Many are the sorrows of the wicked,
    but mercy surrounds him who trusts in the LORD.
Be glad in the LORD and rejoice, you just;
    exult all you upright of heart.

R̸. Let the just exult and rejoice in the Lord.

2

Ps 98:1, 2-3a, 3b-4, 5-6, 7-8, 9

R̸. The Lord has remembered his mercy.

Sing to the LORD a new song,
    for he has done wondrous deeds;
His right hand has won victory for him,
    his holy arm.

℟. The Lord has remembered his mercy.

The LORD has made his salvation known:
  in the sight of the nations he has revealed his justice.
He has remembered his mercy and his faithfulness
  toward the house of Israel.

℟. The Lord has remembered his mercy.

All the ends of the earth have seen
  the salvation by our God.
Sing joyfully to the LORD, all you lands;
  break into song; sing praise.

℟. The Lord has remembered his mercy.

Sing praise to the LORD with the harp,
  with the harp and melodious song.
With trumpets and the sound of the horn
  sing joyfully before the King, the LORD.

℟. The Lord has remembered his mercy.

Let the sea and what fills it resound,
  the world and those who dwell in it;
Let the rivers clap their hands.
  the mountains shout with them for joy.

℟. The Lord has remembered his mercy.

Before the Lord, for he comes,
   for he comes to rule the earth;
He will rule the world with justice
   and the peoples with equity.

R̠. The Lord has remembered his mercy.

3

Ps 100:1b-2, 3, 4, 5

R̠. The Lord is loving and kind: his mercy is for ever.

Sing joyfully to the Lord, all you lands;
   serve the Lord with gladness;
   come before him with joyful song.

R̠. The Lord is loving and kind: his mercy is for ever.

Know that the Lord is God;
   he made us, his we are;
   his people, the flock he tends.

R̠. The Lord is loving and kind: his mercy is for ever.

Enter his gates with thanksgiving,
   his courts with praise;
   Give thanks to him; bless his name.

R̠. The Lord is loving and kind: his mercy is for ever.

The LORD is good:
the LORD, whose kindness endures forever,
and his faithfulness, to all generations.

R̶/. The Lord is loving and kind: his mercy is for ever.

4

Ps 119:1, 10-11, 12-13, 15-16,
18 and 33, 105, 169-170, 174-175

R̶/. Blessed are you, Lord; teach me your decrees.

Blessed are they whose way is blameless.
who walk in the law of the LORD.

R̶/. Blessed are you, Lord; teach me your decrees.

With all my heart I seek you;
let me not stray from your commands.
Within my heart I treasure your promise,
that I may not sin against you.

R̶/. Blessed are you, Lord; teach me your decrees.

Blessed are you, O LORD;
teach me your statutes.
With my lips I declare
all the ordinances of your mouth.

R̶/. Blessed are you, Lord; teach me your decrees.

I will meditate on your precepts
    and consider your ways.
In your statutes I will delight;
    I will not forget your words.

R̽. Blessed are you, Lord; teach me your decrees.

Open my eyes, that I may consider
    the wonders of your law.
Instruct me, O Lord, in the way of your statutes,
    that I may exactly observe them.

R̽. Blessed are you, Lord; teach me your decrees.

A lamp to my feet is your word,
    a light to my path.

R̽. Blessed are you, Lord; teach me your decrees.

Let my cry come before you, O Lord;
    in keeping with your word, give me discernment.
Let my supplication reach you;
    rescue me according to your promise.

R̽. Blessed are you, Lord; teach me your decrees.

I long for your salvation, O Lord,
    and your law is my delight.
Let my soul live to praise you,
    and may your ordinances help me.

R̽. Blessed are you, Lord; teach me your decrees.

5

Ps 103:1-2, 3-4, 8-9, 10-11,
12-13, 14-15, 16-18

℟. The Lord's kindness is everlasting to those who fear him.

Bless the LORD, O my soul;
    and all my being, bless his holy name.
Bless the LORD, O my soul,
    and forget not all his benefits.

℟. The Lord's kindness is everlasting to those who fear him.

He pardons all your iniquities,
    he heals all your ills.
He redeems your life from destruction,
    he crowns you with kindness and compassion.

℟. The Lord's kindness is everlasting to those who fear him.

Merciful and gracious is the LORD,
    slow to anger and abounding in kindness.
He will not always chide,
    nor does he keep his wrath forever.

℟. The Lord's kindness is everlasting to those who fear him.

Not according to our sins does he deal with us,
    nor does he requite us according to our crimes.
For as the heavens are high above the earth,
    so surpassing is his mercy toward those who fear him.

R̷. The Lord's kindness is everlasting to those who fear him.

As a father has compassion on his children,
    so the LORD has compassion on those who fear him.
For he knows how we are formed;
    he remembers that we are dust.

R̷. The Lord's kindness is everlasting to those who fear him.

Man's days are like those of grass;
    like a flower of the field he blooms.
The wind sweeps over him and he is gone,
    and his place knows him no more.

R̷. The Lord's kindness is everlasting to those who fear him.

But the mercy of the LORD is from eternity
    to eternity toward those who fear him.
And his justice toward children's children
    among those who keep his covenant
    and remember to fulfill his precepts.

R̷. The Lord's kindness is everlasting to those who fear him.

6

Ps 145:1-2, 3-4, 5-7, 8-9,
10-11, 12-13a, 13b-14,
15-16, 17-18, 19-20, 21

℟. Day after day I will bless you, Lord; I will praise your
    name for ever.

I will extol you, O my God and King,
    and I will bless your name forever and ever.
Every day will I bless you,
    and I will praise your name forever and ever.

℟. Day after day I will bless you, Lord; I will praise your
    name for ever.

Great is the LORD and highly to be praised;
    his greatness is unsearchable.
Generation after generation praises your works
    and proclaims your might.

℟. Day after day I will bless you, Lord; I will praise your
    name for ever.

They speak of the splendor of your majesty
    and tell of your wondrous works.
They discourse of the power of your terrible deeds
    and declare your greatness.
They publish the fame of your abundant goodness
    and joyfully sing of your justice.

℟. Day after day I will bless you, Lord; I will praise your
      name for ever.

The LORD is gracious and merciful,
    slow to anger and of great mercy.
The LORD is good to all
    and compassionate toward all his works.

℟. Day after day I will bless you, Lord; I will praise your
      name for ever.

Let all your works give you thanks, O LORD,
    and let your faithful ones bless you.
Let them discourse of the glory of your Kingdom
    and speak of your might.

℟. Day after day I will bless you, Lord; I will praise your
      name for ever.

Making known to men your might
    and the glorious splendor of your Kingdom.
Your Kingdom is a Kingdom for all ages,
    and your dominion endures through all generations.

℟. Day after day I will bless you, Lord; I will praise your
      name for ever.

The LORD is faithful in all his words
    and holy in all his works.
The LORD lifts up all who are falling
    and raises up all who are bowed down.

℞. Day after day I will bless you, Lord; I will praise your
    name for ever.

The eyes of all look hopefully to you,
    and you give them food in due season;
You open your hand
    and satisfy the desire of every living thing.

℞. Day after day I will bless you, Lord; I will praise your
    name for ever.

The Lord is just in all his ways
    and holy in all his works.
The Lord is near to all who call upon him
    to all who call upon him in truth.

℞. Day after day I will bless you, Lord; I will praise your
    name for ever.

He fulfills the desire of those who fear him,
    he hears their cry and saves them.
The Lord keeps all who love him,
    but all the wicked he will destroy.

℞. Day after day I will bless you, Lord; I will praise your
    name for ever.

May my mouth speak the praise of the LORD,
   and may all flesh bless his holy name
   forever and ever.

℟. Day after day I will bless you, Lord; I will praise your
      name for ever.

7

Ps 146:1b-2, 3-4, 5-6b,
6c-7a, 7b-8, 9-10

℟. I will sing to my God all the days of my life.

Praise the Lord, O my soul;
   I will praise the LORD all my life;
   I will sing praise to my God while I live.

℟. I will sing to my God all the days of my life.

Put not your trust in princes,
   in man, in whom there is no salvation.
When his spirit departs, he returns to the earth;
   on that day his plans perish.

℟. I will sing to my God all the days of my life.

Blessed he whose help is the God of Jacob,
   whose hope is in the LORD, his God.
Who made heaven and earth,
   the sea and all that is in them.

℟. I will sing to my God all the days of my life.

The LORD keeps faith forever,
    secures justice for the oppressed,
    gives food to the hungry.

℟. I will sing to my God all the days of my life.

The LORD sets captives free;
    the LORD gives sight to the blind.
The LORD raises up those that were bowed down;
    the LORD loves the just.

℟. I will sing to my God all the days of my life.

The LORD protects strangers;
    the fatherless and the widow he sustains,
    but the way of the wicked he thwarts.
The LORD shall reign forever;
    your God, O Zion, through all generations. Alleluia.

℟. I will sing to my God all the days of my life.

8

Is 12:2-3, 4, 5-6

℟. Praise the Lord and call upon his name.

God indeed is my savior;
    I am confident and unafraid.
My strength and my courage is the LORD,
    and he has been my savior.

With joy you will draw water
at the fountain of salvation.

R̶. Praise the Lord and call upon his name.

Give thanks to the LORD, acclaim his name;
among the nations make known his deeds,
proclaim how exalted is his name.

R̶. Praise the Lord and call upon his name.

Sing praise to the LORD for his glorious achievement;
let this be known throughout all the earth.
Shout with exultation, O city of Zion,
for great in your midst
is the Holy One of Israel!

R̶. Praise the Lord and call upon his name.

9

Is 61:10, 11

R̶. My spirit rejoices in my God.

I rejoice heartily in the LORD,
in my God is the joy of my soul;
For he has clothed me with a robe of salvation,
and wrapped me in a mantle of justice,
Like a bridegroom adorned with a diadem,
like a bride bedecked with her jewels.

℟. My spirit rejoices in my God.

As the earth brings forth its plants,
    and a garden makes its growth spring up,
So will the Lord GOD make justice and praise
    spring up before all the nations.

℟. My spirit rejoices in my God.

10

Jer 31:10, 11-12a, 12b-13, 14

℟. The Lord has redeemed his people.

Hear the word of the LORD, O nations,
    proclaim it on distant coasts, and say:
He who scattered Israel, now gathers them together,
    he guards them as a shepherd his flock.

℟. The Lord has redeemed his people.

The LORD shall ransom Jacob,
    he shall redeem him from the hand of his conqueror.
Shouting, they shall mount the heights of Zion,
    they shall come streaming to the LORD's blessings:

℟. The Lord has redeemed his people.

The grain, the wine, and the oil,
    the sheep and the oxen;

They themselves shall be like watered gardens,
    never again shall they languish.

℞. The Lord has redeemed his people.

Then the virgins shall make merry and dance,
    and young men and old as well.
I will turn their mourning into joy,
    I will console and gladden them after their sorrows.

℞. The Lord has redeemed his people.

I will lavish choice portions upon the priests,
    and my people shall be filled with my blessings,
    says the LORD.

℞. The Lord has redeemed his people.

II

Dn 3:52, 53, 54, 55, 56, 57

℞. Bless the Lord, all the works of his hand: praise and
    glorify him for ever.

"Blessed are you, O Lord, the God of our fathers,
    praiseworthy and exalted above all forever;
And blessed is your holy and glorious name,
    praiseworthy and exalted above all for all ages."

℞. Bless the Lord, all the works of his hand: praise and
    glorify him for ever.

"Blessed are you in the temple of your holy glory,
  praiseworthy and glorious above all forever."

℟. Bless the Lord, all the works of his hand: praise and
  glorify him for ever.

"Blessed are you on the throne of your Kingdom,
  praiseworthy and exalted above all forever."

℟. Bless the Lord, all the works of his hand: praise and
  glorify him for ever.

"Blessed are you who look into the depths
  from your throne upon the cherubim,
  praiseworthy and exalted above all forever."

℟. Bless the Lord, all the works of his hand: praise and
  glorify him for ever.

"Blessed are you in the firmament of heaven,
  praiseworthy and glorious forever."

℟. Bless the Lord, all the works of his hand: praise and
  glorify him for ever.

"Bless the Lord, all you works of the Lord,
  praise and exalt him above all forever."

℟. Bless the Lord, all the works of his hand: praise and
  glorify him for ever.

12

Lk 1:46-47, 48-49,
50-51, 52-53, 54-55

℟. The Lord has remembered his mercy.

"My soul proclaims the greatness of the Lord,
　my spirit rejoices in God my Savior."

℟. The Lord has remembered his mercy.

"For he has looked with favor on his lowly servant.
From this day all generations will call me blessed:
　the Almighty has done great things for me,
　and holy is his Name."

℟. The Lord has remembered his mercy.

"He has mercy on those who fear him
　in every generation.
He has shown the strength of his arm,
　and has scattered the proud in their conceit."

℟. The Lord has remembered his mercy.

"He has cast down the mighty from their thrones,
　and has lifted up the lowly.
He has filled the hungry with good things,
　and the rich he has sent away empty."

℞. The Lord has remembered his mercy.

"He has come to the help of his servant Israel
    for he has remembered his promise of mercy,
The promise he made to our fathers,
    to Abraham and his children for ever."

℞. The Lord has remembered his mercy.

13

Eph 1:3-4a, 4b-6, 7-8a, 8b-10

℞. Blessed be God who chose us in Christ.

Blessed be the God and Father of our Lord Jesus Christ,
    who has blessed us in Christ
    with every spiritual blessing in the heavens,
as he chose us in him,
    before the foundation of the world,
    to be holy and without blemish before him.

℞. Blessed be God who chose us in Christ.

In love he destined us for adoption
    to himself through Jesus Christ,
    in accord with the favor of his will,
for the praise of the glory of his grace
    that he granted us in the beloved.

℞. Blessed be God who chose us in Christ.

In him we have redemption by his Blood,
   the forgiveness of transgressions,
in accord with the riches of his grace
   that he lavished upon us.

℟. Blessed be God who chose us in Christ.

In all wisdom and insight, he has made known to us
   the mystery of his will in accord with his favor
that he set forth in him as a plan for the fullness of times,
   to sum up all things in Christ,
   in heaven and on earth.

℟. Blessed be God who chose us in Christ.

14

Rev 15:3, 4

℟. Great and wonderful are your works, Lord.

They sang the song of Moses, the servant of God,
   and the song of the Lamb:
"Great and wonderful are your works,
   Lord God almighty.
Just and true are your ways,
   O king of the nations.

℟. Great and wonderful are your works, Lord.

Who will not fear you, Lord,
  or glorify your name?
For you alone are holy.
    All the nations will come
    and worship before you,
    for your righteous acts have been revealed."

R⁄. Great and wonderful are your works, Lord.

CONCLUDING PRAYERS

207.

Father, all-powerful and ever-living God,
we do well always and everywhere to give you thanks.
When you punish us, you show your justice;
when you pardon us, you show your kindness;
yet always your mercy enfolds us.
When you chastise us, you do not wish to condemn us;
when you spare us, you give us time to make amends
        for our sins
through Christ our Lord.

R⁄. Amen.

208.

Lord God,
creator and ruler of your kingdom of light,
in your great love for this world
you gave up your only Son
for our salvation.

His cross has redeemed us,
his death has given us life,
his resurrection has raised us to glory.
Through him we ask you
to be always present among your family.
Teach us to be reverent in the presence of your glory;
fill our hearts with faith,
our days with good works,
our lives with your love;
may your truth be on our lips
and your wisdom in all our actions,
that we may receive the reward of everlasting life.
We ask this through Christ our Lord.

℟. Amen.

209.
Lord Jesus Christ,
your loving forgiveness knows no limits.
You took our human nature
to give us an example of humility
and to make us faithful in every trial.
May we never lose the gifts you have given us,
but if we fall into sin
lift us up by your gift of repentance,
for you live and reign for ever and ever.

℟. Amen.

210.

**Father,
in your love you have brought us
from evil to good and from misery to happiness.
Through your blessings
give the courage of perseverance
to those you have called and justified by faith.
Grant this through Christ our Lord.**

R/. Amen.

211.

**God and Father of us all,
you have forgiven our sins
and sent us your peace.
Help us to forgive each other
and to work together to establish peace in the world.
We ask this through Christ our Lord.**

R/. Amen.

212.

**And may the blessing of almighty God,
the Father, and the Son, ✠ and the Holy Spirit,
come upon you and remain with you for ever.**

R/. Amen.

213.

**May the Father bless us,
for we are his children, born to eternal life.**

℟. Amen.

**May the Son show us his saving power,
for he died and rose for us.**

℟. Amen.

**May the Spirit give us his gift of holiness
and lead us by the right path,
for he dwells in our hearts.**

℟. Amen.

214.

**May the Father bless us,
for he has adopted us as his children.**

℟. Amen.

**May the Son come to help us,
for he has received us as brothers and sisters.**
℟. Amen.

**May the Spirit be with us,
for he has made us his dwelling place.**

℟. Amen.

APPENDIX I
ABSOLUTION FROM CENSURES

1. The form of absolution is not to be changed when a priest, in keeping with the provision of law, absolves a properly disposed penitent within the sacramental forum from a censure *latae sententiae*. It is enough that the confessor intend to absolve also from censures. Before absolving from sins, however, the confessor may absolve from the censure, using the formula which is given below for absolution from censure outside the sacrament of penance.

2. When a priest, in accordance with the law, absolves a penitent from a censure outside the sacrament of penance, he uses the following formula:

By the power granted to me,
I absolve you
from the bond of excommunication (or **suspension**
      or **interdict**).
In the name of the Father, and of the Son, ✠
and of the Holy Spirit.

The penitent answers:

Amen.

DISPENSATION FROM IRREGULARITY

3. When, in accordance with the law, a priest dispenses a penitent from an irregularity, either during confession, after absolution has been given, or outside the sacrament of penance, he says:

By the power granted to me
I dispense you from the irregularity
which you have incurred.
In the name of the Father, and of the Son, ✠
and of the Holy Spirit.

The penitent answers:

Amen.

APPENDIX II
SAMPLE PENITENTIAL SERVICES

These services have been prepared by the Congregation for Divine Worship to help those who prepare or lead penitential celebrations.

PREPARING PENITENTIAL CELEBRATIONS

1. Penitential celebrations, mentioned in the *Rite of Penance* (nos. 36-37), are beneficial in fostering the spirit and virtue of penance among individuals and communities; they also help in preparing for a more fruitful celebration of the sacrament of penance. However, the faithful must be reminded of the difference between these celebrations and sacramental confession and absolution.[1]

2. The particular conditions of life, the manner of speaking, and the educational level of the congregation or special group should be taken into consideration. Thus liturgical commissions[2] and individual Christian communities preparing these celebrations should choose the texts and format most suited to the circumstances of each particular group.

3. To this end, several examples of penitential celebrations are given below. These are models and should be adapted to the specific conditions and needs of each community.

4. When the sacrament of penance is celebrated in these services, it follows the readings and homily, and the rite of reconciling several penitents with individual confession and absolution is used (nos. 54-59, *Rite of Penance*); when permitted by law, the rite for general confession and absolution is used (nos. 60-63, *Rite of Penance*).

---

1 See Congregation for the Doctrine of the Faith, *Normae pastorales circa absolutionem sacra-mentalem generali modo impertiendam*, June 16, 1972, no. X: AAS 64 (1972) 513.

2 See Congregation of Rites, Instruction *Inter Oecumenici*, September 26, 1964, no. 39: AAS (1964) 110.

I. PENITENTIAL CELEBRATIONS DURING LENT

5. Lent is the principal time of penance both for individual Christians and for the whole Church. It is therefore desirable to prepare the Christian community for a fuller sharing in the paschal mystery by penitential celebrations during Lent.[3]

6. Texts from the lectionary and sacramentary may be used in these penitential celebrations; the penitential nature of the liturgy of the word in the Masses for Lent should be considered.

7. Two outlines of penitential celebrations suitable for Lent are given here. The first emphasizes penance as strengthening or restoring baptismal grace; the second shows penance as a preparation for a fuller sharing in the Easter mystery of Christ and his Church.

FIRST EXAMPLE

Penance Leads to a Strengthening of Baptismal Grace

8. (a) After an appropriate song and the greeting by the minister, the meaning of this celebration is explained to the people. It prepares the Christian community to recall their baptismal grace at the Easter Vigil and to reach newness of life in Christ through freedom from sins.

9. (b) Prayer

My brothers and sisters, we have neglected the gifts of our baptism and fallen into sin. Let us ask God to renew his grace within us as we turn to him in repentance.

Let us kneel (or: **Bow your heads before God**).

---

3   See Second Vatican Council, constitution *Sacrosanctum concilium*, no. 109; Paul VI, Apostolic Constitution *Paenitemini*, February 17, 1966, no. IX: AAS 58 (1966) 185.

All pray in silence for a brief period.

Let us stand (or: **Raise your heads**).

Lord Jesus,
you redeemed us by your passion
and raised us to new life in baptism.
Protect us with your unchanging love
and share with us the joy of your resurrection,
for you live and reign for ever and ever.

R/. Amen.

10. (c) Readings

FIRST READING

A reading from the first Letter of Saint Paul
to the Corinthians   10:1-13

I do not want you to be unaware, brothers and sisters,
    that our ancestors were all under the cloud
    and all passed through the sea,
    and all of them were baptized into Moses
    in the cloud and in the sea.
All ate the same spiritual food,
    and all drank the same spiritual drink,
    for they drank from a spiritual rock that followed them,
    and the rock was the Christ.
Yet God was not pleased with most of them,
    for they were struck down in the desert.

These things happened as examples for us,
    so that we might not desire evil things, as they did.
And do not become idolaters, as some of them did,
    as it is written,
    The people sat down to eat and drink,
    and rose up to revel.
Let us not indulge in immorality as some of them did,
    and twenty-three thousand fell within a single day.
Let us not test Christ as some of them did,
    and suffered death by serpents.
Do not grumble as some of them did,
    and suffered death by the destroyer.
These things happened to them as an example,
    and they have been written down as a warning to us,
    upon whom the end of the ages has come.
Therefore, whoever thinks he is standing secure should
        take care not to fall.
No trial has come to you but what is human.
God is faithful and will not let you be tried
    beyond your strength;
    but with the trial he will also provide a way out,
    so that you may be able to bear it.

The word of the Lord.

RESPONSORIAL PSALM Ps 106:6-10, 13-14, 19-22

℟. Lord, remember us, for the love you bear your people.

We have sinned, we and our fathers;
  we have committed crimes; we have done wrong.
Our fathers in Egypt
  considered not your wonders;
They remembered not your abundant kindness,
  but rebelled against the Most High at the Red Sea.

℟. Lord, remember us, for the love you bear your people.

Yet he saved them for his name's sake,
  to make known his power.
He rebuked the Red Sea, and it was dried up,
  and he led them through the deep as through a desert.
He saved them from hostile hands
  and freed them from the hands of the enemy.

℟. Lord, remember us, for the love you bear your people.

But soon they forgot his works;
  they waited not for his counsel.
They gave way to craving in the desert
  and tempted God in the wilderness.

℟. Lord, remember us, for the love you bear your people.

They made a calf in Horeb
    and adored a molten image;
They exchanged their glory
    for the image of a grass-eating bullock.

R̷. Lord, remember us, for the love you bear your people.

They forgot the God who had saved them,
    who had done great deeds in Egypt,
Wondrous deeds in the land of Ham,
    terrible things at the Red Sea.

R̷. Lord, remember us, for the love you bear your people.

GOSPEL

✠ A reading from the holy Gospel
according to Luke   15:4-7

Jesus addressed this parable to them:
"What man among you having a hundred sheep and
            losing one of them
    would not leave the ninety-nine in the desert
    and go after the lost one until he finds it?
And when he does find it,
    he sets it on his shoulders with great joy
    and, upon his arrival home,
    he calls together his friends and neighbors and says
            to them,
    'Rejoice with me because I have found my lost sheep.'

245

I tell you, in just the same way
    there will be more joy in heaven over one sinner
        who repents
    than over ninety-nine righteous people
    who have no need of repentance."

The Gospel of the Lord.

    Or:

✠ A reading from the holy Gospel according to Luke **15:11-32**

Jesus addressed this parable to them:
"A man had two sons, and the younger son said to
        his father,
    'Father, give me the share of your estate that should
        come to me.'
So the father divided the property between them.
After a few days, the younger son collected all
        his belongings
    and set off to a distant country
    where he squandered his inheritance on a life
        of dissipation.
When he had freely spent everything,
    a severe famine struck that country,
    and he found himself in dire need.
So he hired himself out to one of the local citizens
    who sent him to his farm to tend the swine.
And he longed to eat his fill of the pods on which the
        swine fed,
    but nobody gave him any.

Coming to his senses he thought,
    'How many of my father's hired workers
    have more than enough food to eat,
    but here am I, dying from hunger.
I shall get up and go to my father and I shall say to him,
    "Father, I have sinned against heaven and against you.
I no longer deserve to be called your son;
    treat me as you would treat one of your hired workers."'
So he got up and went back to his father.
While he was still a long way off,
    his father caught sight of him, and was filled
        with compassion.
He ran to his son, embraced him and kissed him.
His son said to him,
    'Father, I have sinned against heaven and against you;
    I no longer deserve to be called your son.'
But his father ordered his servants,
    'Quickly, bring the finest robe and put it on him;
    put a ring on his finger and sandals on his feet.
Take the fattened calf and slaughter it.
Then let us celebrate with a feast,
    because this son of mine was dead, and has come to
        life again;
    he was lost, and has been found.'
Then the celebration began.
Now the older son had been out in the field
    and, on his way back, as he neared the house,
    he heard the sound of music and dancing.
He called one of the servants and asked what this
        might mean.

The servant said to him,
    'Your brother has returned
    and your father has slaughtered the fattened calf
    because he has him back safe and sound.'
He became angry,
    and when he refused to enter the house,
    his father came out and pleaded with him.
He said to his father in reply,
    'Look, all these years I served you
    and not once did I disobey your orders;
    yet you never gave me even a young goat to feast on
        with my friends.
But when your son returns
    who swallowed up your property with prostitutes,
    for him you slaughter the fattened calf.'
He said to him,
    'My son, you are here with me always;
    everything I have is yours.
But now we must celebrate and rejoice,
    because your brother was dead and has come to
        life again;
    he was lost and has been found.'"

The Gospel of the Lord.

11. (d) Homily

The celebrant may speak about:

— the need to fulfill the grace of baptism by living faithfully the Gospel of Christ (see 1 Cor 10:1-13);

— the seriousness of sin committed after baptism (see Heb 6:4-8);

— the unlimited mercy of our God and Father who continually welcomes those who turn back to him after having sinned (see Lk 15);

— Easter as the feast when the Church rejoices over the Christian initiation of catechumens and the reconciliation of penitents.

12. (e) Examination of conscience.

After the homily, the examination of conscience takes place; a sample text is given in Appendix III. A period of silence should always be included so that each person may personally examine his conscience. In a special way the people should examine their conscience on the baptismal promises which will be renewed at the Easter Vigil.

13. (f) Act of repentance

The deacon (or another minister, if there is no deacon) speaks to the assembly:

My brothers and sisters, the hour of God's favor draws near, the day of his mercy and of our salvation, when death was destroyed and eternal life began. This is the season for planting new vines in God's vineyard, the time for pruning the vines to ensure a richer harvest.

We all acknowledge that we are sinners. We are moved to penance, encouraged by the example and prayers of our brothers and sisters. We admit our guilt and say: "Lord, I acknowledge my sins; my offenses are always before me. Turn away your face, Lord, from my sins, and blot out all my wrong-doing. Give me back the joy of your salvation and give me a new and steadfast spirit."

We are sorry for having offended God by our sins. May he be merciful and hear us as we ask to be restored to his friendship and numbered among the living who share the joy of Christ's risen life.

Then the priest sprinkles the congregation with holy water, while all sing (say):

Cleanse us, Lord, from all our sins;
Wash us, and we shall be whiter than snow.

Then the priest says:

Lord our God,
you created us in love
and redeemed us in mercy.
While we were exiled from heaven
by the jealousy of the evil one,
you gave us your only Son,
who shed his blood to save us.
Send now your Holy Spirit
to breathe new life into your children,

for you do not want us to die
but to live for you alone.
You do not abandon those who abandon you;
correct us as a Father
and restore us to your family.

Lord,
your sons and daughters stand before you
in humility and trust.
Look with compassion on us
as we confess our sins.
Heal our wounds;
stretch out a hand of pity
to save us and raise us up.
Keep us free from harm
as members of Christ's body,
as sheep of your flock,
as children of your family.
Do not allow the enemy
to triumph over us
or death to claim us for ever,
for you raised us to new life in baptism.

Hear, Lord, the prayers we offer from contrite hearts.
Have pity on us as we acknowledge our sins.
Lead us back to the way of holiness.
Protect us now and always
from the wounds of sin.

**May we ever keep safe in all its fullness
the gift your love once gave us
and your mercy now restores.**

**We ask this through our Lord Jesus Christ, your Son,
who lives and reigns with you and the Holy Spirit,
one God for ever and ever.**

R̷. Amen.

The celebration ends with an appropriate song and the dismissal of the people.

SECOND EXAMPLE

Penance Prepares for a Fuller Sharing in the Paschal Mystery of Christ for the Salvation of the World

14. (a) After an appropriate song and the greeting by the minister, the faithful are briefly reminded that they are linked with each other in sin and in repentance so that each should take his calling to conversion as an occasion of grace for the whole community.

15. (b) Prayer

**My brothers and sisters, let us pray that by penance
we may be united with Christ, who was crucified
for our sins, and so share with all mankind in his
resurrection.**

Let us kneel (or: **Bow your heads before God**).

All pray in silence for a brief period.

Let us stand (or: **Raise your heads**).

Lord, our God and Father,
through the passion of your Son
you gave us new life.
By our practice of penance
make us one with him in his dying
so that we and all mankind
may be one with him
in his resurrection.
We ask this through Christ our Lord.

R̸. Amen.

Or:

Almighty and merciful Father,
send your Holy Spirit
to inspire and strengthen us,
so that by always carrying
the death of Jesus in our bodies
we may also show forth the power of his risen life.
We ask this through Christ our Lord.

R̸. Amen.

16. (c) Readings

FIRST READING

A reading from the Book of the
Prophet Isaiah   53:1-7, 10-12

Who would believe what we have heard?
    To whom has the arm of the LORD been revealed?
He grew up like a sapling before him,
    like a shoot from the parched earth;
There was in him no stately bearing to make us look
        at him,
    nor appearance that would attract us to him.
He was spurned and avoided by people,
    a man of suffering, accustomed to infirmity,
One of those from whom people hide their faces,
    spurned, and we held him in no esteem.

Yet it was our infirmities that he bore,
    our sufferings that he endured,
While we thought of him as stricken,
    as one smitten by God and afflicted.
But he was pierced for our offenses,
    crushed for our sins;
Upon him was the chastisement that makes us whole,
    by his stripes we were healed.
We had all gone astray like sheep,
    each following his own way;
But the LORD laid upon him
    the guilt of us all.

Though he was harshly treated, he submitted
    and opened not his mouth;
Like a lamb led to the slaughter
    or a sheep before the shearers,
    he was silent and opened not his mouth.

But the LORD was pleased
    to crush him in infirmity.

If he gives his life as an offering for sin,
    he shall see his descendants in a long life,
    and the will of the LORD shall be accomplished
        through him.

Because of his affliction
    he shall see the light in fullness of days;
Through his suffering, my servant shall justify many,
    and their guilt he shall bear.
Therefore I will give him his portion among the great,
    and he shall divide the spoils with the mighty,
Because he surrendered himself to death
    and was counted among the wicked;
And he shall take away the sins of many,
    and win pardon for their offenses.

The word of the Lord.

RESPONSORIAL PSALM

Ps 22:2-3, 7-9, 18-19,
20-22, 23-24, 25, 26-27, 28

R̸. Father, your will be done.

My God, my God, why have you forsaken me,
    far from my prayer, from the words of my cry?
O my God, I cry out by day, and you answer not;
    by night, and there is no relief for me.

R̸. Father, your will be done.

But I am a worm, not a man;
    the scorn of men, despised by the people.
All who see me scoff at me;
    they mock me with parted lips, they wag their heads;
"He relied on the LORD; let him deliver him,
    let him rescue him if he loves him."

R̸. Father, your will be done.

I can count all my bones.
They look on and gloat over me;
    they divide my garments among them,
    and for my vesture they cast lots.

R̸. Father, your will be done.

But you, O Lord, be not far from me;
　O my help, hasten to aid me.
Rescue my soul from the sword,
　my loneliness from the grip of the dog.
Save me from the lion's mouth;
　from the horns of the wild bulls, my wretched life.

℞. Father, your will be done.

I will proclaim your name to my brethren;
　in the midst of the assembly I will praise you;
"You who fear the Lord, praise him;
　all you descendants of Jacob, give glory to him;
　revere him, all you descendants of Israel!"

℞. Father, your will be done.

"For he has not spurned or disdained
　the wretched man in his misery,
Nor did he turn his face away from him
　but when he cried out to him, he heard him."

℞. Father, your will be done.

So by your gift I will utter praise in the vast assembly;
　I will fulfill my vows before those who fear him.
The lowly shall eat their fill;
　they who seek the Lord shall praise him;
　"May your hearts be ever merry!"

R/. Father, your will be done.

All the ends of the earth
    shall remember and turn to the LORD;
All the families of the nations
    shall bow down before him.

R/. Father, your will be done.

SECOND READING

A reading from the first Letter of Saint Peter   **2:20b-25**

Beloved:
If you are patient when you suffer for doing what is good,
    this is a grace before God.
For to this you have been called,
    because Christ also suffered for you,
    leaving you an example that you should follow in
        his footsteps.
He committed no sin, and no deceit was found in his mouth.

When he was insulted, he returned no insult;
    when he suffered, he did not threaten;
    instead, he handed himself over to the one who
        judges justly.
He himself bore our sins in his body upon the Cross,
    so that, free from sin, we might live for righteousness.
By his wounds you have been healed.

For you had gone astray like sheep,
    but you have now returned to the shepherd and
        guardian of your souls.

The word of the Lord.

GOSPEL ACCLAMATION

Glory to you, Lord; you were given up to death
    for our sins and rose again for our justification.
Glory to you, Lord.

GOSPEL

Long Form

✠ A reading from the holy Gospel according to Mark **10:32-45**

The disciples were on the way, going up to Jerusalem,
    and Jesus went ahead of them.
They were amazed, and those who followed were afraid.
Taking the Twelve aside again, he began to tell them
    what was going to happen to him.
"Behold, we are going up to Jerusalem, and the Son of Man
    will be handed over to the chief priests and the scribes,
    and they will condemn him to death
    and hand him over to the Gentiles who will mock him,
    spit upon him, scourge him, and put him to death,
    but after three days he will rise."

Then James and John, the sons of Zebedee,
 came to Jesus and said to him,
  "Teacher, we want you to do for us whatever we ask
   of you."
He replied, "What do you wish me to do for you?"
They answered him,
  "Grant that in your glory
 we may sit one at your right and the other at your left."
Jesus said to them, "You do not know what you are asking.
Can you drink the chalice that I drink
 or be baptized with the baptism with which I
  am baptized?"
They said to him, "We can."
Jesus said to them, "The chalice that I drink, you will drink,
 and with the baptism with which I am baptized, you
  will be baptized;
 but to sit at my right or at my left is not mine to give
 but is for those for whom it has been prepared."
When the ten heard this, they became indignant at James
  and John.
Jesus summoned them and said to them,
 "You know that those who are recognized as rulers
  over the Gentiles
 lord it over them,
 and their great ones make their authority over them felt.
But it shall not be so among you.
Rather, whoever wishes to be great among you will be
  your servant;
 whoever wishes to be first among you will be the slave
  of all.

For the Son of Man did not come to be served but to serve
and to give his life as a ransom for many."

The Gospel of the Lord.

Or:

Short Form

✠ A reading from the holy Gospel
according to Mark   **10:32-34, 42-45**

The disciples were on the way, going up to Jerusalem,
and Jesus went ahead of them.
They were amazed, and those who followed were afraid.
Taking the Twelve aside again, he began to tell them
what was going to happen to him.
"Behold, we are going up to Jerusalem, and the Son of Man
will be handed over to the chief priests and the scribes,
and they will condemn him to death
and hand him over to the Gentiles who will mock him,
spit upon him, scourge him, and put him to death,
but after three days he will rise."

Jesus summoned them and said to them,
"You know that those who are recognized as rulers
over the Gentiles
lord it over them,
and their great ones make their authority over them felt.
But it shall not be so among you.
Rather, whoever wishes to be great among you will be
your servant;

whoever wishes to be first among you will be the slave
of all.
For the Son of Man did not come to be served but to serve
and to give his life as a ransom for many."

The Gospel of the Lord.

17. (d) Homily

The celebrant may speak about:

— sin, by which we offend God and also Christ's body, the Church, whose
members we became in baptism;

— sin as a failure of love for Christ who in the paschal mystery showed his
love for us to the end;

— the way we affect each other when we do good or choose evil;

— the mystery of vicarious satisfaction by which Christ bore the burden of
our sins, so that by his wounds we would be healed (see Is 53; 1 Pt 2:24);

— the social and ecclesial dimension of penance by which individual
Christians share in the work of converting the whole community;

— the celebration of Easter as the feast of the Christian community which
is renewing itself by the conversion or repentance of each member, so
that the Church may become a clearer sign of salvation in the world.

18. (e) Examination of conscience

After the homily, the examination of conscience takes place; a sample
text is given in Appendix III. A period of silence should always be included
so that each person may personally examine his conscience.

19. (f) Act of repentance

After the examination of conscience, all say together:

I confess to almighty God,
and to you, my brothers and sisters,
that I have sinned through my own fault,

They strike their breast:

in my thoughts and in my words,
in what I have done,
and in what I have failed to do;
and I ask blessed Mary, ever virgin,
all the angels and saints,
and you, my brothers and sisters,
to pray for me to the Lord our God.

As a sign of conversion and charity toward others, it should be suggested that the faithful give something to help the poor to celebrate the feast of Easter with joy; or they might visit the sick, or make up for some injustice in the community, or perform similar works.

Then the Lord's Prayer may be said, which the priest concludes in this way:

Deliver us, Father, from every evil
as we unite ourselves through penance
with the saving passion of your Son.
Grant us a share
in the joy of the resurrection of Jesus
who is Lord for ever and ever.

R̸. Amen.

Depending on circumstances, the general confession may be followed by a form of devotion such as adoration of the cross or the way of the cross, according to local customs and the wishes of the people.

At the end, an appropriate song is sung, and the people are sent away with a greeting or blessing.

II. PENITENTIAL CELEBRATIONS DURING ADVENT

20. (a) After an appropriate song and the greeting by the minister, the meaning of the celebration is explained in these or similar words:

My brothers and sisters, Advent is a time of preparation, when we make ready to celebrate the mystery of our Lord's coming as man, the beginning of our redemption. Advent also moves us to look forward with renewed hope to the second coming of Christ, when God's plan of salvation will be brought to fulfillment. We are reminded too of our Lord's coming to each one of us at the hour of our death. We must make sure that he will find us prepared for his coming, as the gospel tells us: "Blessed are those servants who are found awake when the Lord comes" (Lk 12:37). This service of penance is meant to make us ready in mind and heart for the coming of Christ, which we are soon to celebrate in the Mass of Christmas.

Or:

Now it is time for you to wake from sleep, for our salvation is nearer to us than it was when we first believed. The night is ending; the day draws near. Let us then cast off the deeds of darkness and put on the armor of light. Let us live honestly as people do in the daylight, not in carousing and drunkenness, not in lust and debauchery, not in quarreling and jealousy. But rather let us put on the Lord Jesus Christ and give no thought to the desires of the flesh (Rom 13:11-12).

21. (b) Prayer

My brothers and sisters, we look forward to celebrating the mystery of Christ's coming on the feast of Christmas. Let us pray that when he comes he may find us awake and ready to receive him.

All pray in silence for a brief period.

**Lord our God,
maker of the heavens,
as we look forward to the coming of our redeemer
grant us the forgiveness of our sins.**

We ask this through Christ our Lord.

R̸. Amen.

Or:

Eternal Son of God,
creator of the human family
and our redeemer,
come at last among us
as the child of the immaculate Virgin,
and redeem the world.
Reveal your loving presence
by which you set us free from sin
in becoming one like us
in all things but sin,
for you live and reign for ever and ever.

℟. Amen.

22. (c) Readings

FIRST READING

A reading from the Book of the Prophet Malachi   3:1-7a

Lo, I am sending my messenger
    to prepare the way before me;
And suddenly there will come to the temple
    the Lord whom you seek,
And the messenger of the covenant whom you desire.
    Yes, he is coming, says the Lord of hosts.
But who will endure the day of his coming?
    And who can stand when he appears?

For he is like the refiner's fire,
  or like the fuller's lye.
He will sit refining and purifying silver,
  and he will purify the sons of Levi,
Refining them like gold or like silver
  that they may offer due sacrifice to the LORD.
Then the sacrifice of Judah and Jerusalem
  will please the LORD,
  as in days of old, as in years gone by.
I will draw near to you for judgment,
  and I will be swift to bear witness
Against the sorcerers, adulterers, and perjurers,
  those who defraud the hired man of his wages,
Against those who defraud widows and orphans;
  those who turn aside the stranger,
  and those who do not fear me, says the LORD of hosts.

Surely I, the LORD, do not change,
  nor do you cease to be sons of Jacob.
Since the days of your fathers you have turned aside
  from my statutes, and have not kept them.
Return to me, and I will return to you,
  says the LORD of hosts.

The word of the Lord.

RESPONSORIAL PSALM

Ps 85:2-3, 4-5, 6-8,
9-10, 11-12, 13-14

℟. Lord, let us see your kindness, and grant us
    your salvation.

You have favored, O LORD, your land;
    you have restored the well-being of Jacob.
You have forgiven the guilt of your people;
    you have covered all their sins.

℟. Lord, let us see your kindness, and grant us
    your salvation.

You have withdrawn all your wrath;
    you have revoked your burning anger.
Restore us, O God, our savior,
    and abandon your displeasure against us.

℟. Lord, let us see your kindness, and grant us
    your salvation.

Will you be ever angry with us,
    prolonging your anger to all generations?
Will you not instead give us life;
    and shall not your people rejoice in you:
Show us, LORD, your mercy,
    and grant us your salvation.

℟. Lord, let us see your kindness, and grant us
      your salvation.

I will hear what God proclaims;
   the LORD—for he proclaims peace to his people.
Near indeed is his salvation to those who fear him,
   glory dwelling in our land.

℟. Lord, let us see your kindness, and grant us
      your salvation.

Kindness and truth shall meet;
   justice and peace shall kiss.
Truth shall spring out of the earth,
   and justice shall look down from heaven.

℟. Lord, let us see your kindness, and grant us
      your salvation.

The LORD himself will give his benefits;
   our land shall yield its increase.
Justice shall walk before him,
   and prepare the way of his steps.

℟. Lord, let us see your kindness, and grant us
      your salvation.

SECOND READING

A reading from the Book of Revelation   21:1-12

Then I saw a new heaven and a new earth.
The former heaven and the former earth had passed away,
    and the sea was no more.
I also saw the holy city, a new Jerusalem,
    coming down out of heaven from God,
    prepared as a bride adorned for her husband.
I heard a loud voice from the throne saying,
    "Behold, God's dwelling is with the human race.
He will dwell with them and they will be his people
    and God himself will always be with them as their God.
He will wipe every tear from their eyes,
    and there shall be no more death or mourning, wailing
        or pain,
    for the old order has passed away."

The one who sat on the throne said,
    "Behold, I make all things new."
Then he said, "Write these words down,
    for they are trustworthy and true."
He said to me, "They are accomplished.
I am the Alpha and the Omega,
    the beginning and the end.
To the thirsty I will give a gift from the spring of life-
        giving water.
The victor will inherit these gifts,
    and I shall be his God,
    and he will be my son.

But as for cowards, the unfaithful, the depraved, murderers,
the unchaste, sorcerers, idol-worshipers, and deceivers
of every sort,
their lot is in the burning pool of fire and sulfur, which
is the second death."

One of the seven angels who held the seven bowls
filled with the seven last plagues
came and said to me,
"Come here. I will show you the bride, the wife of
the Lamb."
He took me in spirit to a great, high mountain
and showed me the holy city Jerusalem
coming down out of heaven from God.
It gleamed with the splendor of God.
Its radiance was like that of a precious stone,
like jasper, clear as crystal.
It had a massive, high wall, with twelve gates
where twelve angels were stationed
and on which names were inscribed,
the names of the twelve tribes of the children of Israel.

The word of the Lord.

GOSPEL ACCLAMATION

I am coming quickly, says the Lord, and I will repay
each man.
Come, Lord Jesus.

Or:

The Spirit and the Bride say: "Come."
Let all who hear answer: "Come."
Come, Lord Jesus.

GOSPEL

✠ A reading from the holy Gospel
according to Matthew   3:1-12

John the Baptist appeared, preaching in the desert
        of Judea
    and saying, "Repent, for the Kingdom of heaven is
        at hand!"
It was of him that the prophet Isaiah had spoken when
        he said:
    A voice of one crying out in the desert,
    Prepare the way of the Lord,
        make straight his paths.
John wore clothing made of camel's hair
    and had a leather belt around his waist.
His food was locusts and wild honey.
At that time Jerusalem, all Judea,
    and the whole region around the Jordan
    were going out to him
    and were being baptized by him in the Jordan River
    as they acknowledged their sins.

When he saw many of the Pharisees and Sadducees
    coming to his baptism, he said to them, "You brood
        of vipers!
Who warned you to flee from the coming wrath?
Produce good fruit as evidence of your repentance.
And do not presume to say to yourselves,
    'We have Abraham as our father.'
For I tell you,
    God can raise up children to Abraham from
        these stones.
Even now the ax lies at the root of the trees.
Therefore every tree that does not bear good fruit
    will be cut down and thrown into the fire.
I am baptizing you with water, for repentance,
    but the one who is coming after me is mightier than I.
I am not worthy to carry his sandals.
He will baptize you with the Holy Spirit and fire.
His winnowing fan is in his hand.
He will clear his threshing floor
    and gather his wheat into his barn,
    but the chaff he will burn with unquenchable fire."

The Gospel of the Lord.

Or:

✠ A reading from the holy Gospel according to Luke   3:1-17

In the fifteenth year of the reign of Tiberius Caesar,
    when Pontius Pilate was governor of Judea,
    and Herod was tetrarch of Galilee,

and his brother Philip tetrarch of the region of Ituraea
and Trachonitis,
and Lysanias was tetrarch of Abilene,
during the high priesthood of Annas and Caiaphas,
the word of God came to John the son of Zechariah in
the desert.
John went throughout the whole region of the Jordan,
proclaiming a baptism of repentance for the forgiveness
of sins,
as it is written in the book of the words of the prophet
Isaiah:
A voice of one crying out in the desert:
"Prepare the way of the Lord,
make straight his paths.
Every valley shall be filled
and every mountain and hill shall be
made low.
The winding roads shall be made straight,
and the rough ways made smooth,
and all flesh shall see the salvation of God."
The crowds asked John the Baptist,
"What should we do?"
He said to them in reply,
"Whoever has two cloaks
should share with the person who has none.
And whoever has food should do likewise."
Even tax collectors came to be baptized and they said
to him,
"Teacher, what should we do?"

He answered them,
  "Stop collecting more than what is prescribed."
Soldiers also asked him,
  "And what is it that we should do?"
He told them,
  "Do not practice extortion,
  do not falsely accuse anyone,
  and be satisfied with your wages."

Now the people were filled with expectation,
  and all were asking in their hearts
  whether John might be the Christ.
John answered them all, saying,
  "I am baptizing you with water,
  but one mightier than I is coming.
I am not worthy to loosen the thongs of his sandals.
He will baptize you with the Holy Spirit and fire.
His winnowing fan is in his hand to clear his
          threshing floor
  and to gather the wheat into his barn,
  but the chaff he will burn with unquenchable fire."

The Gospel of the Lord.

23. (d) Examination of conscience

  After the homily, the examination of conscience takes place; a sample text is given in Appendix III. A period of silence should always be included so that each person may personally examine his conscience.

24. (e) Act of repentance

The act of repentance follows the examination of conscience. All may say the **I confess to almighty God** or the intercessions as in no. 60.

The Lord's Prayer is said or sung, and is concluded by the presiding minister in this way:

Lord our God,
on the first day of creation
you made the light
that scatters all darkness.
Let Christ, the light of lights,
hidden from all eternity,
shine at last on your people
and free us from the darkness of sin.
Fill our lives with good works
as we go out to meet your Son,
so that we may give him a fitting welcome.
We ask this through Christ our Lord.

℟. Amen.

Or:

Almighty and eternal God,
you sent your only-begotten Son
to reconcile the world to yourself.
Lift from our hearts
the oppressive gloom of sin,

**so that we may celebrate
the approaching dawn of Christ's birth
with fitting joy.
We ask this through Christ our Lord.**

℟. Amen.

At the end, a song is sung, and the people are sent away with a greeting or blessing.

III. COMMON PENITENTIAL CELEBRATIONS

I. SIN AND CONVERSION

25. (a) After an appropriate song (for example Ps 139:1-12, 16, 23-24) and greeting, the minister who presides briefly explains the meaning of the readings. Then he invites all to pray. After a period of silence, he concludes the prayer in this way:

**Lord Jesus,
you turned and looked on Peter
when he denied you for the third time.
He wept for his sin
and turned again to you in sincere repentance.
Look now on us and touch our hearts,
so that we also may turn back to you
and be always faithful in serving you,
for you live and reign for ever and ever.**

℟. Amen.

26. (b) Readings

✠ A reading from the holy Gospel according to Luke **22:31-34**

"I tell you, Peter, before the cock crows this day,
you will deny three times that you know me."

Jesus said,
"Simon, Simon, behold Satan has demanded
   to sift all of you like wheat,
   but I have prayed that your own faith may not fail;
   and once you have turned back,
   you must strengthen your brothers."
He said to him,
   "Lord, I am prepared to go to prison and to die with you."
But he replied,
"I tell you, Peter, before the cock crows this day,
   you will deny three times that you know me."

The Gospel of the Lord.

✠ A reading from the holy Gospel according to Luke **22:54-62**

Peter went out and began to weep bitterly.

After arresting Jesus they led him away
   and took him into the house of the high priest;
   Peter was following at a distance.
They lit a fire in the middle of the courtyard and sat
            around it,
   and Peter sat down with them.

When a maid saw him seated in the light,
  she looked intently at him and said,
  "This man too was with him."
But he denied it saying,
  "Woman, I do not know him."
A short while later someone else saw him and said,
  "You too are one of them";
  but Peter answered, "My friend, I am not."
About an hour later, still another insisted,
  "Assuredly, this man too was with him,
  for he also is a Galilean."
But Peter said,
  "My friend, I do not know what you are talking about."
Just as he was saying this, the cock crowed,
  and the Lord turned and looked at Peter;
  and Peter remembered the word of the Lord,
  how he had said to him,
  "Before the cock crows today, you will deny me
      three times."
He went out and began to weep bitterly.

The Gospel of the Lord.

Ps 31:10, 15-17, 20

℞. My trust is in you, O God.

Have pity on me, O Lord, for I am in distress;
  with sorrow my eye is consumed; my soul also, and
      my body.

℞. My trust is in you, O God.

But my trust is in you, O LORD;
I say, "You are my God."
In your hands is my destiny; rescue me
    from the clutches of my enemies and my persecutors.
Let your face shine upon your servant;
    save me in your mercy.

℞. My trust is in you, O God.

How great is the goodness, O LORD,
    which you have in store for those who fear you,
And which, toward those who take refuge in you,
    you show in the sight of men.

℞. My trust is in you, O God.

**Ps 51:3-4, 5-6ab, 7-8, 9-11,
12-13, 14 and 17, 19**

℞. (see 14a) Give me back the joy of your salvation.

Have mercy on me, O God, in your goodness;
    in the greatness of your compassion wipe out
        my offense.
Thoroughly wash me from my guilt
    and of my sin cleanse me.

℞. Give me back the joy of your salvation.

For I acknowledge my offense,
    and my sin is before me always:
"Against you only have I sinned,
    and done what is evil in your sight."

℟. Give me back the joy of your salvation.

Indeed, in guilt was I born,
    and in sin my mother conceived me;
Behold, you are pleased with sincerity of heart,
    and in my inmost being you teach me wisdom.

℟. Give me back the joy of your salvation.

Cleanse me of sin with hyssop, that I may be purified;
    wash me, and I shall be whiter than snow.
Let me hear the sounds of joy and gladness;
    the bones you have crushed shall rejoice.
Turn away your face from my sins,
    and blot out all my guilt.

℟. Give me back the joy of your salvation.

A clean heart create for me, O God,
    and a steadfast spirit renew within me.
Cast me not out from your presence,
    and your Holy Spirit take not from me.

℟. Give me back the joy of your salvation.

Give me back the joy of your salvation,
   and a willing spirit sustain in me.
O Lord, open my lips,
   and my mouth shall proclaim your praise.

R⁄. Give me back the joy of your salvation.

My sacrifice, O God, is a contrite spirit;
   a heart contrite and humbled, O God, you will not spurn.

R⁄. Give me back the joy of your salvation.

✠ A reading from the holy Gospel according to John 21:15-19

Feed my lambs, feed my sheep.

After Jesus had revealed himself to his disciples and eaten
         breakfast with them,
      he said to Simon Peter,
      "Simon, son of John, do you love me more than these?"
Simon Peter answered him, "Yes, Lord, you know that I
         love you."
Jesus said to him, "Feed my lambs."
He then said to Simon Peter a second time,
      "Simon, son of John, do you love me?"
Simon Peter answered him, "Yes, Lord, you know that I
         love you."
He said to him, "Tend my sheep."
He said to him the third time,
      "Simon, son of John, do you love me?"

Peter was distressed that he had said to him a third time,
    "Do you love me?" and he said to him,
    "Lord, you know everything; you know that I love you."
Jesus said to him, "Feed my sheep.
Amen, amen, I say to you, when you were younger,
    you used to dress yourself and go where you wanted;
    but when you grow old, you will stretch out your hands,
    and someone else will dress you
    and lead you where you do not want to go."
He said this signifying by what kind of death he would
          glorify God.
And when he had said this, he said to him, "Follow me."

The Gospel of the Lord.

27. (c) Homily

The celebrant may speak about:

— the trust we must put in God's grace, not in our own powers;

— the faithfulness by which we as baptized Christians must live as true
and faithful followers of the Lord;

— our weakness by which we often fall into sin and refuse to give witness
to the gospel;

— the mercy of the Lord, who welcomes as a friend the one who turns to
him with his whole heart.

28. (d) Examination of conscience

After the homily, the examination of conscience takes place; a sample text is given in Appendix III. A period of silence should always be included so that each person may personally examine his conscience.

29. (e) Act of repentance

After the examination of conscience, the presiding minister invites all to prayer in these or similar words:

God gives us an example of love: when we were sinners he first loved us and took pity on us. Let us turn to him with a sincere heart, and in the words of Peter say to him:

℟. Lord, you know all things; you know that I love you.

A short period of silence should follow each invocation.

Each invocation may be said by different individuals, the rest answering.

—Lord, like Peter we have relied on our own strength rather than on grace. Look on us, Lord, and have mercy.

℟. Lord, you know all things; you know that I love you.

—Our pride and foolishness have led us into temptation. Look on us, Lord, and have mercy.

℟. Lord, you know all things; you know that I love you.

—We have been vain and self-important. Look on us, Lord, and have mercy.

R̸. Lord, you know all things; you know that I love you.

—We have at times been pleased rather than saddened by the misfortunes of others. Look on us, Lord, and have mercy.

R̸. Lord, you know all things; you know that I love you.

—We have shown indifference for those in need instead of helping them. Look on us, Lord, and have mercy.

R̸. Lord, you know all things; you know that I love you.

—We have been afraid to stand up for justice and truth. Look on us, Lord, and have mercy.

R̸. Lord, you know all things; you know that I love you.

—We have repeatedly broken the promises of our baptism and failed to be your disciples. Look on us, Lord, and have mercy.

R̸. Lord, you know all things; you know that I love you.

—Let us now pray to the Father in the words Christ gave us and ask forgiveness for our sins:

Our Father . . .

30. (f) After an appropriate song, the presiding minister says the final prayer and dismisses the people:

Lord Jesus, our Savior,
you called Peter to be an apostle;
when he repented of his sin
you restored him to your friendship
and confirmed him as first of the apostles.
Turn to us with love
and help us to imitate Peter's example.
Give us strength to turn from our sins
and to serve you in the future
with greater love and devotion,
for you live and reign for ever and ever.

℟. Amen.

II. THE SON RETURNS TO THE FATHER

31. (a) After an appropriate song and the greeting by the minister, the theme of the celebration is explained to the community. Then he invites all to pray. After a period of silence, he says:

Almighty God,
you are the Father of us all.
You created the human family
to dwell for ever with you
and to praise your glory.
Open our ears to hear your voice
so that we may return to you
with sincere repentance for our sins.

Teach us to see in you our loving Father,
full of compassion for all who call to you for help.
We know that you punish us only to set us free from evil
and that you are ready to forgive us our sins.
Restore your gift of salvation
which alone brings true happiness,
so that we may all return to our Father's house
and share your table
now and for ever.

℟. Amen.

32. (b) Readings

FIRST READING

A reading from the Letter of Saint Paul to
the Ephesians   1:3-7

He destined us for adoption to himself.

Blessed be the God and Father of our Lord Jesus Christ,
    who has blessed us in Christ
    with every spiritual blessing in the heavens,
    as he chose us in him, before the foundation of
        the world,
    to be holy and without blemish before him.

In love he destined us for adoption to himself through
       Jesus Christ,
   in accord with the favor of his will,
   for the praise of the glory of his grace
   that he granted us in the beloved.

The word of the Lord.

RESPONSORIAL PSALM   Ps 27:1, 4, 7-10, 13-14

R̷. The Lord is my light and my salvation.

The Lord is my light and my salvation;
   whom should I fear?
The Lord is my life's refuge;
   of whom should I be afraid?

R̷. The Lord is my light and my salvation.

One thing I ask of the Lord;
   this I seek:
To dwell in the house of the Lord
   all the days of my life,
That I may gaze on the loveliness of the Lord
   and contemplate his temple.

R̷. The Lord is my light and my salvation.

Hear, O LORD, the sound of my call;
  have pity on me, and answer me.
Of you my heart speaks; you my glance seeks;
  your presence, O LORD, I seek.

R̷. The Lord is my light and my salvation.

Hide not your face from me;
  do not in anger repel your servant.
You are my helper; cast me not off;
  forsake me not, O God my savior.
Though my father and mother forsake me,
  yet will the LORD receive me.

R̷. The Lord is my light and my salvation.

I believe that I shall see the bounty of the LORD
  in the land of the living.
Wait for the LORD with courage
  be stouthearted, and wait for the LORD.

R̷. The Lord is my light and my salvation.

GOSPEL

✠ A reading from the holy Gospel
according to Luke   15:11-32

His father caught sight of him, and was filled with compassion.

Jesus addressed this parable to them:
"A man had two sons, and the younger son said to
          his father,
     'Father, give me the share of your estate that should
          come to me.'
So the father divided the property between them.
After a few days, the younger son collected all
          his belongings
     and set off to a distant country
     where he squandered his inheritance on a life
          of dissipation.
When he had freely spent everything,
     a severe famine struck that country,
     and he found himself in dire need.
So he hired himself out to one of the local citizens
     who sent him to his farm to tend the swine.
And he longed to eat his fill of the pods on which the
          swine fed,
     but nobody gave him any.
Coming to his senses he thought,
     'How many of my father's hired workers
     have more than enough food to eat,
     but here am I, dying from hunger.

I shall get up and go to my father and I shall say to him,
   "Father, I have sinned against heaven and against you.
I no longer deserve to be called your son;
   treat me as you would treat one of your hired workers.'"
So he got up and went back to his father.
While he was still a long way off,
   his father caught sight of him, and was filled
      with compassion.
He ran to his son, embraced him and kissed him.
His son said to him,
   'Father, I have sinned against heaven and against you;
   I no longer deserve to be called your son.'
But his father ordered his servants,
   'Quickly, bring the finest robe and put it on him;
   put a ring on his finger and sandals on his feet.
Take the fattened calf and slaughter it.
Then let us celebrate with a feast,
   because this son of mine was dead, and has come to
      life again;
   he was lost, and has been found.'
Then the celebration began.
Now the older son had been out in the field
   and, on his way back, as he neared the house,
   he heard the sound of music and dancing.
He called one of the servants and asked what this
      might mean.
The servant said to him,
   'Your brother has returned
   and your father has slaughtered the fattened calf
   because he has him back safe and sound.'

He became angry,
    and when he refused to enter the house,
    his father came out and pleaded with him.
He said to his father in reply,
    'Look, all these years I served you
    and not once did I disobey your orders;
    yet you never gave me even a young goat to feast on
            with my friends.
But when your son returns
    who swallowed up your property with prostitutes,
    for him you slaughter the fattened calf.'
He said to him,
    'My son, you are here with me always;
    everything I have is yours.
But now we must celebrate and rejoice,
    because your brother was dead and has come to
            life again;
    he was lost and has been found.'"

The Gospel of the Lord.

33. (c) Homily

The minister may speak about:

— sin as a turning away from the love that we should have for God our Father;

— the limitless mercy of our Father for his children who have sinned;

— the nature of true conversion;

— the forgiveness we should extend to our brothers;

— the eucharistic banquet as the culmination of our reconciliation with the Church and with God.

34. (d) Examination of conscience

After the homily, the examination of conscience takes place; a sample text is given in Appendix III. A period of silence should always be included so that each person may personally examine his conscience.

35. (e) Act of repentance

After the examination of conscience, the presiding minister invites all to pray:

Our God is a God of mercy, slow to anger and full of patience. He is the father who welcomes his son when he returns from a distant country. Let us pray to him with trust in his goodness:

R̸. We are not worthy to be called your children.

—By our misuse of your gifts we have sinned against you.

R̸. We are not worthy to be called your children.

—By straying from you in mind and heart we have sinned against you.

R̸. We are not worthy to be called your children.

—By forgetting your love we have sinned against you.

R̸. We are not worthy to be called your children.

—By indulging ourselves, while neglecting our true good and the good of our neighbor, we have sinned against you.

℟. We are not worthy to be called your children.

—By failing to help our neighbor in his need we have sinned against you.

℟. We are not worthy to be called your children.

—By being slow to forgive we have sinned against you.

℟. We are not worthy to be called your children.

—By failing to remember your repeated forgiveness we have sinned against you.

℟. We are not worthy to be called your children.

Members of the congregation may add other invocations. A brief period of silence should follow each invocation. It may be desirable to have different individuals say each invocation.

—Let us now call upon our Father in the words that Jesus gave us, and ask him to forgive us our sins: Our Father . . .

36. (f) After an appropriate song, the presiding minister says the final prayer and dismisses the people:

God our Father,
you chose us to be your children,
to be holy in your sight
and happy in your presence.
Receive us as a loving Father
so that we may share the joy and love
of your holy Church.
We ask this through Christ our Lord.

R̷. Amen.

III. THE BEATITUDES

37. (a) After an appropriate song and greeting of the minister, the person presiding explains briefly the meaning of the readings. Then he invites all to pray. After a period of silence, he says:

Lord,
open our ears and our hearts today
to the message of your Son,
so that through the power of his death and resurrection
we may walk in newness of life.
We ask this through Christ our Lord.

R̷. Amen.

38. (b) Readings

FIRST READING

A reading from the first Letter of Saint John   1:5-9

If we say, "We are without sin," we deceive ourselves.

Beloved:
This is the message that we have heard from Jesus Christ
    and proclaim to you: God is light,
    and in him there is no darkness at all.
If we say, "We have fellowship with him,"
    while we continue to walk in darkness,
    we lie and do not act in truth.
But if we walk in the light as he is in the light,
    then we have fellowship with one another,
    and the Blood of his Son Jesus cleanses us from all sin.
If we say, "We are without sin," we deceive ourselves,
    and the truth is not in us.
If we acknowledge our sins, he is faithful and just
    and will forgive our sins and cleanse us from
        every wrongdoing.

The word of the Lord.

RESPONSORIAL PSALM　　　Ps 146:5-6b, 6c-7a, 7b-8, 9-10

R/. Lord, come and save us.

Blessed he whose help is the God of Jacob,
　　whose hope is in the LORD, his God.
Who made heaven and earth,
　　the sea and all that is in them.

R/. Lord, come and save us.

The LORD keeps faith forever,
　　secures justice for the oppressed,
　　gives food to the hungry.

R/. Lord, come and save us.

The LORD sets captives free;
　　the LORD gives sight to the blind.
The LORD raises up those that were bowed down;
　　the LORD loves the just.

R/. Lord, come and save us.

The LORD protects strangers;
　　the fatherless and the widow he sustains,
　　but the way of the wicked he thwarts.
The LORD shall reign forever;
　　your God, O Zion, through all generations. Alleluia.

R/. Lord, come and save us.

GOSPEL

✠ A reading from the holy Gospel
according to Matthew   5:1-10

Blessed are the poor in spirit, for theirs is the Kingdom of heaven.

When Jesus saw the crowds, he went up the mountain,
    and after he had sat down, his disciples came to him.
He began to teach them, saying:

"Blessed are the poor in spirit,
    for theirs is the Kingdom of heaven.
Blessed are they who mourn,
    for they will be comforted.
Blessed are the meek,
    for they will inherit the land.
Blessed are they who hunger and thirst for righteousness,
    for they will be satisfied.
Blessed are the merciful,
    for they will be shown mercy.
Blessed are the clean of heart,
    for they will see God.
Blessed are the peacemakers,
    for they will be called children of God.
Blessed are they who are persecuted for the sake
        of righteousness,
    for theirs is the Kingdom of heaven."

The Gospel of the Lord.

Or:

✠ A reading from the holy Gospel according to Luke 15:1-10

Tax collectors and sinners were all drawing near to listen
        to Jesus,
    but the Pharisees and scribes began to complain, saying,
    "This man welcomes sinners and eats with them."
So to them he addressed this parable.
"What man among you having a hundred sheep and
        losing one of them
    would not leave the ninety-nine in the desert
    and go after the lost one until he finds it?
And when he does find it,
    he sets it on his shoulders with great joy
    and, upon his arrival home,
    he calls together his friends and neighbors and says
        to them,
    'Rejoice with me because I have found my lost sheep.'
I tell you, in just the same way
    there will be more joy in heaven over one sinner
        who repents
    than over ninety-nine righteous people
    who have no need of repentance."

The Gospel of the Lord.

39. (c) Homily

The minister may speak about:

— sin, by which we ignore the commandments of Christ and act contrary to the teaching of the beatitudes;

— the firmness of our faith in the words of Jesus;

— our faithfulness in imitating Christ in our private lives, in the Christian community, and in human society;

— each beatitude.

40. (d) Examination of conscience

After the homily, the examination of conscience takes place; a sample text is given in Appendix III. A period of silence should always be included so that each person may personally examine his conscience.

41. (e) Act of repentance

After the examination of conscience, the presiding minister invites all to pray in these or similar words:

My brothers and sisters, Jesus Christ has left an example for us to follow. Humbly and confidently let us ask him to renew us in spirit so that we may shape our lives according to the teaching of his Gospel.

—Lord Jesus Christ, you said:
"Blessed are the poor in spirit,
for theirs is the kingdom of heaven."
Yet we are preoccupied with money and worldly goods

and even try to increase them at the expense of justice.
Lamb of God, you take away the sin of the world:

R⁄. Have mercy on us.

—Lord Jesus Christ, you said:
"Blessed are the gentle,
for they shall inherit the earth."
Yet we are ruthless with each other,
and our world is full of discord and violence.
Lamb of God, you take away the sin of the world:

R⁄. Have mercy on us.

—Lord Jesus Christ, you said:
"Blessed are those who mourn,
for they shall be comforted."
Yet we are impatient under our own burdens
and unconcerned about the burdens of others.
Lamb of God, you take away the sin of the world:

R⁄. Have mercy on us.

—Lord Jesus Christ, you said:
"Blessed are those who hunger and thirst for justice,
for they shall be filled."
Yet we do not thirst for you, the fountain of all holiness,
and are slow to spread your influence
in our private lives or in society.
Lamb of God, you take away the sin of the world:

R⁄. Have mercy on us.

—Lord Jesus Christ, you said:
"Blessed are the merciful,
for they shall receive mercy."
Yet we are slow to forgive
and quick to condemn.
Lamb of God, you take away the sin of the world:

R̸. Have mercy on us.

—Lord Jesus Christ, you said:
"Blessed are the clean of heart,
for they shall see God."
Yet we are prisoners of our senses and evil desires
and dare not raise our eyes to you.
Lamb of God, you take away the sin of the world:

R̸. Have mercy on us.

—Lord Jesus Christ, you said:
"Blessed are the peacemakers,
for they shall be called children of God."
Yet we fail to make peace in our families,
in our country, and in the world.
Lamb of God, you take away the sin of the world:

R̸. Have mercy on us.

—Lord Jesus Christ, you said:
"Blessed are those who are persecuted
for the sake of justice,
for the kingdom of heaven is theirs."

**Yet we prefer to practice injustice
rather than suffer for the sake of right;
we discriminate against our neighbors
and oppress and persecute them.
Lamb of God, you take away the sin of the world:**

R̷. Have mercy on us.

**—Now let us turn to God our Father and ask him to
free us from evil and prepare us for the coming of
his kingdom:**

Our Father . . .

42. (f) After an appropriate song, the presiding minister says the final prayer
and dismisses the people:

**Lord Jesus Christ,
gentle and humble of heart,
full of compassion and maker of peace,
you lived in poverty
and were persecuted in the cause of justice.
You chose the cross as the path to glory
to show us the way to salvation.
May we receive with joyful hearts
the word of your Gospel
and live by your example
as heirs and citizens of your kingdom,
where you live and reign for ever and ever.**

R̷. Amen.

IV. FOR CHILDREN

43. This service is suitable for younger children, including those who have not yet participated in the sacrament of penance.

Theme: *God Comes to Look for Us*

44. The penitential celebration should be prepared with the children so that they will understand its meaning and purpose, be familiar with the songs, have at least an elementary knowledge of the biblical text to be read, and know what they are to say and in what order.

45. (a) Greeting

When the children have come together in the church or some other suitable place, the celebrant greets them in a friendly manner. Briefly he reminds them why they have come together and recounts the theme of the service. After the greeting, an opening song may be sung.

46. (b) Reading

The celebrant may give a short introduction to the reading in these or similar words:

My dear children, each one of us has been baptized, and so we are all sons and daughters of God. God loves us as a Father, and he asks us to love him with all our hearts. He also wants us to be good to each other, so that we may all live happily together.

But people do not always do what God wants. They say: "I will not obey! I am going to do as I please." They disobey God and do not want to listen to him. We, too, often act like that.

That is what we call sin. When we sin we turn our backs on God. If we do something really bad we cut ourselves off from God; we are complete strangers to him.

What does God do when someone turns away from him? What does he do when we leave the path of goodness that he has shown us, when we run the risk of losing the life of grace he has given us? Does God turn away from us when we turn away from him by our sins?

Here is what God does, in the words of Jesus himself:

47. Only one text of Scripture should be read.

48. (c) Homily

The homily should be short, proclaiming God's love for us and preparing the ground for the examination of conscience.

49. (d) Examination of conscience

The celebrant should adapt the examination to the children's level of understanding by brief comments. There should be a suitable period of silence (see Appendix III).

50. (e) Act of repentance

This litany may be said by the celebrant or by one or more of the children, alternating with all present. Before the response, which may be sung, all should observe a brief pause.

God our Father,

—Sometimes we have not behaved as your children should.

R/. But you love us and come to us.

—We have given trouble to our parents and teachers.

R/. But you love us and come to us.

—We have quarrelled and called each other names.

R/. But you love us and come to us.

—We have been lazy at home and in school, and have not been helpful to our parents (brothers, sisters, friends).

R/. But you love us and come to us.

—We have thought too much of ourselves and have told lies.

R/. But you love us and come to us.

—We have not done good to others when we had the chance.

R/. But you love us and come to us.

Now with Jesus, our brother, we come before our Father in heaven and ask him to forgive our sins:

Our Father . . .

51. (f) Act of contrition and purpose of amendment

Sorrow may be shown by some sign, for example, individual children may come to the altar or another suitable place with a candle, and light it there; if necessary, a server may help. Each child says in his own words:

Father,
I am sorry for all my sins:
for what I have done
and for what I have failed to do.
I will sincerely try to do better
especially . . . (he mentions his particular resolution).
Help me to walk by your light.

In place of the candle, or in addition to it, the children may prepare a written prayer or resolution and place it on the altar or on a table designated for this purpose.

If the number of children or other circumstances do not allow for this, the celebrant asks the children present to say the above prayer together, along with a general resolution.

52. (g) Prayer of the celebrant

God our Father always seeks us out
when we walk away from the path of goodness.
He is always ready to forgive
when we have sinned.
May almighty God have mercy on us,
forgive us our sins,
and bring us to everlasting life.

℞. Amen.

53. The minister invites the children to express their thanks to God. They may do this by an appropriate hymn.

Then he dismisses them.

V. FOR YOUNG PEOPLE

54. The penitential celebration should be prepared with the young people so that with the celebrant, they may choose or compose the texts and songs. The readers, cantors or choir should be chosen from among them.

Theme: *Renewal of Our Lives According to the Christian Vocation*

55. (a) Greeting

This may be given in these or similar words:

Dear friends, we have come here to do penance and to make a fresh start as Christians. Many people see in penance only its difficult side, and its emphasis on sorrow. But it has also a more joyful side, and it looks more to the future than to the past.

Through penance God calls us to a new beginning. He helps us to find our true freedom as his sons and daughters. When Jesus invites us to repentance, he is inviting us to take our place in his Father's kingdom. This is what he teaches us in the parable about the merchant who came across a pearl of great value and sold everything he had in order to buy it.

If we follow our Lord's advice we exchange our past life for one far more valuable.

Then a song is sung; it should stress the call to a new life or following God's call with an eager heart (for example, Psalm 40:1-9).

℟. Here am I, Lord; I come to do your will.

56. (b) Prayer

Lord our God,
you call us out of darkness into light,
out of self-deception into truth,
out of death into life.
Send us your Holy Spirit
to open our ears to your call.
Fill our hearts with courage
to be true followers of your Son.
We ask this through Christ our Lord.

℟. Amen.

57. (c) Readings

FIRST READING

A reading from the Letter of Saint Paul to
the Romans   7:18-25a

Brothers and sisters:
I know that good does not dwell in me, that is, in my flesh.
The willing is ready at hand, but doing the good is not.

For I do not do the good I want,
   but I do the evil I do not want.
Now if I do what I do not want, it is no longer I who do it,
   but sin that dwells in me.
So, then, I discover the principle
   that when I want to do right, evil is at hand.
For I take delight in the law of God, in my inner self,
   but I see in my members another principle
   at war with the law of my mind,
      taking me captive to the law of sin that dwells in
         my members.
Miserable one that I am!
Who will deliver me from this mortal body?
Thanks be to God through Jesus Christ our Lord.

The word of the Lord.

Or:

A reading from the Letter of Saint Paul
to the Romans   8:18-25

Brothers and sisters:
I consider that the sufferings of this present time are
         as nothing
   compared with the glory to be revealed for us.
For creation awaits with eager expectation
   the revelation of the children of God;
   for creation was made subject to futility,
   not of its own accord but because of the one who
      subjected it,

in hope that creation itself
would be set free from slavery to corruption
and share in the glorious freedom of the children of God.
We know that all creation is groaning in labor pains even
        until now;
and not only that, but we ourselves,
who have the firstfruits of the Spirit,
we also groan within ourselves
as we wait for adoption, the redemption of our bodies.
For in hope we were saved.
Now hope that sees for itself is not hope.
For who hopes for what one sees?
But if we hope for what we do not see, we wait
        with endurance.

The word of the Lord.

GOSPEL

✠ A reading from the holy Gospel
according to Matthew   **13:44-46**

Jesus said to his disciples:
"The Kingdom of heaven is like a treasure buried in
        a field,
    which a person finds and hides again,
    and out of joy goes and sells all that he has and buys
        that field.
Again, the Kingdom of heaven is like a merchant
    searching for fine pearls.

When he finds a pearl of great price,
he goes and sells all that he has and buys it."

The Gospel of the Lord.

58. (d) Homily

The celebrant may speak about:

— the law of sin which in us struggles against God;

— the necessity of giving up the way of sin so that we may enter the kingdom of God.

59. (e) Examination of conscience

After the homily, the examination of conscience takes place; a sample text is given in Appendix III. A period of silence should always be included so that each person may personally examine his conscience.

60. (f) Act of repentance

Christ our Lord came to call sinners into his Father's kingdom. Let us now make an act of sorrow in our hearts and resolve to avoid sin in the future.

After a brief period of silence, all say together:

I confess to almighty God,
and to you, my brothers and sisters,
that I have sinned through my own fault,

They strike their breast:

in my thoughts and in my words,
in what I have done,
and in what I have failed to do;
and I ask blessed Mary, ever virgin,
all the angels and saints,
and you, my brothers and sisters,
to pray for me to the Lord our God.

Minister:

Lord our God,
you know all things.
You know that we want to be more generous
in serving you and our neighbor.
Look on us with love and hear our prayer.

Reader:

Give us the strength to turn away from sin.

R̷. Hear our prayer.

Help us to be sorry for our sins and to keep our
**   resolutions.**

R̷. Hear our prayer.

Forgive our sins and have pity on our weakness.

R̷. Hear our prayer.

Give us trust in your goodness and make us generous
**   in serving you.**

R̷. Hear our prayer.

Help us to be true followers of your Son and living members of his Church.

℞. Hear our prayer.

Minister:

God does not want the sinner to die, but to turn to him and live. May he be pleased that we have confessed our sinfulness, and may he show us his mercy as we pray in obedience to his Son.

All say together:

Our Father . . .

61. The celebration ends with an appropriate song and the dismissal.

VI. FOR THE SICK

62. According to the condition of the sick people and the suitability of the place, the minister goes to the sick, gathered in one room, or else he brings them together in the sanctuary or church. He should adapt carefully the texts and their number to the condition of those who take part in the service. Since in most instances none of the sick will be able to act as reader, the minister should, if possible, invite another person to carry out this office.

Theme: *The Time of Sickness Is a Time of Grace*

63. (a) Greeting

He may greet them in these or similar words:

My dear friends, when Jesus came to preach repentance, he was bringing us good news, for he was proclaiming to us God's love and mercy. Again and again God comes to our help so that we may turn to him and live our lives entirely in his service. Penance is his gift, a gift we should accept with gratitude. Keeping this in mind, let us open our hearts to God with great simplicity and humility and ask to be reconciled with him as we now forgive each other.

If possible, a penitential song is sung by the sick persons, or by a choir.

64. (b) Prayer

Lord our God,
source of all goodness and mercy,
we come together as your family
to ask your forgiveness
and the forgiveness of each other.
Give us true sorrow for our sins
and loving trust in your compassion
so that we may acknowledge our sins
with sincere hearts.
Through this celebration
restore us to fuller union with yourself
and with our neighbor
so that we may serve you with greater generosity.
We ask this through Christ our Lord.

℟. Amen.

65. (c) Readings

The readings may be introduced in these or similar words:

Many people enjoy good health and other blessings and accept them as a matter of course, with no sense of gratitude. In time of sickness we discover that all these are great gifts, and that without them we easily lose heart. God allows us to experience sickness in order to test our faith. What is more, if we see our suffering as a share in Christ's suffering, it can be of great value both to ourselves and to the Church. The time of sickness is not then wasted or meaningless. It is in fact a time of grace if we accept it as God wants us to accept it. This celebration is meant to help us to do so. We shall therefore listen to God's word, examine our conscience, and pray with sincere hearts.

66.

FIRST READING

A reading from the Letter of Saint James   5:13-16

Beloved:
Is anyone among you suffering?
He should pray.
Is anyone in good spirits?
He should sing a song of praise.
Is anyone among you sick?

He should summon the presbyters of the Church,
    and they should pray over him
    and anoint him with oil in the name of the Lord.
The prayer of faith will save the sick person,
    and the Lord will raise him up.
If he has committed any sins, he will be forgiven.

Therefore, confess your sins to one another
    and pray for one another, that you may be healed.
The fervent prayer of a righteous person is very powerful.

The word of the Lord.

RESPONSORIAL PSALM   **Ps 130:1-2, 3-4, 5-6, 7-8**

R̹. (7bc) With the Lord there is mercy and fullness
      of redemption.

Out of the depths I cry to you, O LORD;
    LORD, hear my voice!
Let your ears be attentive
    to my voice in supplication.

R̹. With the Lord there is mercy and fullness of redemption.

If you, O LORD, mark iniquities,
    LORD, who can stand?
But with you is forgiveness,
    that you may be revered.

℟. With the Lord there is mercy and fullness of redemption.

I trust in the LORD;
   my soul trusts in his word.
More than sentinels wait for the dawn,
   let Israel wait for the LORD.

℟. With the Lord there is mercy and fullness of redemption.

For with the LORD is kindness
   and with him is plenteous redemption;
And he will redeem Israel
   from all their iniquities.

℟. With the Lord there is mercy and fullness of redemption.

Or:

Ps 51:3-4, 5-6ab, 7-8, 9-11,
12-13, 14 and 17, 19

℟. (see 14a) Give me back the joy of your salvation.

Have mercy on me, O God, in your goodness;
   in the greatness of your compassion wipe out
      my offense.
Thoroughly wash me from my guilt
   and of my sin cleanse me.

℟. Give me back the joy of your salvation.

For I acknowledge my offense,
    and my sin is before me always:
"Against you only have I sinned,
    and done what is evil in your sight."

℟. Give me back the joy of your salvation.

Indeed, in guilt was I born,
    and in sin my mother conceived me;
Behold, you are pleased with sincerity of heart,
    and in my inmost being you teach me wisdom.

℟. Give me back the joy of your salvation.

Cleanse me of sin with hyssop, that I may be purified;
    wash me, and I shall be whiter than snow.
Let me hear the sounds of joy and gladness;
    the bones you have crushed shall rejoice.
Turn away your face from my sins,
    and blot out all my guilt.

℟. Give me back the joy of your salvation.

A clean heart create for me, O God,
    and a steadfast spirit renew within me.
Cast me not out from your presence,
    and your Holy Spirit take not from me.

℟. Give me back the joy of your salvation.

Give me back the joy of your salvation,
> and a willing spirit sustain in me.

O Lord, open my lips,
> and my mouth shall proclaim your praise.

R̸. Give me back the joy of your salvation.

My sacrifice, O God, is a contrite spirit;
> a heart contrite and humbled, O God, you will not spurn.

R̸. Give me back the joy of your salvation.

GOSPEL

✠ A reading from the holy Gospel
according to Mark   2:1-12

When Jesus returned to Capernaum after some days,
> it became known that he was at home.

Many gathered together so that there was no longer room
> > for them,
> not even around the door,
> and he preached the word to them.

They came bringing to him a paralytic carried by four men.
Unable to get near Jesus because of the crowd,
> they opened up the roof above him.

After they had broken through,
> they let down the mat on which the paralytic was lying.

When Jesus saw their faith, he said to him,
> "Child, your sins are forgiven."

Now some of the scribes were sitting there asking themselves,
    "Why does this man speak that way? He is blaspheming.
Who but God alone can forgive sins?"
Jesus immediately knew in his mind what
    they were thinking to themselves,
    so he said, "Why are you thinking such things in
        your hearts?
Which is easier, to say to the paralytic,
    'Your sins are forgiven,'
    or to say, 'Rise, pick up your mat and walk'?
But that you may know
    that the Son of Man has authority to forgive sins on earth"
    —he said to the paralytic,
    "I say to you, rise, pick up your mat, and go home."
He rose, picked up his mat at once,
    and went away in the sight of everyone.
They were all astounded
    and glorified God, saying, "We have never seen
        anything like this."

The Gospel of the Lord.

67. (d) Homily

It is fitting that the celebrant speak of sickness, dwelling not so much on sickness of the body as on sickness of the soul. He should emphasize the power of Jesus and his Church to forgive sins and the value of suffering offered for others.

68. (e) Examination of conscience

After the homily, the examination of conscience takes place; a sample text is given in Appendix III. A period of silence should always be included so that each person may personally examine his conscience.

The following questions may be added but adapted to the condition of the sick:

— Do I trust God's goodness and providence, even in times of stress and illness?
— Do I give in to sickness, to despair, to other unworthy thoughts and feelings?
— Do I fill my empty moments with reflection on life and with prayer to God?
— Do I accept my illness and pain as an opportunity for suffering with Christ, who redeemed us by his passion?
— Do I live by faith, confident that patience in suffering is of great benefit to the Church?
— Am I thoughtful of others and attentive to my fellow patients and their needs?
— Am I grateful to those who look after me and visit me?
— Do I give a good Christian example to others?
— Am I sorry for my past sins, and do I try to make amends for them by my patient acceptance of weakness and illness.

69. (f) Act of repentance

After a moment of silence, all say together:

I confess to almighty God,
and to you, my brothers and sisters,
that I have sinned through my own fault

They strike their breast:

in my thoughts and in my words,
in what I have done,
and in what I have failed to do;
and I ask blessed Mary, ever virgin,
all the angels and saints,
and you, my brothers and sisters,
to pray for me to the Lord our God.

Reader:

Lord our God, we bear the name of your Son and call you Father. We are sorry for our sins against you and against our brothers and sisters.

℟. Give us true repentance and sincere love for you and
for our neighbor.

Lord Jesus Christ, you redeemed us by your passion and cross and gave us an example of patience and love. We are sorry for our sins against you, and especially for failing to serve you and our brothers and sisters.

℟. Give us true repentance and sincere love for you and
for our neighbor.

Holy Spirit, Lord, you speak to us in the Church and in our conscience and inspire within us the desire to do good. We are sorry for our sins against you, and especially for our obstinate refusal to obey you.

℞. Give us true repentance and sincere love for you and for our neighbor.

Minister:

Let us ask God our Father to forgive us and to free us from evil:

Our Father . . .

70. Then, if possible, the choir or the assembled people sing a song, and the service concludes with a prayer of thanksgiving:

71.

**God of consolation and Father of mercies,
you forgive the sinner who acknowledges his guilt:**

℞. We praise you and thank you.

**God of consolation and Father of mercies,
you give to those who suffer hardship or pain
a share in the sufferings of your Son
for the salvation of the world:**

℞. We praise you and thank you.

**God of consolation and Father of mercies,
you look with love on those who are troubled or
in sorrow;**

**you give them hope of salvation
and the promise of eternal life:**

℟. We praise you and thank you.

**Let us pray.
Lord,
your goodness and mercy are boundless.
Look on your sons and daughters
gathered here in the name of your Son.
We thank you for all your gifts
and ask you to keep us always as your family,
full of living faith, firm hope,
and sincere love for you and for our neighbor.
We ask this through Christ our Lord.**

℟. Amen.

72. In place of the prayer, the service may end with a blessing.

**May the God of peace
fill your hearts with every blessing.
May he sustain you
with his gifts of hope and consolation,
help you to offer your lives in his service,
and bring you safely to eternal glory.
May almighty God,
the Father, and the Son, ✠ and the Holy Spirit,
grant you all that is good.**

℟. Amen.

73. The minister dismisses the assembly, or invites those present to a friendly visit with the sick.

APPENDIX III

FORM OF EXAMINATION OF CONSCIENCE

1. This suggested form for an examination of conscience should be completed and adapted to meet the needs of different individuals and to follow local usages.

2. In an examination of conscience, before the sacrament of penance, each individual should ask himself these questions in particular:

1. What is my attitude to the sacrament of penance? Do I sincerely want to be set free from sin, to turn again to God, to begin a new life, and to enter into a deeper friendship with God? Or do I look on it as a burden, to be undertaken as seldom as possible?
2. Did I forget to mention, or deliberately conceal, any grave sins in past confessions?
3. Did I perform the penance I was given? Did I make reparation for any injury to others? Have I tried to put into practice my resolution to lead a better life in keeping with the Gospel?

3. Each individual should examine his life in the light of God's word.

I. The Lord says: "You shall love the Lord your God with your whole heart."

1. Is my heart set on God, so that I really love him above all things and am faithful to his commandments, as a son loves his father? Or am I more concerned about the things of this world? Have I a right intention in what I do?
2. God spoke to us in his Son. Is my faith in God firm and secure? Am I wholehearted in accepting the Church's teaching? Have I been careful to grow in my understanding of the faith, to hear God's word, to listen to instructions on the faith, to avoid dangers to faith? Have I been always strong and fearless in professing my faith in God and the Church? Have I been willing to be known as a Christian in private and public life?

3. Have I prayed morning and evening? When I pray, do I really raise my mind and heart to God or is it a matter of words only? Do I offer God my difficulties, my joys, and my sorrows? Do I turn to God in time of temptation?

4. Have I love and reverence for God's name? Have I offended him in blasphemy, swearing falsely, or taking his name in vain? Have I shown disrespect for the Blessed Virgin Mary and the saints?

5. Do I keep Sundays and feast days holy by taking a full part, with attention and devotion, in the liturgy, and especially in the Mass? Have I fulfilled the precept of annual confession and of communion during the Easter season?

6. Are there false gods that I worship by giving them greater attention and deeper trust than I give to God: money, superstition, spiritism, or other occult practices?

II. The Lord says: "Love one another as I have loved you."

1. Have I a genuine love for my neighbors? Or do I use them for my own ends, or do to them what I would not want done to myself? Have I given grave scandal by my words or actions?

2. In my family life, have I contributed to the well-being and happiness of the rest of the family by patience and genuine love? Have I been obedient to parents, showing them proper respect and giving them help in their spiritual and material needs? Have I been careful to give a Christian upbringing to my children, and to help them by good example and by exercising authority as a parent? Have I been faithful to my husband (wife) in my heart and in my relations with others?

3. Do I share my possessions with the less fortunate? Do I do my best to help the victims of oppression, misfortune, and poverty? Or do I look down on my neighbor, especially the poor, the sick, the elderly, strangers, and people of other races?

4. Does my life reflect the mission I received in confirmation? Do I share in the apostolic and charitable works of the Church and in the life of my parish? Have I helped to meet the needs of the Church and of the world and prayed for them: for unity in the Church, for the spread of the Gospel among the nations, for peace and justice, etc.?

5. Am I concerned for the good and prosperity of the human community in which I live, or do I spend my life caring only for myself? Do I share to the best of my ability in the work of promoting justice, morality, harmony, and love in human relations? Have I done my duty as a citizen? Have I paid my taxes?

6. In my work or profession am I just, hard-working, honest, serving society out of love for others? Have I paid a fair wage to my employees? Have I been faithful to my promises and contracts?

7. Have I obeyed legitimate authority and given it due respect?

8. If I am in a position of responsibility or authority, do I use this for my own advantage or for the good of others, in a spirit of service?

9. Have I been truthful and fair, or have I injured others by deceit, calumny, detraction, rash judgment, or violation of a secret?

10. Have I done violence to others by damage to life or limb, reputation, honor, or material possessions? Have I involved them in loss? Have I been responsible for advising an abortion or procuring one? Have I kept up hatred for others? Am I estranged from others through quarrels, enmity, insults, anger? Have I been guilty of refusing to testify to the innocence of another because of selfishness?

11. Have I stolen the property of others? Have I desired it unjustly and inordinately? Have I damaged it? Have I made restitution of other people's property and made good their loss?

12. If I have been injured, have I been ready to make peace for the love of Christ and to forgive, or do I harbor hatred and the desire for revenge?

III. Christ our Lord says: "Be perfect as your Father is perfect."

1. Where is my life really leading me? Is the hope of eternal life my inspiration? Have I tried to grow in the life of the Spirit through prayer, reading the word of God and meditating on it, receiving the sacraments, self-denial? Have I been anxious to control my vices, my bad inclinations and passions, e.g., envy, love of food and drink? Have I been proud and boastful, thinking myself better in the sight of God and despising others as less important than myself? Have I imposed my own will on others, without respecting their freedom and rights?

2. What use have I made of time, of health and strength, of the gifts God has given me to be used like the talents in the Gospel? Do I use them to become more perfect every day? Or have I been lazy and too much given to leisure?

3. Have I been patient in accepting the sorrows and disappointments of life? How have I performed mortification so as to "fill up what is wanting to the sufferings of Christ"? Have I kept the precept of fasting and abstinence?

4. Have I kept my senses and my whole body pure and chaste as a temple of the Holy Spirit consecrated for resurrection and glory, and as a sign of God's faithful love for men and women, a sign that is seen most perfectly in the sacrament of matrimony? Have I dishonored my body by fornication, impurity, unworthy conversation or thoughts, evil desires, or actions? Have I given in to sensuality? Have I indulged in reading, conversation, shows, and entertainments that offend against Christian and

human decency? Have I encouraged others to sin by my own failure to maintain these standards? Have I been faithful to the moral law in my married life?

5. Have I gone against my conscience out of fear or hypocrisy?
6. Have I always tried to act in the true freedom of the sons of God according to the law of the Spirit, or am I the slave of forces within me?

APPENDIX IV

APOSTOLIC LETTER IN THE FORM OF MOTU PROPRIO MISERICORDIA DEI

ON CERTAIN ASPECTS OF THE CELEBRATION OF THE SACRAMENT OF PENANCE

By the mercy of God, the Father who reconciles us to himself, the Word took flesh in the spotless womb of the Blessed Virgin Mary to save "his people from their sins" (Mt 1:21) and to open for them "the way of eternal salvation."[1] By identifying Jesus as "the Lamb of God, who takes away the sin of the world" (Jn 1:29), Saint John the Baptist confirms this mission. In all his deeds and preaching, the Precursor issues a fervent and energetic summons to repentance and conversion, the sign of which is the baptism administered in the waters of the Jordan. Jesus himself underwent this penitential rite (cf. Mt 3:13-17), not because he had sinned, but because "he allows himself to be numbered among sinners; he is already 'the Lamb of God who takes away the sin of the world' (Jn 1:29); already he is anticipating the 'baptism' of his bloody death."[2]

Salvation is therefore and above all redemption from sin, which hinders friendship with God, a liberation from the state of slavery in which man finds himself ever since he succumbed to the temptation of the Evil One and lost the freedom of the children of God (cf. Rom 8:21).

Christ entrusts to the Apostles the mission of proclaiming the Kingdom of God and preaching the Gospel of conversion (cf. Mk 16:15; Mt 28:18-20). On the evening of the day of his Resurrection, as the apostolic mission is about to begin, Jesus grants the Apostles, through the power of the Holy Spirit, the authority to reconcile repentant sinners with God and the Church: "Receive the Holy Spirit. If you forgive the sins of any, they are forgiven; if you retain the sins of any, they are retained" (Jn 20:22-23).[3]

Down through history in the constant practice of the Church, the "ministry of reconciliation" (2 Cor 5:18), conferred through the Sacraments of Baptism and Penance, has always been seen as an essential and highly esteemed pastoral duty of the priestly ministry, performed in obedience to the command of Jesus. Through the centuries, the celebration of the Sacrament of Penance has developed in different forms, but it has always kept the same basic structure: it necessarily entails not only the action of the minister—only a Bishop or priest, who judges and absolves, tends and heals in the name of Christ—but also the actions of the penitent: contrition, confession and satisfaction.

I wrote in my Apostolic Letter *Novo Millennio Ineunte*: "I am asking for renewed pastoral courage in ensuring that the day-to-day teaching of Christian communities persuasively and effectively presents the practice of the Sacrament of Reconciliation. As you will recall, in 1984 I dealt with this subject in the Post-Synodal Exhortation *Reconciliatio et Paenitentia*, which synthesized the results of a General Assembly of the Synod of Bishops devoted to this question. My invitation then was to make every effort to face the crisis of 'the sense of sin' apparent in today's culture. But I was even more insistent in calling for a rediscovery of Christ as *mysterium pietatis*, the one in whom God shows us his compassionate heart and reconciles us fully with himself. It is this face of Christ that must be rediscovered through the Sacrament of Penance, which for the faithful is 'the ordinary way of obtaining forgiveness and the remission of serious sins committed after Baptism.' When the Synod addressed the problem, the crisis of the Sacrament was there for all to see, especially in some parts of the world. The causes of the crisis have not disappeared in the brief span of time since then. But the Jubilee Year, which has been particularly marked by a return to the Sacrament of Penance, has given us an encouraging message, which should not be ignored: if many people, and among them also many young people, have benefited from approaching this Sacrament, it is probably necessary that Pastors should arm themselves with more confidence, creativity and perseverance in presenting it and leading people to appreciate it."[4]

With these words, I intended, as I do now, to encourage my Brother Bishops and earnestly appeal to them—and, through them, to all priests—to undertake a vigorous revitalization of the Sacrament of Reconciliation. This is a requirement of genuine charity and true pastoral justice,[5] and we should remember that the faithful, when they have the proper interior dispositions, have the right to receive personally the sacramental gift.

In order that the minister of the Sacrament may know the dispositions of penitents with a view to granting or withholding absolution and imposing a suitable penance, it is necessary that the faithful, as well as being aware of the sins they have committed, of being sorry for them and resolved not to fall into them again,[6] should also confess their sins. In this sense, the Council of Trent declared that it is necessary "by divine decree to confess each and every mortal sin."[7] The Church has always seen an essential link between the judgment entrusted to the priest in the Sacrament and the need for penitents to name their own sins,[8] except where this is not possible. Since, therefore, the integral confession of serious sins is by divine decree a constitutive part of the Sacrament, it is in no way subject to the discretion of pastors (dispensation, interpretation, local customs, etc.). In the relevant disciplinary norms, the competent ecclesiastical authority merely indicates the criteria for distinguishing a real impossibility of confessing one's sins from other situations in which the impossibility is only apparent or can be surmounted.

In the present circumstances of the care of souls and responding to the concerned requests of many Brothers in the Episcopate, I consider it useful to recall some of the canonical laws in force regarding the celebration of this Sacrament and clarify certain aspects of them—in a spirit of communion with the responsibility proper to the entire Episcopate[9] with a view to a better administration of the Sacrament. It is a question of ensuring an ever more faithful, and thus more fruitful, celebration of the gift entrusted to the Church by the Lord Jesus after his Resurrection (cf. Jn 20:19-23). This seems especially necessary, given that in some places there has been a tendency to abandon individual confession and wrongly to resort to "general" or "communal" absolution. In this case general absolution is no longer seen as an extraordinary means to be used in wholly exceptional situations. On the basis of an arbitrary extension of the conditions required for *grave necessity*,[10] in practice there is a lessening of fidelity to the divine configuration of the Sacrament, and specifically regarding the need for individual confession, with consequent serious harm to the spiritual life of the faithful and to the holiness of the Church.

Thus, after consultation with the Congregation for the Doctrine of the Faith, the Congregation for Divine Worship and the Discipline of the Sacraments, and the Pontifical Council for Legislative Texts, and after hearing the views of venerable Brother Cardinals in charge of the dicasteries of the Roman Curia, and reaffirming Catholic doctrine on the Sacrament of Penance and Reconciliation as summarized in the *Catechism of the Catholic Church*,[11] conscious of my pastoral responsibility and fully aware of the need for this Sacrament and of its enduring efficacy, I decree the following:

1. Ordinaries are to remind all the ministers of the Sacrament of Penance that the universal law of the Church, applying Catholic doctrine in this area, has established that:

    a. "Individual and integral confession and absolution are the sole ordinary means by which the faithful, conscious of grave sin, are reconciled with God and the Church; only physical or moral impossibility excuses from such confession, in which case reconciliation can be obtained in other ways."[12]

    b. Therefore, "all those of whom it is required by virtue of their ministry in the care of souls are obliged to ensure that the confessions of the faithful entrusted to them are heard when they reasonably ask, and that they are given the opportunity to approach individual confession, on days and at times set down for their convenience."[13]

    Moreover, all priests with faculties to administer the Sacrament of Penance are always to show themselves wholeheartedly disposed to administer it whenever the faithful make a reasonable request.[14] An unwillingness to welcome the wounded sheep, and even to go out to them in order to bring them back into the fold, would be a sad sign of a lack of pastoral sensibility in those who, by priestly Ordination, must reflect the image of the Good Shepherd.

2. Local Ordinaries, and parish priests and rectors of churches and shrines, should periodically verify that the greatest possible provision is in fact being made for the faithful to confess their sins. It is particularly recommended that in places of worship confessors be visibly present at the advertised times, that these times be adapted to the real circumstances of penitents, and that confessions be especially available before Masses, and even during Mass if there are other priests available, in order to meet the needs of the faithful.[15]

3. Since "the faithful are obliged to confess, according to kind and number, all grave sins committed after Baptism of which they are conscious after careful examination and which have not yet been directly remitted by the Church's power of the keys, nor acknowledged in individual confession,"[16] any practice which restricts confession to a generic accusation of sin or of only one or two sins judged to be more important is to be reproved. Indeed, in view of the fact that all the faithful are called to holiness, it is recommended that they confess venial sins also.[17]

4. In the light of and within the framework of the above norms, the absolution of a number of penitents at once without previous confession, as envisaged by Can. 961 of the Code of Canon Law, is to be correctly understood and administered.

Such absolution is in fact "exceptional in character"[18] and "cannot be imparted in a general manner unless:

1. *the danger of death is imminent* and there is not time for the priest or priests to hear the confessions of the individual penitents;
2. a *grave necessity* exists, that is, when in light of the number of penitents a supply of confessors is not readily available to hear the confessions of individuals in an appropriate way within an appropriate time, so that the penitents would be deprived of sacramental grace or Holy Communion for a long time through no fault of their own; it is not considered sufficient necessity if confessors cannot be readily available only because of the great number of penitents, as can occur on the occasion of some great feast or pilgrimage."[19]

With reference to the case of *grave necessity*, the following clarification is made:

a. It refers to situations which are objectively exceptional, such as can occur in mission territories or in isolated communities of the faithful, where the priest can visit only once or very few times a year, or when war or weather conditions or similar factors permit.
b. The two conditions set down in the Canon to determine grave necessity are inseparable. Therefore, it is never just a question of whether individuals can have their confession heard "in an appropriate way" and "within an appropriate time" because of the shortage of priests; this must be combined with the fact that penitents would otherwise be forced to remain deprived of sacramental grace "for a long time," through no fault of their own. Therefore, account must be taken of the overall circumstances of the penitents and of the Diocese, in what refers to its pastoral organization and the possibility of the faithful having access to the Sacrament of Penance.
c. The first condition, the impossibility of hearing confessions "in an appropriate way" "within an appropriate time," refers only to the time reasonably required for the elements of a valid and worthy celebration of the Sacrament. It is not a question here of a more extended pastoral conversation, which can be left to more favorable circumstances. The reasonable and appropriate time within which confessions can be heard will depend upon the real possibilities of the confessor or confessors, and of the penitents themselves.
d. The second condition calls for a prudential judgment in order to assess how long penitents can be deprived of sacramental grace for there to be a true

impossibility as described in Can. 960, presuming that there is no imminent danger of death. Such a judgment is not prudential if it distorts the sense of physical or moral impossibility, as would be the case, for example, if it was thought that a period of less than a month means remaining "for a long time" in such a state of privation.

e. It is not acceptable to contrive or to allow the contrivance of situations of apparent *grave necessity*, resulting from not administering the Sacrament in the ordinary way through a failure to implement the above mentioned norms,[20] and still less because of penitents' preference for general absolution, as if this were a normal option equivalent to the two ordinary forms set out in the Ritual.

f. The large number of penitents gathered on the occasion of a great feast or pilgrimage, or for reasons of tourism or because of today's increased mobility of people, does not in itself constitute sufficient necessity.

5. Judgment as to whether there exist the conditions required by Can. 961 §1, 2 is not a matter for the confessor but for "the diocesan Bishop who can determine cases of such necessity in the light of criteria agreed upon with other members of the Episcopal Conference."[21] These pastoral criteria must embody the pursuit of total fidelity, in the circumstances of their respective territories, to the fundamental criteria found in the universal discipline of the Church, which are themselves based upon the requirements deriving from the Sacrament of Penance itself as a divine institution.

6. Given the fundamental importance of full harmony among the Bishops' Conferences of the world in a matter so essential to the life of the Church, the various Conferences, observing Can. 455 § 2 of the Code of Canon Law, shall send as soon as possible to the Congregation for Divine Worship and the Discipline of the Sacraments the text of the norms which they intend to issue or update in the light of this *Motu Proprio* on the application of Can. 961. This will help to foster an ever greater communion among the Bishops of the Church as they encourage the faithful everywhere to draw abundantly from the fountains of divine mercy which flow unceasingly in the Sacrament of Reconciliation.

In this perspective of communion it will also be appropriate for Diocesan Bishops to inform their respective Bishops' Conferences whether or not cases of *grave necessity* have occurred in their jurisdictions. It will then be the task of each Conference to inform the above-mentioned Congregation about the real situation in their regions and about any changes subsequently taking place.

7. As regards the personal disposition of penitents, it should be reiterated that:

   a. "For the faithful to avail themselves validly of sacramental absolution given to many at one time, it is required that they not only be suitably disposed but also at the same time intend to confess individually the serious sins which at present cannot be so confessed."[22]

   b. As far as possible, including cases of imminent danger of death, there should be a preliminary exhortation to the faithful "that each person take care to make an act of contrition."[23]

   c. It is clear that penitents living in a habitual state of serious sin and who do not intend to change their situation cannot validly receive absolution.

8. The obligation "to confess serious sins at least once a year"[24] remains, and therefore "a person who has had serious sins remitted by general absolution is to approach individual confession as soon as there is an opportunity to do so before receiving another general absolution, unless a just cause intervenes."[25]

9. Concerning the *place* and *confessional* for the celebration of the Sacrament, it should be remembered that:

   a. "The proper place to hear sacramental confessions is a church or an oratory,"[26] though it remains clear that pastoral reasons can justify celebrating the Sacrament in other places.[27]

   b. Confessionals are regulated by the norms issued by the respective Episcopal Conferences, who shall ensure that confessionals are located "in an open area" and have "a fixed grille," so as to permit the faithful and confessors themselves who may wish to make use of them to do so freely.[28]

I decree that everything I have set down in this Apostolic Letter issued *Motu Proprio* shall have full and lasting force and be observed from this day forth, notwithstanding any provisions to the contrary. All that I have decreed in this Letter is, by its nature, valid for the venerable Oriental Catholic Churches in conformity with the respective Canons of their own Code.

Given in Rome, at Saint Peter's, on April 7, the Second Sunday of Easter, the Feast of Divine Mercy, in the year of our Lord 2002, the twenty-fourth of my Pontificate.

Joannes Paulus II

NOTES

1   *Roman Missal*, Advent Preface I.

2   *Catechism of the Catholic Church*, no. 536.

3   Cf. Ecumenical Council of Trent, Session XIV, *De Sacramento Paenitentiae*, Can. 3: DS 1703.

4   No. 37: AAS 93 (2001) 292.

5   Cf. *Code of Canon Law*, Cans. 213 and 843 § 1.

6   Cf. Ecumenical Council of Trent, Session XIV, *Doctrina de Sacramento Paenitentiae*, Chap. 4: DS 1676.

7   *Ibid.*, Can. 7: DS 1707.

8   *Ibid.*, Chap. 5: DS 1679; Ecumenical Council of Florence, Decree for the Armenians (November 22, 1439): DS 1323.

9   Cf. Can. 392; Second Vatican Ecumenical Council, Dogmatic Constitution on the Church *Lumen Gentium*, nos. 23, 27; Decree on the Pastoral Ministry of Bishops *Christus Dominus*, no. 16.

10   Cf. Can. 961, § 1, 2.

11   Cf. nos. 980-987; 1114-1134; 1420-1498.

12   Can. 960.

13   Can. 986, § 1.

14   Cf. Second Vatican Ecumenical Council, Decree on the Ministry and Life of Priests *Presbyterorum Ordinis*, no. 13; *Ordo Paenitentiae*, editio typica, 1974, *Praenotanda*, No. 10, b.

15   Cf. Congregation for Divine Worship and the Discipline of the Sacraments, *Responsa ad dubia proposita: Notitiae*, 37 (2001) 259-260

16   Can. 988, § 1.

17   Cf. Can. 988, § 2: John Paul II, Post-Synodal Apostolic Exhortation *Reconciliatio et Paenitentia* (December 2, 1984), no. 32: AAS 77 (1985) 267; *Catechism of the Catholic Church*, no. 1458.

18   John Paul II, Post-Synodal Apostolic Exhortation *Reconciliatio et Paenitentia* (December 2, 1984), no. 32: AAS 77 (1985) 267.

19   Can. 961, § 1.

20   Cf. above nos. 1 and 2.

21   Can. 961, § 2.

22   Can. 962, § 1.

23   Can. 962, § 2.

24   Can. 989.

25   Can. 963.

26   Can 964, § 1.

27   Cf. Can. 964 § 3.

28   Pontifical Council for the Interpretation of Legislative Texts, *Responsa ad propositum dubium: de loco excipiendi sacramentales confessiones* (July 7, 1998): AAS 90 (1998) 711.

APPENDIX V

POST-SYNODAL APOSTOLIC EXHORTATION RECONCILIATION AND PENANCE

OF JOHN PAUL II TO THE BISHOPS, CLERGY, AND FAITHFUL ON RECONCILIATION AND PENANCE IN THE MISSION OF THE CHURCH TODAY

INTRODUCTION: ORIGIN AND MEANING OF THE DOCUMENT

1. To speak of reconciliation and penance is for the men and women of our time an invitation to rediscover, translated into their own way of speaking, the very words with which our savior and teacher Jesus Christ began his preaching: "Repent, and believe in the Gospel,"[1] that is to say, accept the good news of love, of adoption as children of God and hence of brotherhood.

Why does the church put forward once more this subject and this invitation?

The concern to know better and to understand modern man and the contemporary world, to solve their puzzle and reveal their mystery, to discern the ferments of good and evil within them, has long caused many people to direct at man and the world a questioning gaze. It is the gaze of the historian and sociologist, philosopher and

338

theologian, psychologist and humanist, poet and mystic: Above all, it is the gaze, anxious yet full of hope, of the pastor.

In an exemplary fashion this is shown on every page of the important pastoral constitution of the Second Vatican Council *Gaudium et Spes* on the church in the modern world, particularly in its wide-ranging and penetrating introduction. It is likewise shown in certain documents issued through the wisdom and charity of my esteemed predecessors, whose admirable pontificates were marked by the historic and prophetic event of that ecumenical council.

In common with others, the pastor too can discern among the various unfortunate characteristics of the world and of humanity in our time the existence of many deep and painful divisions.

A Shattered World

2. These divisions are seen in the relationships between individuals and groups, and also at the level of larger groups: nations against nations and blocs of opposing countries in a headlong quest for domination. At the root of this alienation it is not hard to discern conflicts which, instead of being resolved through dialogue, grow more acute in confrontation and opposition.

Careful observers, studying the elements that cause division, discover reasons of the most widely differing kinds: from the growing disproportion between groups, social classes and countries, to ideological rivalries that are far from dead; from the opposition between economic interests to political polarization; from tribal differences to discrimination for social and religious reasons. Moreover, certain facts that are obvious to all constitute as it were the pitiful face of the division of which they are the fruit and demonstrate its seriousness in an inescapably concrete way. Among the many other painful social phenomena of our times one can note:

- The trampling upon the basic rights of the human person, the first of these being the right to life and to a worthy quality of life, which is all the more scandalous in that it coexists with a rhetoric never before known on these same rights.
- Hidden attacks and pressures against the freedom of individuals and groups, not excluding the freedom which is most offended against and threatened: the freedom to have, profess and practice one's own faith.
- The various forms of discrimination: racial, cultural, religious, etc.
- Violence and terrorism.
- The use of torture and unjust and unlawful methods of repression.

- The stockpiling of conventional or atomic weapons, the arms race with the spending on military purposes of sums which could be used to alleviate the undeserved misery of peoples that are socially and economically depressed.
- An unfair distribution of the world's resources and of the assets of civilization, which reaches its highest point in a type of social organization whereby the distance between the human conditions of the rich and the poor becomes ever greater.[2] The overwhelming power of this division makes the world in which we live a world shattered[3] to its very foundations.

Moreover, the church—without identifying herself with the world or being of the world—is in the world and is engaged in dialogue with the world.[4] It is therefore not surprising if one notices in the structure of the church herself repercussions and signs of the division affecting human society. Over and above the divisions between the Christian communions that have afflicted her for centuries, the church today is experiencing within herself sporadic divisions among her own members, divisions caused by differing views or options in the doctrinal and pastoral field.[5] These divisions too can at times seem incurable.

However disturbing these divisions may seem at first sight, it is only by a careful examination that one can detect their root: It is to be found in a wound in man's inmost self. In the light of faith we call it sin: beginning with original sin, which all of us bear from birth as an inheritance from our first parents, to the sin which each one of us commits when we abuse our own freedom.

Longing for Reconciliation

3. Nevertheless, that same inquiring gaze, if it is discerning enough, detects in the very midst of division an unmistakable desire among people of good will and true Christians to mend the divisions, to heal the wounds and to reestablish at all levels an essential unity. This desire arouses in many people a real longing for reconciliation even in cases where there is no actual use of this word.

Some consider reconciliation as an impossible dream which ideally might become the lever for a true transformation of society. For others it is to be gained by arduous efforts and therefore a goal to be reached through serious reflection and action. Whatever the case, the longing for sincere and consistent reconciliation is without a shadow of doubt a fundamental driving force in our society, reflecting an irrepressible desire for peace. And it is as strongly so as the factors of division, even though this is a paradox.

But reconciliation cannot be less profound than the division itself. The longing for reconciliation and reconciliation itself will be complete and effective only to the extent that they reach—in order to heal it—that original wound which is the root of all other wounds: namely sin.

The Synod's View

4. Therefore every institution or organization concerned with serving people and saving them in their fundamental dimensions must closely study reconciliation in order to grasp more fully its meaning and significance and in order to draw the necessary practical conclusions.

The church of Jesus Christ could not fail to make this study. With the devotion of a mother and the understanding of a teacher, she earnestly and carefully applies herself to detecting in society not only the signs of division but also the no less eloquent and significant signs of the quest for reconciliation. For she knows that she especially has been given the ability and assigned the mission to make known the true and profoundly religious meaning of reconciliation and its full scope. She is thereby already helping to clarify the essential terms of the question of unity and peace.

My predecessors constantly preached reconciliation and invited to reconciliation the whole of humanity and every section and portion of the human community that they saw wounded and divided.[6] And I myself, by an interior impulse which—I am certain—was obeying both an inspiration from on high and the appeals of humanity, decided to emphasize the subject of reconciliation and to do this in two ways, each of them solemn and exacting. In the first place, by convoking the Sixth General Assembly of the Synod of Bishops; in the second place, by making reconciliation the center of the jubilee year called to celebrate the 1,950th anniversary of the redemption.[7] Having to assign a theme to the synod, I found myself fully in accord with the one suggested by many of my brothers in the episcopate, namely, the fruitful theme of reconciliation in close connection with the theme of penance.[8]

The term and the very concept of penance are very complex. If we link penance with the *metanoia* which the synoptics refer to, it means the inmost change of heart under the influence of the word of God and in the perspective of the kingdom.[9] But penance also means changing one's life in harmony with the change of heart, and in this sense doing penance is completed by bringing forth fruits worthy of penance:[10] It is one's whole existence that becomes penitential, that is to say, directed toward a continuous striving for what is better. But doing penance is something authentic and effective only if it is translated into deeds and acts of penance. In this sense penance means, in the Christian theological and spiritual vocabulary, asceticism, that is to say, the concrete daily effort of a person, supported by God's lose his or her own life for Christ as the only means of gaining it;[11] an effort to put off the old man and put on the new;[12] an effort to overcome in oneself what is of the flesh in order that what is spiritual[13] may prevail; a continual effort to rise from the things of here below to the things of above, where Christ is.[14] Penance is therefore a conversion that passes from the heart to deeds and then to the Christian's whole life.

In each of these meanings penance is closely connected with reconciliation, for reconciliation with God, with oneself and with others implies overcoming that radical break which is sin. And this is achieved only through the interior transformation or conversion which bears fruit in a person's life through acts of penance.

The basic document of the synod (also called the lineamenta), which was prepared with the sole purpose of presenting the theme while stressing certain fundamental aspects of it, enabled the ecclesial communities throughout the world to reflect for almost two years on these aspects of a question—that of conversion and reconciliation—which concerns everyone. It also enabled them to draw from it a fresh impulse for the Christian life and Apostolate. That reflection was further deepened in the more immediate preparation for the work of the synod, thanks to the *instrumentum laboris* which was sent in due course to the bishops and their collaborators. After that, the synod fathers, assisted by all those called to attend the actual sessions, spent a whole month assiduously dealing with the theme itself and with the numerous and varied questions connected with it. There emerged from the discussions, from the common study and from the diligent and accurate work done, a large and precious treasure which the final propositions sum up in their essence.

The synod's view does not ignore the acts of reconciliation (some of which pass almost unobserved in their daily ordinariness) which, though in differing degrees, serve to resolve the many tensions, to overcome the many conflicts and to conquer the divisions both large and small by restoring unity. But the synod's main concern was to discover in the depth of these scattered acts the hidden root "reconciliation so to speak at the source," which takes place in people's hearts and minds.

The church's charism and likewise her unique nature vis-à-vis reconciliation, at whatever level it needs to be achieved, lie in the fact that she always goes back to that reconciliation at the source. For by reason of her essential mission, the church feels an obligation to go to the roots of that original wound of sin in order to bring healing and to reestablish, so to speak, an equally original reconciliation which will be the effective principle of all true reconciliation. This is the reconciliation which the church had in mind and which she put forward through the synod.

Sacred Scripture speaks to us of this reconciliation, inviting us to make every effort to attain it.[15] But Scripture also tells us that it is above all a merciful gift of

God to humanity.[16] The history of salvation—the salvation of the whole of humanity as well as of every human being of whatever period—is the wonderful history of a reconciliation: the reconciliation whereby God, as Father, in the blood and the cross of his Son made man, reconciles the world to himself and thus brings into being a new family of those who have been reconciled.

Reconciliation becomes necessary because there has been the break of sin from which derive all the other forms of break within man and about him. Reconciliation, therefore, in order to be complete necessarily requires liberation from sin, which is to be rejected in its deepest roots. Thus a close internal link unites conversion and reconciliation. It is impossible to split these two realities or to speak of one and say nothing of the other.

The synod at the same time spoke about the reconciliation of the whole human family and of the conversion of the heart of every individual, of his or her return to God: It did so because it wished to recognize and proclaim the fact that there can be no union among people without an internal change in each individual. Personal conversion is the necessary path to harmony between individuals.[17] When the church proclaims the good news of reconciliation or proposes achieving it through the sacraments, she is exercising a truly prophetic role, condemning the evils of man in their infected source, showing the root of divisions and bringing hope in the possibility of overcoming tensions and conflict and reaching brotherhood, concord and peace at all levels and in all sections of human society. She is changing a historical condition of hatred and violence into a civilization of love. She is offering to everyone the evangelical and sacramental principle of that reconciliation at the source, from which comes every other gesture or act of reconciliation, also at the social level.

It is this reconciliation, the result of conversion, which is dealt with in the present apostolic exhortation. For, as happened at the end of the three previous assemblies of the synod, this time too the fathers who had taken part presented the conclusions of the synod's work to the bishop of Rome, the universal pastor of the church and the head of the College of Bishops, in his capacity as president of the synod. I accepted as a serious and welcome duty of my ministry the task of drawing from the enormous abundance of the synod in order to offer to the people of God, as the fruit of the same synod, a doctrinal and pastoral message on the subject of penance and reconciliation. In the first part I shall speak of the church in the carrying out of her mission of reconciliation, in the work of the conversion of hearts in order to bring about a renewed embrace between man and God, man and his brother, man and the whole of creation. In the second part there will be indicated the radical cause of all wounds and divisions between people, and in the first place between people and God: namely sin. Afterward I shall indicate the means that enable the church to promote and encourage full reconciliation between people and God and, as a consequence, of people with one another.

The document which I now entrust to the sons and daughters of the church and also to all those who, whether they are believers or not, look to the church with interest and sincerity, is meant to be a fitting response to what the synod asked of me. But it is also—and I wish to say this dearly as a duty to truth and justice—something produced by the synod itself. For the contents of these pages come from the synod: from its remote and immediate preparation, from the *instrumentum laboris*, from the interventions in the Synod Hall and the *circuli minores*, and especially from the sixty-three propositions. Here we have the result of the joint work of the fathers, who included the representatives of the Eastern churches, whose theological, spiritual and liturgical heritage is so rich and venerable, also with regard to the subject that concerns us here. Furthermore, it was the Council of the Synod Secretariat which evaluated, in two important sessions, the results and orientations of the synod assembly just after it had ended, which highlighted the dynamics of the already mentioned propositions and which then indicated the lines considered most suitable for the preparation of the present document. I am grateful to all those who did this work and, in fidelity to my mission, I wish here to pass on the elements from the doctrinal and pastoral treasure of the synod which seem to me providential for people's lives at this magnificent yet difficult moment in history.

It is appropriate—and very significant—to do this while there remains fresh in people's minds the memory of the Holy Year, which was lived in the spirit of penance, conversion and reconciliation. May this exhortation, entrusted to my brothers in the episcopate and to their collaborators, the priests and deacons, to men and women religious, and to all men and women of upright conscience, be a means of purification, enrichment and deepening in personal faith. May it also be a leaven capable of encouraging the growth in the midst of the world of peace and brotherhood, hope and joy—values which spring from the Gospel as it is accepted, meditated upon and lived day by day after the example of Mary, mother of our Lord Jesus Christ, through whom it pleased God to reconcile all things to himself.[18]

PART ONE:
CONVERSION AND RECONCILIATION—THE CHURCH'S TASK AND COMMITMENT

CHAPTER ONE:
A PARABLE OF RECONCILIATION

5. At the beginning of this apostolic exhortation there comes into my mind that extraordinary passage in St. Luke, the deeply religious as well as human substance of which I have already sought to illustrate in a previous document.[19] I refer to the parable of the prodigal son.[20]

From the Brother Who Was Lost . . .

"There was a man who had two sons; the younger of them said to his father, 'Father, give me the share of property that falls to me,'" says Jesus as he begins the dramatic story of that young man: the adventurous departure from his father's house, the squandering of all his property in a loose and empty life, the dark days of exile and hunger, but even more of lost dignity, humiliation and shame and then nostalgia for his own home, the courage to go back, the father's welcome. The father had certainly not forgotten his son, indeed he had kept unchanged his affection and esteem for him. So he had always waited for him, and now he embraces him and he gives orders for a great feast to celebrate the return of him who "was dead, and is alive; he was lost, and is found."

This prodigal son is man—every human being: bewitched by the temptation to separate himself from his Father in order to lead his own independent existence; disappointed by the emptiness of the mirage which had fascinated him; alone, dishonored, exploited when he tries to build a world all for himself, sorely tried, even in the depths of his own misery, by the desire to return to communion with his Father. Like the father in the parable, God looks out for the return of his child, embraces him when he arrives and orders the banquet of the new meeting with which the reconciliation is celebrated.

The most striking element of the parable is the father's festive and loving welcome of the returning son: It is a sign of the mercy of God, who is always willing to forgive. Let us say at once: Reconciliation is principally a gift of the heavenly Father.

345

. . . To the Brother Who Stayed at Home

6. But the parable also brings into the picture the elder brother, who refuses to take his place at the banquet. He rebukes his younger brother for his dissolute wanderings, and he rebukes his father for the welcome given to the prodigal son while he himself, a temperate and hard-working person, faithful to father and home, has never been allowed—he says—to have a celebration with his friends. This is a sign that he does not understand the father's goodness. To the extent that this brother, too sure of himself and his own good qualities, jealous and haughty, full of bitterness and anger, is not converted and is not reconciled with his father and brother, the banquet is not yet fully the celebration of a reunion and rediscovery.

Man—every human being—is also this elder brother. Selfishness makes him jealous, hardens his heart, blinds him and shuts him off from other people and from God. The loving kindness and mercy of the father irritate and enrage him; for him the happiness of the brother who has been found again has a bitter taste.[21] From this point of view he too needs to be converted in order to be reconciled. The parable of the prodigal son is above all the story of the inexpressible love of a Father-God who offers to his son when he comes back to him the gift of full reconciliation. But when the parable evokes, in the figure of the elder son, the selfishness which divides the brothers, it also becomes the story of the human family: It describes our situation and shows the path to be followed. The prodigal son, in his anxiety for conversion, to return to the arms of his father and to be forgiven, represents those who are aware of the existence in their inmost hearts of a longing for reconciliation at all levels and without reserve, and who realize with an inner certainty that this reconciliation is possible only if it derives from a first and fundamental reconciliation—the one which brings a person back from distant separation to filial friendship with God, whose infinite mercy is clearly known. But if the parable is read from the point of view of the other son, it portrays the situation of the human family, divided by forms of selfishness. It throws light on the difficulty involved in satisfying the desire and longing for one reconciled and united family. It therefore reminds us of the need for a profound transformation of hearts through the rediscovery of the Father's mercy and through victory over misunderstanding and over hostility among brothers and sisters.

In the light of this inexhaustible parable of the mercy that wipes out sin, the church takes up the appeal that the parable contains and grasps her mission of working, in imitation of the Lord, for the conversion of hearts and for the reconciliation of people with God and with one another—these being two realities that are intimately connected.

CHAPTER TWO:
AT THE SOURCES OF RECONCILIATION

In the Light of Christ the Reconciler

7. As we deduce from the parable of the prodigal son, reconciliation is a gift of God, an initiative on his part. But our faith teaches us that this initiative takes concrete form in the mystery of Christ the redeemer, the reconciler and the liberator of man from sin in all its forms. St. Paul likewise does not hesitate to sum up in this task and function the incomparable mission of Jesus of Nazareth, the word and the Son of God made man.

We too can start with this central mystery of the economy of salvation, the key to St. Paul's Christology. "If while we were enemies we were reconciled to God by the death of his Son," writes St. Paul, "much more, now that we are reconciled, shall we be saved by his life. Not only so, but we also rejoice in God through our Lord Jesus Christ, through whom we have now received our reconciliation."[22] Therefore, since "God was in Christ reconciling the world to himself," Paul feels inspired to exhort the Christians of Corinth: "Be reconciled to God."[23]

This mission of reconciliation through death on the cross is spoken of in another terminology by the evangelist John, when he observes that Christ had to die "to gather into one the children of God who are scattered abroad."[24]

But it is once more St. Paul who enables us to broaden our vision of Christ's work to cosmic dimensions when he writes that in Christ the Father has reconciled to himself all creatures, those in heaven and those on earth.[25] It can rightly be said of Christ the redeemer that "in the time of wrath he was taken in exchange"[26] and that, if he is "our peace,"[27] he is also our reconciliation.

With every good reason his passion and death, sacramentally renewed in the eucharist, are called by the liturgy the "sacrifice of reconciliation":[28] reconciliation with God and with the brethren, since Jesus teaches that fraternal reconciliation must take place before the sacrifice is offered.[29]

Beginning with these and other significant passages in the New Testament, we can therefore legitimately relate all our reflections on the whole mission of Christ to his mission as the one who reconciles. Thus there must be proclaimed once more the church's belief in Christ's redeeming act, in the paschal mystery of his death and resurrection, as the cause of man's reconciliation in its twofold aspect of liberation from sin and communion of grace with God.

It is precisely before the sad spectacle of the divisions and difficulties in the way of reconciliation between people that I invite all to look to the *mysterium crucis* as the loftiest drama in which Christ perceives and suffers to the greatest possible extent the tragedy of the division of man from God, so that he cries out in the words of the psalmist: "My God, my God, why have you forsaken me?"[30] and at the same time accomplishes our reconciliation. With our eyes fixed on the mystery of Golgotha we should be reminded always of that "vertical" dimension of division and reconciliation concerning the relationship between man and God, a dimension which in the eyes of faith always prevails over the "horizontal" dimension, that is to say, over the reality of division between people and the need for reconciliation between them. For we know that reconciliation between people is and can only be the fruit of the redemptive act of Christ, who died and rose again to conquer the kingdom of sin, to reestablish the covenant with God and thus break down the dividing wall[31] which sin had raised up between people.

The Reconciling Church

8. But, as Pope St. Leo said, speaking of Christ's passion, "Everything that the Son of God did and taught for the reconciliation of the world we know not only from the history of his past actions, but we experience it also in the effectiveness of what he accomplishes in the present."[32] We experience the reconciliation which he accomplished in his humanity in the efficacy of the sacred mysteries which are celebrated by his church, for which he gave his life and which he established as the sign and also the means of salvation.

This is stated by St. Paul when he writes that God has given to Christ's apostles a share in his work of reconciliation. He says: "God . . . gave us the ministry of reconciliation . . . and the message of reconciliation."[33]

To the hands and lips of the apostles, his messengers, the Father has mercifully entrusted a ministry of reconciliation, which they carry but in out in a singular way by virtue of the power to act "in persona Christi." But the message of reconciliation has also been entrusted to the whole community of believers, to the whole fabric of the church, that is to say, the task of doing everything possible to witness to reconciliation and to bring it about in the world.

It can be said that the Second Vatican Council too, in defining the church as a "sacrament—a sign and instrument, that is, of communion with God and of unity among all people," and in indicating as the church's function that of obtaining "full unity in Christ" for the "people of the present day . . . drawn ever more closely together by social, technical and cultural bonds,"[34] recognized that the church must strive above all to bring all people to full reconciliation.

In intimate connection with Christ's mission, one can therefore sum up the church's mission, rich and complex as it is, as being her central task of reconciling people: with God, with themselves, with neighbor, with the whole of creation; and this in a permanent manner since, as I said on another occasion, "the church is also by her nature always reconciling."[35]

The church is reconciling inasmuch as she proclaims the message of reconciliation as she has always done throughout her history, from the apostolic Council of Jerusalem[36] down to the latest synod and the recent jubilee of the redemption. The originality of this proclamation is in the fact that for the church reconciliation is closely linked with conversion of heart: This is the necessary path to understanding among human beings.

The church is also reconciling inasmuch as she shows man the paths and offers the means for reaching this fourfold reconciliation. The paths are precisely those of conversion of heart and victory over sin, whether this latter is selfishness or injustice, arrogance or exploitation of others, attachment to material goods or the unrestrained quest for pleasure. The means are those of faithful and loving attention to God's word; personal and community prayer; and in particular the sacraments, true signs and instruments of reconciliation, among which there excels, precisely under this aspect, the one which we are rightly accustomed to call the sacrament of reconciliation or penance and to which we shall return later on.

The Reconciled Church

9. My venerable predecessor Paul VI commendably highlighted the fact that the church, in order to evangelize, must begin by showing that she herself has been evangelized, that is to say, that she is open to the full and complete proclamation of the good news of Jesus Christ in order to listen to it and put it into practice.[37] I too, by bringing together in one document the reflections of the fourth general assembly of the synod, have spoken of a church that is catechized to the extent that she carries out catechesis.[38]

I now do not hesitate to resume the comparison, insofar as it applies to the theme I am dealing with, in order to assert that the church, if she is to be reconciling, must begin by being a reconciled church. Beneath this simple and indicative expression lies the conviction that the church, in order ever more effectively to proclaim and propose reconciliation to the world, must become ever more genuinely a community of disciples of Christ (even though it were only "the little flock" of the first days), united in the commitment to be continually converted to the Lord and to live as new people in the spirit and practice of reconciliation.

To the people of our time, so sensitive to the proof of concrete living witness, the church is called upon to give an example of reconciliation particularly within herself. And for this purpose we must all work to bring peace to people's minds, to reduce tensions, to overcome divisions and to heal wounds that may have been inflicted by brother on brother when the contrast of choices in the field of what is optional becomes acute; and on the contrary we must try to be united in what is essential for Christian faith and life, in accordance with the ancient maxim: In what is doubtful, freedom; in what is necessary, unity; in all things, charity.

It is in accordance with this same criterion that the church must conduct her ecumenical activity. For in order to be completely reconciled, she knows that she must continue the quest for unity among those who are proud to call themselves Christians but who are separated from one another, also as churches or communions, and from the church of Rome. The latter seeks a unity which, if it is to be the fruit and expression of true reconciliation, is meant to be based neither upon a disguising of the points that divide nor upon compromises which are as easy as they are superficial and fragile. Unity must be the result of a true conversion of everyone, the result of mutual forgiveness, of theological dialogue and fraternal relations, of prayer and of complete docility to the action of the Holy Spirit, who is also the Spirit of reconciliation.

Finally, in order that the church may say that she is completely reconciled, she feels that it is her duty to strive ever harder, by promoting the "dialogue of salvation,"[39] to bring the Gospel to those vast sections of humanity in the modern world that do not share her faith, but even, as a result of growing secularism, keep their distance from her and oppose her with cold indifference when they do not actually hinder and persecute her. She feels the duty to say once more to everyone in the words of St. Paul: "Be reconciled to God."[40]

At any rate, the church promotes reconciliation in the truth, knowing well that neither reconciliation nor unity is possible outside or in opposition to the truth.

CHAPTER THREE:
GOD'S INITIATIVE AND THE CHURCH'S MINISTRY

10. The church, as a reconciled and reconciling community, cannot forget that at the source of her gift and mission of reconciliation is the initiative, full of compassionate love and mercy, of that God who is love[41] and who out of love created human beings;[42] and he created them so that they might live in friendship with him and in communion with one another.

Reconciliation Comes from God

God is faithful to his eternal plan even when man, under the impulse of the evil one[43] and carried away by his own pride, abuses the freedom given to him in order to love and generously seek what is good, and refuses to obey his Lord and Father. God is faithful even when man, instead of responding with love to God's love, opposes him and treats him like a rival, deluding himself and relying on his own power, with the resulting break of relationship with the one who created him. In spite of this transgression on man's part, God remains faithful in love. It is certainly true that the story of the Garden of Eden makes us think about the tragic consequences of rejecting the Father, which becomes evident in man's inner disorder and in the breakdown of harmony between man and woman, brother and brother.[44] Also significant is the gospel parable of the two brothers who, in different ways, distance themselves from their father and cause a rift between them. Refusal of God's fatherly love and of his loving gifts is always at the root of humanity's divisions.

But we know that God, "rich in mercy,"[45] like the father in the parable, does not close his heart to any of his children. He waits for them, looks for them, goes to meet them at the place where the refusal of communion imprisons them in isolation and division. He calls them to gather about his table in the joy of the feast of forgiveness and reconciliation.

This initiative on God's part is made concrete and manifest in the redemptive act of Christ, which radiates through the world by means of the ministry of the church.

For, according to our faith, the word of God became flesh and came to dwell in the world; he entered into the history of the world, summing it up and recapitulating it in himself.[46] He revealed to us that God is love, and he gave us the "new commandment" of love,[47] at the same time communicating to us the certainty that the path of love is open for all people, so that the effort to establish universal brotherhood is not a vain one.[48] By conquering through his death on the cross evil and the power of sin, by his loving obedience, he brought salvation to all and became "reconciliation" for all. In him God reconciled man to himself.

The church carries on the proclamation of reconciliation which Christ caused to echo through the villages of Galilee and all Palestine[49] and does not cease to invite all humanity to be converted and to believe in the good news. She speaks in the name of Christ, making her own the appeal of St. Paul which we have already recalled: "We are ambassadors for Christ, God making his appeal through us. We beseech you on behalf of Christ, be reconciled to God."[50]

Those who accept this appeal enter into the economy of reconciliation and experience the truth contained in that other affirmation of St. Paul, that Christ "is our peace, who has made us both one, and has broken down the dividing wall of hostility . . . , so making peace" that he "might reconcile us both to God."[51] This text directly concerns the overcoming of the religious division between Israel—as the chosen people of the Old Testament—and the other peoples, all called to form part of the new covenant. Nevertheless it contains the affirmation of the new spiritual universality desired by God and accomplished by him through the sacrifice of his Son, the word made man, without limits or exclusions of any sort, for all those who are converted and who believe in Christ. We are all therefore called to enjoy the fruits of this reconciliation desired by God: every individual and every people.

The Church, the Great Sacrament of Reconciliation

11. The church has the mission of proclaiming this reconciliation and as it were of being its sacrament in the world. The church is the sacrament, that is to say, the sign and means of reconciliation in different ways which differ in value but which all come together to obtain what the divine initiative of mercy desires to grant to humanity.

She is a sacrament in the first place by her very existence as a reconciled community which witnesses to and represents in the world the work of Christ.

She is also a sacrament through her service as the custodian and interpreter of sacred Scripture, which is the good news of reconciliation inasmuch as it tells each succeeding generation about God's loving plan and shows to each generation the paths to universal reconciliation in Christ.

Finally she is a sacrament by reason of the seven sacraments which, each in its own way, "make the church."[52] For since they commemorate and renew Christ's paschal mystery, all the sacraments are a source of life for the church and in the church's hands they are means of conversion to God and of reconciliation among people.

Other Means of Reconciliation

12. The mission of reconciliation is proper to the whole church, also and especially to that church which has already been admitted to the full sharing in divine glory with the Virgin Mary, the angels and the saints, who contemplate and adore the thrice-holy God. The church in heaven, the church on earth and the church in purgatory are mysteriously united in this cooperation with Christ in reconciling the world to God.

The first means of this salvific action is that of prayer. It is certain that the Blessed Virgin, mother of Christ and of the church,[53] and the saints, who have now reached the end of their earthly journey and possess God's glory, sustain by their intercession their brethren who are on pilgrimage through the world, in the commitment to conversion, to faith, to getting up again after every fall, to acting in order to help the growth of communion and peace in the church and in the world. In the mystery of the communion of saints, universal reconciliation is accomplished in its most profound form, which is also the most fruitful for the salvation of all.

There is yet another means: that of preaching. The church, since she is the disciple of the one teacher Jesus Christ, in her own turn as mother and teacher untiringly exhorts people to reconciliation. And she does not hesitate to condemn the evil of sin, to proclaim the need for conversion, to invite and ask people to "let themselves be reconciled." In fact, this is her prophetic mission in today's world, just as it was in the world of yesterday. It is the same mission as that of her teacher and head, Jesus. Like him, the church will always carry out this mission with sentiments of merciful love and will bring to all people those words of forgiveness and that invitation to hope which come from the cross.

There is also the often so difficult and demanding means of pastoral action aimed at bringing back every individual—whoever and wherever he or she may be—to the path, at times a long one, leading back to the Father in the communion of all the brethren.

Finally there is the means of witness, which is almost always silent. This is born from a twofold awareness on the part of the church: that of being in herself "unfailingly holy,"[54] but also the awareness of the need to go forward and "daily be further purified and renewed, against the day when Christ will present her to himself in all her glory without spot or wrinkle," for, by reason of her sins, sometimes "the radiance of the church's face shines less brightly" in the eyes of those who behold her.[55] This witness cannot fail to assume two fundamental aspects. This first aspect is that of being the sign of that universal charity which Jesus Christ left as an inheritance to his followers, as a proof of belonging to his kingdom. The second aspect is translation into ever new manifestations of conversion and reconciliation both within the church and outside her, by the overcoming of tensions, by mutual forgiveness, by growth in the spirit of brotherhood and peace which is to be spread throughout the world. By this means the church will effectively be able to work for the creation of what my predecessor Paul VI called the "civilization of love."

PART TWO:
THE LOVE THAT IS GREATER THAN SIN

The Tragedy of Man

13. In the words of St. John the apostle, "If we say we have no sin, we deceive ourselves, and the truth is not in us. If we confess our sins, he is faithful and just and will forgive our sins."[56] Written at the very dawn of the church, these inspired words introduce better than any other human expression the theme of sin, which is intimately connected with that of reconciliation. These words present the question of sin in its human dimension: sin as an integral part of the truth about man. But they immediately relate the human dimension to its divine dimension, where sin is countered by the truth of divine love, which is just, generous and faithful, and which reveals itself above all in forgiveness and redemption. Thus St. John also writes a little further on that "whatever accusations (our conscience) may raise against us, God is greater than our conscience."[57]

To acknowledge one's sin, indeed—penetrating still more deeply into the consideration of one's own personhood—to recognize oneself as being a sinner, capable of sin and inclined to commit sin, is the essential first step in returning to God. For example, this is the experience of David, who "having done what is evil in the eyes of the Lord" and having been rebuked by the prophet Nathan,[58] exclaims: "For I know my transgressions, and my sin is ever before me. Against you, you alone, have I sinned and done what is evil in your sight."[59] Similarly, Jesus himself puts the following significant words on the lips and in the heart of the prodigal son: "Father, I have sinned against heaven and before you."[60]

In effect, to become reconciled with God presupposes and includes detaching oneself consciously and with determination from the sin into which one has fallen. It presupposes and includes, therefore, doing penance in the fullest sense of the term: repenting, showing this repentance, adopting a real attitude of repentance—which is the attitude of the person who starts out on the road of return to the Father. This is a general law and one which each individual must follow in his or her particular situation. For it is not possible to deal with sin and conversion only in abstract terms.

In the concrete circumstances of sinful humanity, in which there can be no conversion without the acknowledgment of one's own sin, the church's ministry of reconciliation intervenes in each individual case with a precise penitential purpose. That is, the church's ministry intervenes in order to bring the person to the "knowledge of self"—in the words of St. Catherine of Siena[61]—to the rejection of evil, to the reestablishment of friendship with God, to a new interior ordering, to a fresh ecclesial conversion. Indeed, even beyond the boundaries of the church and the community of believers, the message and ministry of penance are addressed to all men and women, because all need conversion and reconciliation.[62]

In order to carry out this penitential ministry adequately, we shall have to evaluate the consequences of sin with "eyes enlightened"[63] by faith. These consequences of sin are the reasons for division and rupture not only within each person, but also within the various circles of a person's life: in relation to the family, to the professional and social environment, as can often be seen from experience; it is confirmed by the passage in the Bible about the city of Babel and its tower.[64] Intent on building what was to be at once a symbol and a source of unity, those people found themselves more scattered than before, divided in speech, divided among themselves, incapable of consensus and agreement.

Why did the ambitious project fail? Why did "the builders labor in vain?"[65] They failed because they had set up as a sign and guarantee of the unity they desired a work of their own hands alone and had forgotten the action of the Lord. They had attended only to the horizontal dimension of work and social life, forgetting the vertical dimension by which they would have been rooted in God, their creator and Lord, and would have been directed toward him as the ultimate goal of their progress.

Now it can be said that the tragedy of humanity today, as indeed of every period in history, consists precisely in its similarity to the experience of Babel.

CHAPTER ONE:
THE MYSTERY OF SIN

14. If we read the passage in the Bible on the city and tower of Babel in the new light offered by the Gospel and if we compare it with the other passage on the fall of our first parents, we can draw from it valuable elements for an understanding of the mystery of sin. This expression, which echoes what St. Paul writes concerning the mystery of evil,[66] helps us to grasp the obscure and intangible element hidden in sin. Clearly sin is a product of man's freedom. But deep within its human reality there are factors at work which place it beyond the merely human, in the border area where man's conscience, will and sensitivity are in contact with the dark forces which, according to St. Paul, are active in the world almost to the point of ruling it.[67]

Disobedience to God

A first point which helps us to understand sin emerges from the biblical narrative on the building of the tower of Babel: The people sought to build a city, organize themselves into a society and to be strong and powerful without God, if not precisely against God.[68] In this sense the story of the first sin in Eden and the story of Babel, in spite of notable differences in content and form, have one thing in common: In both there is an exclusion of God through direct opposition to one of his commandments, through an act of rivalry, through the mistaken pretension of being "like him."[69] In the story of Babel the exclusion of God is presented not so much under the aspect of opposition to him as of forgetfulness and indifference toward him, as if God were of no relevance in the sphere of man's joint projects. But in both cases the relationship to God is severed with violence. In the case of Eden there appears in all its seriousness and tragic reality that which constitutes the ultimate essence and darkness of sin: disobedience to God, to His law, to the moral norm that he has given man, inscribing it in his heart and confirming and perfecting it through revelation.

Exclusion of God, rupture with God, disobedience to God: Throughout the history of mankind this has been and is, in various forms, sin. It can go as far as a very denial of God and his existence: This is the phenomenon called atheism.

It is the disobedience of a person who, by a free act, does not acknowledge God's sovereignty over his or her life, at least at that particular moment in which he or she transgresses God's law.

Division Between Brothers

15. In the biblical narratives mentioned above, man's rupture with God leads tragically to divisions between brothers.

In the description of the "first sin," the rupture with Yahweh simultaneously breaks the bond of friendship that had united the human family. Thus the subsequent pages of Genesis show us the man and the woman as it were pointing an accusing finger at each other.[70] Later we have the brother hating his brother and finally taking his life.[71]

According to the Babel story, the result of sin is the shattering of the human family, already begun with the first sin and now reaching its most extreme form on the social level.

No one wishing to investigate the mystery of sin can ignore this link between cause and effect. As a rupture with God, sin is an act of disobedience by a creature who rejects, at least implicitly, the very one from whom he came and who sustains him in life. It is therefore a suicidal act. Since by sinning man refuses to submit to God, his internal balance is also destroyed and it is precisely within himself that contradictions and conflicts arise. Wounded in this way, man almost inevitably causes damage to the fabric of his relationship with others and with the created world. This is an objective law and an objective reality, verified in so many ways in the human psyche and in the spiritual life as well as in society, where it is easy to see the signs and effects of internal disorder.

The mystery of sin is composed of this twofold wound which the sinner opens in himself and in his relationship with his neighbor. Therefore one can speak of personal and social sin: From one point of view, every sin is personal; from another point of view, every sin is social insofar as and because it also has social repercussions.

Personal Sin and Social Sin

16. Sin, in the proper sense, is always a personal act, since it is an act of freedom on the part of an individual person and not properly of a group or community. This individual may be conditioned, incited and influenced by numerous and powerful external factors. He may also be subjected to tendencies, defects and habits linked with his personal condition. In not a few cases such external and internal factors may attenuate, to a greater or lesser degree, the person's freedom and therefore his responsibility and guilt. But it is a truth of faith, also confirmed by our experience and reason, that the human person is free. This truth cannot be disregarded in order to place the blame for individuals' sins on external factors such as structures, systems or other people. Above all, this would be to deny the person's dignity and freedom, which are manifested—even though in a negative and disastrous way—also in this responsibility for sin committed. Hence there is nothing so personal and untransferable in each individual as merit for virtue or responsibility for sin.

As a personal act, sin has its first and most important consequences in the sinner himself: that is, in his relationship with God, who is the very foundation of human life; and also in his spirit, weakening his will and clouding his intellect.

At this point we must ask what was being referred to by those who during the preparation of the synod and in the course of its actual work frequently spoke of social sin.

The expression and the underlying concept in fact have various meanings.

To speak of social sin means in the first place to recognize that, by virtue of human solidarity which is as mysterious and intangible as it is real and concrete, each individual's sin in some way affects others. This is the other aspect of that solidarity which on the religious level is developed in the profound and magnificent mystery of the communion of saints, thanks to which it has been possible to say that "every soul that rises above itself, raises up the world."[72] To this law of ascent there unfortunately corresponds the law of descent. Consequently one can speak of a communion of sin, whereby a soul that lowers itself through sin drags down with itself the church and, in some way, the whole world. In other words, there is no sin, not even the most intimate and secret one, the most strictly individual one, that exclusively concerns the person committing it. With greater or lesser violence, with greater or lesser harm, every sin has repercussions on the entire ecclesial body and the whole human family. According to this first meaning of the term, every sin can undoubtedly be considered as social sin.

Some sins, however, by their very matter constitute a direct attack on one's neighbor and more exactly, in the language of the Gospel, against one's brother or sister. They are an offense against God because they are offenses against one's neighbor. These sins are usually called social sins, and this is the second meaning of the term. In this sense social sin is sin against love of neighbor, and in the law of Christ it is all the more serious in that it involves the Second Commandment, which is "like unto the first."[73] Likewise, the term social applies to every sin against justice in interpersonal relationships, committed either by the individual against the community or by the community against the individual. Also social is every sin against the rights of the human person, beginning with the right to and including the life of the unborn or against a person's physical integrity. Likewise social is every sin against others' freedom, especially against the supreme freedom to believe in God and adore him; social is every sin against the dignity and honor of one's neighbor. Also social is every sin against the common good and its exigencies in relation to the whole broad spectrum of the rights and duties of citizens. The term social can be applied to sins of commission or omission—on the part of political, economic or trade union leaders, who though in a position to do so, do not work diligently and wisely for the improvement and transformation of society according to the requirements and potential of the given historic moment; as also on the part of workers who through absenteeism or non-cooperation fail to ensure that their industries can continue to advance the well-being of the workers themselves, of their families and of the whole of society.

The third meaning of social sin refers to the relationships between the various human communities. These relationships are not always in accordance with the plan of God, who intends that there be justice in the world and freedom and peace between individuals, groups and peoples. Thus the class struggle, whoever the person who leads it or on occasion seeks to give it a theoretical justification, is a social evil. Likewise obstinate confrontation between blocs of nations, between one nation and another, between different groups within the same nation—all this too is a social evil. In both cases one may ask whether moral responsibility for these evils, and therefore sin, can be attributed to any person in particular. Now it has to be admitted that realities and situations such as those described, when they become generalized and reach vast proportions as social phenomena, almost always become anonymous, just as their causes are complex and not always identifiable. Hence if one speaks of social sin here, the expression obviously has an analogical meaning. However, to speak even analogically of social sins must not cause us to underestimate the responsibility of the individuals involved. It is meant to be an appeal to the consciences of all, so that each may shoulder his or her responsibility seriously and courageously in order to change those disastrous conditions and intolerable situations.

Having said this in the clearest and most unequivocal way, one must add at once that there is one meaning sometimes given to social sin that is not legitimate or acceptable even though it is very common in certain quarters today.[74] This usage contrasts social sin and personal sin, not without ambiguity, in a way that leads more or less unconsciously to the watering down and almost the abolition of personal sin, with the recognition only of social guilt and responsibilities. According to this usage, which can readily be seen to derive from non-Christian ideologies and systems— which have possibly been discarded today by the very people who formerly officially upheld them—practically every sin is a social sin, in the sense that blame for it is to be placed not so much on the moral conscience of an individual, but rather on some vague entity or anonymous collectivity such as the situation, the system, society, structures or institutions.

Whenever the church speaks of situations of sin or when she condemns as social sins certain situations or the collective behavior of certain social groups, big or small, or even of whole nations and blocs of nations, she knows and she proclaims that such cases of social sin are the result of the accumulation and concentration of many personal sins. It is a case of the very personal sins of those who cause or support evil or who exploit it; of those who are in a position to avoid, eliminate or at least limit certain social evils but who fail to do so out of laziness, fear or the conspiracy of silence, through secret complicity or indifference; of those who take refuge in the supposed impossibility of changing the world and also of those who sidestep the effort and sacrifice required, producing specious reasons of higher order. The real responsibility, then, lies with individuals.

A situation—or likewise an institution, a structure, society itself—is not in itself the subject of moral acts. Hence a situation cannot in itself be good or bad.

At the heart of every situation of sin are always to be found sinful people. So true is this that even when such a situation can be changed in its structural and institutional aspects by the force of law or—as unfortunately more often happens by the law of force, the change in fact proves to be incomplete, of short duration and ultimately vain and ineffective—not to say counterproductive if the people directly or indirectly responsible for that situation are not converted.

Mortal and Venial

17. But here we come to a further dimension in the mystery of sin, one on which the human mind has never ceased to ponder: the question of its gravity. It is a question which cannot be overlooked and one which the Christian conscience has never refused to answer. Why and to what degree is sin a serious matter in the offense it commits against God and in its effects on man? The church has a teaching on this matter which she reaffirms in its essential elements, while recognizing that it is not always easy in concrete situations to define clear and exact limits.

Already in the Old Testament, individuals guilty of several kinds of sins—sins committed deliberately,[75] the various forms of impurity,[76] idolatry,[77] the worship of false gods[78]—were ordered to be "taken away from the people," which could also mean to be condemned to death.[79] Contrasted with these were other sins, especially sins committed through ignorance, that were forgiven by means of a sacrificial offering.[80]

In reference also to these texts, the church has for centuries spoken of mortal sin and venial sin. But it is above all the New Testament that sheds light on this distinction and these terms. Here there are many passages which enumerate and strongly reprove sins that are particularly deserving of condemnation.[81] There is also the confirmation of the Decalogue by Jesus himself.[82] Here I wish to give special attention to two passages that are significant and impressive.

In a text of his First Letter, St. John speaks of a sin which leads to death (*pros thanaton*), as opposed to a sin which does not lead to death (*me pros thanaton*).[83] Obviously, the concept of death here is a spiritual death. It is a question of the loss of the true life or "eternal life," which for John is knowledge of the Father and the Son,[84] and communion and intimacy with them. In that passage the sin that leads to death seems to be the denial of the Son[85] or the worship of false gods.[86] At any rate, by this distinction of concepts John seems to wish to emphasize the incalculable seriousness of what constitutes the very essence of sin, namely the rejection of God. This is manifested above all in apostasy and idolatry: repudiating faith in revealed truth and making certain created realities equal to God, raising them to the status of idols or false gods.[87] But in this passage the apostle's intention is also to underline the certainty that comes to the Christian from the fact of having been "born of God" through the coming of the Son: The Christian possesses a power that preserves him from falling into sin; God protects him, and "the evil one does not touch him." If he should sin through weakness or ignorance, he has confidence in being forgiven, also because he is supported by the joint prayer of the community.

In another passage of the New Testament, namely in St. Matthew's Gospel,[88] Jesus himself speaks of a "blasphemy against the Holy Spirit" that "will not be forgiven" by reason of the fact that in its manifestation, it is an obstinate refusal to be converted to the love of the Father of mercies.

Here of course it is a question of external radical manifestations: rejection of God, rejection of his grace and therefore opposition to the very source of salvation[89]—these are manifestations whereby a person seems to exclude himself voluntarily from the path of forgiveness. It is to be hoped that very few persist to the end in this attitude of rebellion or even defiance of God. Moreover, God in his merciful love is greater than our hearts, as St. John further teaches us,[90] and can overcome all our psychological and spiritual resistance. So that, as St. Thomas writes, "considering the omnipotence and mercy of God, no one should despair of the salvation of anyone in this life."[91]

But when we ponder the problem of a rebellious will meeting the infinitely just God, we cannot but experience feelings of salutary "fear and trembling," as St. Paul suggests.[92] Moreover, Jesus' warning about the sin "that will not be forgiven" confirms the existence of sins which can bring down on the sinner the punishment of "eternal death."

In the light of these and other passages of sacred Scripture, doctors and theologians, spiritual teachers and pastors have divided sins into mortal and venial. St. Augustine, among others, speaks of *letalia* or *mortifera crimina*, contrasting them with *venialia*, *levia* or *quotidiana*.[93] The meaning which he gives to these adjectives was to influence the successive magisterium of the church. After him, it was St. Thomas who was to formulate in the clearest possible terms the doctrine which became a constant in the church.

In defining and distinguishing between mortal and venial sins, St. Thomas and the theology of sin that has its source in him could not be unaware of the biblical reference and therefore of the concept of spiritual death. According to St. Thomas, in order to live spiritually man must remain in communion with the supreme principle of life, which is God, since God is the ultimate end of man's being and acting. Now sin is a disorder perpetrated by the human being against this life-principle. And when "through sin, the soul commits a disorder that reaches the point of turning away from its ultimate end God to which it is bound by charity, then the sin is mortal; on the other hand, whenever the disorder does not reach the point of a turning away from God, the sin is venial."[94] For this reason venial sin does not deprive the sinner of sanctifying grace, friendship with God, charity and therefore eternal happiness, whereas just such a deprivation is precisely the consequence of mortal sin.

Furthermore, when sin is considered from the point of view of the punishment it merits, for St. Thomas and other doctors mortal sin is the sin which, if unforgiven, leads to eternal punishment; whereas venial sin is the sin that merits merely temporal punishment (that is, a partial punishment which can be expiated on earth or in purgatory).

Considering sin from the point of view of its matter, the ideas of death, of radical rupture with God, the supreme good, of deviation from the path that leads to God or interruption of the journey toward him (which are all ways of defining mortal sin) are linked with the idea of the gravity of sin's objective content. Hence, in the church's doctrine and pastoral action, grave sin is in practice identified with mortal sin.

Here we have the core of the church's traditional teaching, which was reiterated frequently and vigorously during the recent synod. The synod in fact not only reaffirmed the teaching of the Council of Trent concerning the existence and nature of mortal and venial sins,[95] but it also recalled that mortal sin is sin whose object is grave matter and which is also committed with full knowledge and deliberate consent. It must be added—as was likewise done at the synod—that some sins are intrinsically grave and mortal by reason of their matter. That is, there exist acts which, per se and in themselves, independently of circumstances, are always seriously wrong by reason of their object. These acts, if carried out with sufficient awareness and freedom, are always gravely sinful.[96]

This doctrine, based on the Decalogue and on the preaching of the Old Testament, and assimilated into the *kerygma* of the apostles and belonging to the earliest teaching of the church, and constantly reaffirmed by her to this day, is exactly verified in the experience of the men and women of all times. Man knows well by experience that along the road of faith and justice which leads to the knowledge and love of God in this life and toward perfect union with him in eternity, he can cease to go forward or can go astray without abandoning the way of God; and in this case there occurs venial sin. This however must never be underestimated, as though it were automatically something that can be ignored or regarded as "a sin of little importance."

For man also knows, through painful experience, that by a conscious and free act of his will he can change course and go in a direction opposed to God's will, separating himself from God (*aversio a Deo*), rejecting loving communion with him, detaching himself from the life principle which God is and consequently choosing death.

With the whole tradition of the church, we call mortal sin the act by which man freely and consciously rejects God, his law, the covenant of love that God offers, preferring to turn in on himself or to some created and finite reality, something contrary to the divine will (*conversio ad creaturam*). This can occur in a direct and formal way in the sins of idolatry, apostasy and atheism; or in an equivalent way as in every act of disobedience to God's commandments in a grave matter. Man perceives that this disobedience to God destroys the bond that unites him with his life principle:

It is a mortal sin, that is, an act which gravely offends God and ends in turning against man himself with a dark and powerful force of destruction.

During the synod assembly some fathers proposed a threefold distinction of sins, classifying them as venial, grave and mortal. This threefold distinction might illustrate the fact that there is a scale of seriousness among grave sins. But it still remains true that the essential and decisive distinction is between sin which destroys charity and sin which does not kill the supernatural life: There is no middle way between life and death.

Likewise, care will have to be taken not to reduce mortal sin to an act of "fundamental option"—as is commonly said today—against God, intending thereby an explicit and formal contempt for God or neighbor. For mortal sin exists also when a person knowingly and willingly, for whatever reason, chooses something gravely disordered. In fact, such a choice already includes contempt for the divine law, a rejection of God's love for humanity and the whole of creation; the person turns away from God and loses charity. Thus the fundamental orientation can be radically changed by individual acts. Clearly there can occur situations which are very complex and obscure from a psychological viewpoint and which have an influence on the sinner's subjective culpability. But from a consideration of the psychological sphere one cannot proceed to the construction of a theological category, which is what the "fundamental option" precisely is, understanding it in such a way that it objectively changes or casts doubt upon the traditional concept of mortal sin.

While every sincere and prudent attempt to clarify the psychological and theological mystery of sin is to be valued, the church nevertheless has a duty to remind all scholars in this field of the need to be faithful to the word of God that teaches us also about sin. She likewise has to remind them of the risk of contributing to a further weakening of the sense of sin in the modern world.

The Loss of the Sense of Sin

18. Over the course of generations, the Christian mind has gained from the Gospel as it is read in the ecclesial community a fine sensitivity and an acute perception of the seeds of death contained in sin, as well as a sensitivity and an acuteness of perception for identifying them in the thousand guises under which sin shows itself. This is what is commonly called the sense of sin.

This sense is rooted in man's moral conscience and is as it were its thermometer. It is linked to the sense of God, since it derives from man's conscious relationship with God as his Creator, Lord and Father. Hence, just as it is impossible to eradicate completely the sense of God or to silence the conscience completely, so the sense of sin is never completely eliminated.

Nevertheless, it happens not infrequently in history, for more or less lengthy periods and under the influence of many different factors, that the moral conscience of many people becomes seriously clouded. "Have we the right idea of conscience?"—I asked two years ago in an address to the faithful. "Is it not true that modern man is threatened by an eclipse of conscience? By a deformation of conscience? By a numbness or 'deadening' of conscience?"[97] Too many signs indicate that such an eclipse exists in our time. This is all the more disturbing in that conscience, defined by the council as "the most secret core and sanctuary of a man,"[98] is "strictly related to human freedom. . . . For this reason conscience, to a great extent, constitutes the basis of man's interior dignity and, at the same time, of his relationship to God."[99] It is inevitable therefore that in this situation there is an obscuring also of the sense of sin, which is closely connected with the moral conscience, the search for truth and the desire to make a responsible use of freedom. When the conscience is weakened the sense of God is also obscured, and as a result, with the loss of this decisive inner point of reference, the sense of sin is lost. This explains why my predecessor Pius XI, one day declared, in words that have almost become proverbial, that "the sin of the century is the loss of the sense of sin."[100]

Why has this happened in our time. A glance at certain aspects of contemporary culture can help us to understand the progressive weakening of the sense of sin, precisely because of the crisis of conscience and crisis of the sense of God already mentioned.

"Secularism" is by nature and definition a movement of ideas and behavior which advocates a humanism totally without God, completely centered upon the cult of action and production and caught up in the heady enthusiasm of consumerism and pleasure seeking, unconcerned with the danger of "losing one's soul." This secularism cannot but undermine the sense of sin. At the very most, sin will be reduced to what offends man. But it is precisely here that we are faced with the bitter experience which I already alluded to in my first encyclical namely, that man can build a world without God, but this world will end by turning against him.[101] In fact, God is the origin and the supreme end of man, and man carries in himself a divine seed.[102] Hence it is the reality of God that reveals and illustrates the mystery of man. It is therefore vain to hope that there will take root a sense of sin against man and against human values, if there is no sense of offense against God, namely the true sense of sin.

Another reason for the disappearance of the sense of sin in contemporary society is to be found in the errors made in evaluating certain findings of the human sciences. Thus on the basis of certain affirmations of psychology, concern to avoid creating feelings of guilt or to place limits on freedom leads to a refusal ever to admit any shortcoming. Through an undue extrapolation of the criteria of the science of sociology, it finally happens—as I have already said—that all failings are blamed upon society, and the individual is declared innocent of them. Again, a certain cultural anthropology so emphasizes the undeniable environmental and historical conditioning and influences which act upon man, that it reduces his responsibility to the point of not acknowledging his ability to perform truly human acts and therefore his ability to sin.

The sense of sin also easily declines as a result of a system of ethics deriving from a certain historical relativism. This may take the form of an ethical system which relativizes the moral norm, denying its absolute and unconditional value, and as a consequence denying that there can be intrinsically illicit acts independent of the circumstances in which they are performed by the subject. Herein lies a real "overthrowing and downfall of moral values," and "the problem is not so much one of ignorance of Christian ethics," but ignorance "rather of the meaning, foundations and criteria of the moral attitude."[103] Another effect of this ethical turning upside down is always such an attenuation of the notion of sin as almost to reach the point of saying that sin does exist, but no one knows who commits it.

Finally the sense of sin disappears when—as can happen in the education of youth, in the mass media and even in education within the family—it is wrongly identified with a morbid feeling of guilt or with the mere transgression of legal norms and precepts.

The loss of the sense of sin is thus a form or consequence of the denial of God: not only in the form of atheism but also in the form of secularism. If sin is the breaking off of one's filial relationship to God in order to situate one's life outside of obedience to him, then to sin is not merely to deny God. To sin is also to live as if he did not exist, to eliminate him from one's daily life. A model of society which is mutilated or distorted in one sense or another, as is often encouraged by the mass media, greatly favors the gradual loss of the sense of sin. In such a situation the obscuring or weakening of the sense of sin comes from several sources: from a rejection of any reference to the transcendent in the name of the individual's aspiration to personal independence; from acceptance of ethical models imposed by general consensus and behavior, even when condemned by the individual conscience; from the tragic social and economic conditions that oppress a great part of humanity, causing a tendency to see errors and faults only in the context of society; finally and especially, from the obscuring of the notion of God's fatherhood and dominion over man's life.

Even in the field of the thought and life of the church certain trends inevitably favor the decline of the sense of sin. For example, some are inclined to replace exaggerated attitudes of the past with other exaggerations: From seeing sin everywhere they pass to not recognizing it anywhere; from too much emphasis on the fear of eternal punishment they pass to preaching a love of God that excludes any punishment deserved by sin; from severity in trying to correct erroneous consciences they pass to a kind of respect for conscience which excludes the duty of telling the truth. And should it not be added that the confusion caused in the consciences of many of the faithful by differences of opinions and teachings in theology, preaching, catechesis and spiritual direction on serious and delicate questions of Christian morals ends by diminishing the true sense of sin almost to the point of eliminating it altogether? Nor can certain deficiencies in the practice of sacramental penance be overlooked. These include the tendency to obscure the ecclesial significance of sin and of conversion and to reduce them to merely personal matters; or vice versa, the tendency to nullify the personal value of good and evil and to consider only their community dimension. There also exists the danger, never totally eliminated, of routine ritualism that deprives the sacrament of its full significance and formative effectiveness.

The restoration of a proper sense of sin is the first way of facing the grave spiritual crisis looming over man today. But the sense of sin can only be restored through a clear reminder of the unchangeable principles of reason and faith which the moral teaching of the church has always upheld.

There are good grounds for hoping that a healthy sense of sin will once again flourish, especially in the Christian world and in the church. This will be aided by sound catechetics, illuminated by the biblical theology of the covenant, by an attentive listening and trustful openness to the magisterium of the church, which; never ceases to enlighten consciences, and by an ever more careful practice of the sacrament of penance.

CHAPTER TWO:
"MYSTERIUM PIETATIS"

19. In order to understand sin we have had to direct our attention to its nature as made known to us by the revelation of the economy of salvation: This is the *mysterium iniquitatis*. But in this economy sin is not the main principle, still less the victor. Sin fights against another active principle which—to use a beautiful and evocative expression of St. Paul—we can call the *mysterium* or *sacramentum pietatis*. Man's sin would be the winner and in the end destructive, God's salvific plan would remain incomplete or even totally defeated, if this *mysterium pietatis* were not made part of the dynamism of history in order to conquer man's sin.

We find this expression in one of St. Paul's pastoral letters, the First Letter to Timothy. It appears unexpectedly, as if by an exuberant inspiration. The apostle had previously devoted long paragraphs of his message to his beloved disciple to an explanation of the meaning of the ordering of the community (the liturgical order and the related hierarchical one). Next he had spoken of the role of the heads of the community, before turning to the conduct of Timothy himself in the church of the living God, the pillar and bulwark of the truth." Then at the end of the passage suddenly, but with a profound purpose, he evokes the element which gives meaning to everything that he has written: "Great indeed, we confess, is the mystery of our religion."[104]

Without in the least betraying the literal sense of the text, we can broaden this magnificent theological insight of St. Paul into a more complete vision of the role which the truth proclaimed by him plays in the economy of salvation: "Great indeed," we repeat with him, "is the mystery of our religion," because it conquers sin.

But what is the meaning of this expression, in Paul's mind?

It Is Christ Himself

20. It is profoundly significant that when Paul presents this *mysterium pietatis* he simply transcribes, without making a grammatical link with what he has just written,[105] three lines of a Christological hymn which—in the opinion of authoritative scholars—has been used in the Greek-speaking Christian communities.

In the words of that hymn, full of theological content and rich in noble beauty, those first-century believers professed their faith in the mystery of Christ, whereby:

- He was made manifest in the reality of human flesh and was constituted by the Holy Spirit as the Just One who offers himself for the unjust.
- He appeared to the angels, having been made greater than them, and he was preached to the nations as the bearer of salvation.
- He was believed in, in the world, as the one sent by the Father, and by the same Father assumed into heaven as Lord.[106]

The mystery or sacrament of pietas, therefore, is the very mystery of Christ. It is, in a striking summary, the mystery of the incarnation and redemption, of the full passover of Jesus, the Son of God and son of Mary: the mystery of his passion and death, of his resurrection and glorification. What St. Paul in quoting the phrases of the hymn wished to emphasize was that this mystery is the hidden vital principle which makes the church the house of God, the pillar and bulwark of the truth. Following the Pauline teaching, we can affirm that this same mystery of God's infinite loving kindness toward us is capable of penetrating to the hidden roots of our iniquity in order to evoke in the soul a movement of conversion, in order to redeem it and set it on course toward reconciliation.

St. John too undoubtedly referring to this mystery, but in his own characteristic language which differs from St. Paul's, was able to write that "anyone born of God does not sin, but he who was born of God keeps him, and the evil one does not touch him."[107] In this Johannine affirmation there is an indication of hope, based on the divine promises: The Christian has received the guarantee and the necessary strength not to sin. It is not a question therefore of a sinlessness acquired through one's own virtue or even inherent in man, as the Gnostics thought. It is a result of God's action. In order not to sin the Christian has knowledge of God, as St. John reminds us in this same passage. But a little before he had written: "No one born of God commits sin; for God's seed abides in him."[108] If by "God's seed" we understand, as some commentators suggest, Jesus the Son of God, then we can say that in order not to sin or in order to gain freedom from sin the Christian has within himself the presence of Christ and the mystery of Christ, which is the mystery of God's loving kindness.

The Effort of the Christian

21. But there is another aspect to the *mysterium pietatis*: The loving kindness of God toward the Christian must be matched by the piety of the Christian toward God. In this second meaning of the word, piety (*eusebeia*) means precisely the conduct of the Christian who responds to God's fatherly loving kindness with his own filial Piety.

In this sense too we can say with St. Paul that "great indeed is the mystery of our religion." In this sense too piety, as a force for conversion and reconciliation, confronts iniquity and sin. In this case too the essential aspects of the mystery of Christ are the object of piety in the sense that the Christian accepts the mystery, contemplates it and draws from it the spiritual strength necessary for living according to the Gospel. Here too one must say that "no one born of God commits sin"; but the expression has an imperative sense: Sustained by the mystery of Christ as by an interior source of spiritual energy, the Christian, being a child of God, is warned not to sin and indeed receives the commandment not to sin but to live in a manner worthy of "the house of God, that is, the church of the living God."[109]

Toward a Reconciled Life

22. Thus the word of Scripture, as it reveals to us the mystery of pietas, opens the intellect to conversion and reconciliation, understood not as lofty abstractions but as concrete Christian values to be achieved in our daily lives.

Deceived by the loss of the sense of sin and at times tempted by an illusion of sinlessness which is not at all Christian, the people of today too need to listen again to St. John's admonition, as addressed to each one of them personally: "If we say we have no sin, we deceive ourselves, and the truth is not in us,"[110] and indeed, "the whole world is in the power of the evil one."[111] Every individual therefore is invited by the voice of divine truth to examine realistically his or her conscience and to confess that he or she has been brought forth in iniquity, as we say in the Miserere psalm."[112]

Nevertheless, though threatened by fear and despair, the people of today can feel uplifted by the divine promise which opens to them the hope of full reconciliation.

The mystery of pietas, on God's part, is that mercy in which our Lord and Father—I repeat it again—is infinitely rich.[113] As I said in my encyclical on the subject of divine mercy,[114] it is a love more powerful than sin, stronger than death. When we realize that God's love for us does not cease in the face of our sin or recoil before our offenses, but becomes even more attentive and generous; when we realize that this love went so far as to cause the passion and death of the Word made flesh who consented to redeem us at the price of his own blood, then we exclaim in gratitude: "Yes, the Lord is rich in mercy," and even: "The Lord is mercy."

The mystery of pietas is the path opened by divine mercy to a reconciled life.

PART THREE:
THE PASTORAL MINISTRY OF PENANCE AND RECONCILIATION

Promoting Penance and Reconciliation

23. To evoke conversion and penance in man's heart and to offer him the gift of reconciliation is the specific mission of the church as she continues the redemptive work of her divine founder. It is not a mission which consists merely of a few theoretical statements and the putting forward of an ethical ideal unaccompanied by the energy with which to carry it out. Rather it seeks to express itself in precise ministerial functions directed toward a concrete practice of penance and reconciliation.

We can call this ministry, which is founded on and illumined by the principles of faith which we have explained and which is directed toward precise objectives and sustained by adequate means, the pastoral activity of penance and reconciliation. Its point of departure is the church's conviction that man, to whom every form of pastoral activity is directed but principally that of penance and reconciliation, is the man marked by sin whose striking image is to be found in King David. Rebuked by the prophet Nathan, David faces squarely his own iniquity and confesses: "I have sinned against the Lord,"[115] and proclaims: "I know my transgressions, and my sin is ever before me."[116] But he also prays: "Purge me with hyssop, and I shall be clean; wash me, and I shall be whiter than snow,"[117] and he receives the response of the divine mercy: "The Lord has put away your sin; you shall not die."[118]

The church thus finds herself face to face with man—with the whole human world—wounded by sin and affected by sin in the innermost depths of his being. But at the same time he is moved by an unrestrainable desire to be freed from sin and, especially if he is a Christian, he is aware that the mystery of pietas, Christ the Lord, is already acting in him and in the world by the power of the redemption.

The church's reconciling role must therefore be carried out in accordance with that intimate link which closely connects the forgiveness and remission of the sin of each person with the fundamental and full reconciliation of humanity which took place with the redemption. This link helps us to understand that, since sin is the active principle of division—division between man and the nature created by God—only conversion from sin is capable of bringing about a profound and lasting reconciliation wherever division has penetrated.

I do not need to repeat what I have already said about the importance of this "ministry of reconciliation,"[119] and of the pastoral activity whereby it is carried out in the church's consciousness and life. This pastoral activity would be lacking an essential aspect of its being and failing in an indispensable function if the "message of reconciliation"[120] were not proclaimed with clarity and tenacity in season and out of season, and if the gift of reconciliation were not offered to the world. But it is worth repeating that the importance of the ecclesial service of reconciliation extends beyond the confines of the church to the whole world.

To speak of the pastoral activity of penance and reconciliation, then, is to refer to all the tasks incumbent on the church, at all levels, for their promotion. More concretely, to speak of this pastoral activity is to evoke all the activities whereby the church, through each and every one of her members—pastors and faithful, at all levels and in all spheres, and with all the means at her disposal, words and actions, teaching and prayer—leads people individually or as groups to true penance and thus sets them on the path to full reconciliation.

The fathers of the synod, as representatives of their brother bishops and as leaders of the people entrusted to them, concerned themselves with the most practical and concrete elements of this pastoral activity. And I am happy to echo their concerns by associating myself with their anxieties and hopes, by receiving the results of their research and experiences, and by encouraging them in their plans and achievements. May they find in this part of the present apostolic exhortation the contribution which they themselves made to the synod, a contribution the usefulness of which I wish to extend, through these pages, to the whole church.

I therefore propose to call attention to the essentials of the pastoral activity of penance and reconciliation by emphasizing, with the synod assembly, the following two points:

1. The means used and the paths followed by the church in order to promote penance and reconciliation.
2. The sacrament par excellence of penance and reconciliation.

CHAPTER ONE:
THE PROMOTION OF PENANCE AND RECONCILIATION—WAYS AND MEANS

24. In order to promote penance and reconciliation, the church has at her disposal two principal means which were entrusted to her by her founder himself: catechesis and the sacraments. Their use has always been considered by the church as fully in harmony with the requirements of her salvific mission and at the same time as corresponding to the requirements and spiritual needs of people in all ages. This use can be in forms and ways both old and new, among which it will be a good idea to remember in particular what we can call, in the expression of my predecessor Paul VI, the method of dialogue.

Dialogue

25. For the church, dialogue is in a certain sense a means and especially a way of carrying out her activity in the modern world.

The Second Vatican Council proclaims that "the church, by virtue of her mission to shed on the whole world the radiance of the gospel message, and to unify under one Spirit all people . . . stands forth as a sign of that fraternal solidarity which allows honest dialogue and invigorates it." The council adds that the church should be capable of "establishing an ever more fruitful dialogue among all those who compose the one people of God,"[121] and also of "establishing a dialogue with human society."[122]

My predecessor Paul VI devoted to dialogue a considerable part of his first encyclical, *Ecclesiam Suam*, in which he describes it and significantly characterizes it as the dialogue of salvation.[123]

The church in fact uses the method of dialogue in order the better to lead people—both those who through baptism and the profession of faith acknowledge their membership of the Christian community and also those who are outside— to conversion and repentance, along the path of a profound renewal of their own consciences and lives in the light of the mystery of the redemption and salvation accomplished by Christ and entrusted to the ministry of his church. Authentic dialogue, therefore, is aimed above all at the rebirth of individuals through interior conversion and repentance, but always with profound respect for consciences and with patience and at the step-by-step pace indispensable for modern conditions.

Pastoral dialogue aimed at reconciliation continues to be today a fundamental task of the church in different spheres and at different levels.

The church in the first place promotes an ecumenical dialogue, that is, with churches and ecclesial communities which profess faith in Christ, the Son of God and only savior. She also promotes dialogue with the other communities of people who are seeking God and wish to have a relationship of communion with him.

At the basis of this dialogue with the other churches and Christian communities and with the other religions, and as a condition of her credibility and effectiveness, there must be a sincere effort of permanent and renewed dialogue within the Catholic Church herself. She is aware that, by her nature, she is the sacrament of the universal communion of charity;[124] but she is equally aware of the tensions within her, tensions which risk becoming factors of division.

The heartfelt and determined invitation which was already extended by my predecessor in preparation for the 1975 Holy Year[125] is also valid at the present moment. In order to overcome conflicts and to ensure that normal tensions do not prove harmful to the unity of the church, we must all apply to ourselves the word of God; we must relinquish our own subjective views and seek the truth where it is to be found, namely in the divine word itself and in the authentic interpretation of that word provided by the magisterium of the church. In this light, listening to one another, respect, refraining from all hasty judgments, patience, the ability to avoid subordinating the faith which unites to the opinions, fashions and ideological choices which divide—these are all qualities of a dialogue within the church which must be persevering, open and sincere. Obviously dialogue would not have these qualities and would not become a factor of reconciliation if the magisterium were not heeded and accepted.

Thus actively engaged in seeking her own internal communion, the Catholic Church can address an appeal for reconciliation to the other churches with which there does not exist full communion, as well as to the other religions and even to all those who are seeking God with a sincere heart. This she has been doing for some time.

In the light of the council and of the magisterium of my predecessors, whose precious inheritance I have received and am making every effort to preserve and put into effect, I can affirm that the Catholic Church at every level is committed to frank ecumenical dialogue, without facile optimism but also without distrust and without hesitation or delays. The fundamental laws which she seeks to follow in this dialogue are, on the one hand, the conviction that only a spiritual ecumenism—namely an ecumenism founded on common prayer and in a common docility to the one Lord—enables us to make a sincere and serious response to the other exigencies of ecumenical action.[126] The other law is the conviction that a certain facile irenicism in doctrinal and especially dogmatic matters could perhaps lead to a form of superficial and short-lived coexistence, but it could not lead to that profound and stable communion which we all long for. This communion will be reached at the hour willed by divine providence. But in order to reach it, the Catholic Church, for her part, knows that she must be open and sensitive to all "the truly Christian endowments from our common heritage which are to be found among our separated brethren";[127] but she also knows that she must likewise base a frank and constructive dialogue upon a clarity regarding her own positions and upon fidelity and consistency with the faith transmitted and defined in accordance with the perennial tradition of her magisterium. Notwithstanding the threat of a certain defeatism and despite the inevitable slowness which rashness could never correct, the Catholic Church continues with all other Christian brethren to seek the paths to unity, and with the followers of the other religions she continues to seek to have sincere dialogue. May this inter-religious dialogue lead to the overcoming of all attitudes of hostility, distrust, mutual condemnation and even mutual invective, which is the precondition for encounter at least in faith in one God and in the certainty of eternal life for the immortal soul. May the Lord especially grant that ecumenical dialogue will also lead to a sincere reconciliation concerning everything that we already have in common with the other Christian churches—faith in Jesus Christ, the Son of God made man, our savior and Lord; a listening to the word; the study of revelation and the sacrament of baptism.

To the extent to which the church is capable of generating active harmony—unity in variety—within herself and of offering herself as a witness to and humble servant of reconciliation with the other churches and ecclesial communities and the other religions, she becomes, in the expressive definition of St. Augustine, a "reconciled world."[128] Then she will be able to be a sign of reconciliation in the world and for the world.

The church is aware of the extreme seriousness of the situation created by the forces of division and war, which today constitute a grave threat not only to the balance and harmony of nations but to the very survival of humanity, and she feels it her duty to offer and suggest her own unique collaboration for the overcoming of conflicts and the restoration of concord.

It is a complex and delicate dialogue of reconciliation in which the church is engaged, especially through the work of the Holy See and its different organisms. The Holy See already endeavors to intervene with the leaders of nations and the heads of the various international bodies or seeks to associate itself with them, conduct a dialogue with them and encourage them to dialogue with one another for the sake of reconciliation in the midst of the many conflicts. It does this not for ulterior motives or hidden interests—since it has none—but "out of a humanitarian concern,"[129] placing its institutional structure and moral authority, which are altogether unique, at the service of concord and peace. It does this in the conviction that as "in war two parties rise against one another" so "in the question of peace there are also necessarily two parties which must know how to commit themselves," and in this "one finds the true meaning of a dialogue for peace."[130] The church engages in dialogue for reconciliation also through the bishops in the competency and responsibility proper to them, either individually in the direction of their respective local churches or united in their episcopal conferences, with the collaboration of the priests and of all those who make up the Christian communities. They truly fulfill their task when they promote this indispensable dialogue and proclaim the human and Christian need for reconciliation and peace. In communion with their pastors, the laity who have as "their own field of evangelizing activity . . . the vast and complicated world of politics, society . . . economics . . . (and) international life,"[131] are called upon to engage directly in dialogue or to work for dialogue aimed at reconciliation. Through them too the church carries out her reconciling activity. Thus the fundamental presupposition and secure basis for any lasting renewal of society and for peace between nations lies in the regeneration of hearts through conversion and penance.

It should be repeated that, on the part of the church and her members, dialogue, whatever form it takes (and these forms can be and are very diverse since the very concept of dialogue has an analogical value) can never begin from an attitude of indifference to the truth. On the contrary, it must begin from a presentation of the truth, offered in a calm way, with respect for the intelligence and consciences of others. The dialogue of reconciliation can never replace or attenuate the proclamation of the truth of the Gospel, the precise goal of which is conversion from sin and communion with Christ and the church. It must be at the service of the transmission and realization of that truth through the means left by Christ to the church for the pastoral activity of reconciliation, namely catechesis and penance.

Catechesis

26. In the vast area in which the church has the mission of operating through dialogue, the pastoral ministry of penance and reconciliation is directed to the members of the body of the church principally through an adequate catechesis concerning the two distinct and complementary realities to which the synod fathers gave a particular importance and which they emphasized in some of the concluding propositions: These are penance and reconciliation. Catechesis is therefore the first means to be used.

At the basis of the synod's very opportune recommendation is a fundamental presupposition: What is pastoral is not opposed to what is doctrinal. Nor can pastoral action prescind from doctrinal content, from which in fact it draws its substance and real validity. Now if the church is the pillar and bulwark of the truth[132] and is placed in the world as mother and teacher, how could she neglect the task of teaching the truth which constitutes a path of life?

From the pastors of the church one expects, first of all, catechesis on reconciliation. This must be founded on the teaching of the Bible, especially the New Testament, on the need to rebuild the covenant with God in Christ the redeemer and reconciler. And in the light of this new communion and friendship, and as an extension of it, it must be founded on the teaching concerning the need to be reconciled with one's brethren, even if this means interrupting the offering of the sacrifice.[133] Jesus strongly insists on this theme of fraternal reconciliation: for example, when he invites us to turn the other cheek to the one who strikes us, and to give our cloak too to the one who has taken our coat,[134] or when he instills the law of forgiveness: forgiveness which each one receives in the measure that he or she forgives,[135] forgiveness to be offered even to enemies,[136] forgiveness to be granted seventy times seven times,[137] which means in practice without any limit. On these conditions, which are realizable only in a genuinely evangelical climate, it is possible to have a true reconciliation between individuals, families, communities, nations and peoples. From these biblical data on reconciliation there will naturally derive a theological catechesis, which in its synthesis will also integrate the elements of psychology, sociology and the other human sciences which can serve to clarify situations, describe problems accurately and persuade listeners or readers to make concrete resolutions.

The pastors of the church are also expected to provide catechesis on penance. Here too the richness of the biblical message must be its source. With regard to penance this message emphasizes particularly its value for conversion, which is the term that attempts to translate the word in the Greek text, *metanoia*,[138] which literally means to allow the spirit to be overturned in order to make it turn toward God. These are also the two fundamental elements which emerge from the parable of the son who was lost and found: his "coming to himself"[139] and his decision to return to his father. There can be no reconciliation unless these attitudes of conversion come first, and catechesis should explain them with concepts and terms adapted to people's various ages and their differing cultural, moral and social backgrounds. This is a first value of penance and it extends into a second: Penance also means repentance. The two meanings of *metanoia* appear in the significant instruction given by Jesus: "If your brother repents (returns to you), forgive him; and if he sins against you seven times in the day, and turns to you seven times and says, 'I repent,' you must forgive him."[140] A good catechesis will show how repentance, just like conversion, is far from being a superficial feeling but a real overturning of the soul.

A third value is contained in penance, and this is the movement whereby the preceding attitudes of conversion and repentance are manifested externally: This is doing penance. This meaning is clearly perceptible in the term *metanoia*, as used by John the Baptist in the texts of the synoptics.[141] To do penance means above all to reestablish the balance and harmony broken by sin, to change direction even at the cost of sacrifice.

A catechesis on penance, therefore, and one that is as complete and adequate as possible, is absolutely essential at a time like ours when dominant attitudes in psychology and social behavior are in such contrast with the threefold value just illustrated. Contemporary man seems to find it harder than ever to recognize his own mistakes and to decide to retrace his steps and begin again after changing course. He seems very reluctant to say "I repent" or "I am sorry." He seems to refuse instinctively and often irresistibly anything that is penance in the sense of a sacrifice accepted and carried out for the correction of sin. In this regard I would like to emphasize that the church's penitential discipline, even though it has been mitigated for some time, cannot be abandoned without grave harm both to the interior life of individual Christians and of the ecclesial community and also to their capacity for missionary influence. It is not uncommon for non-Christians to be surprised at the negligible witness of true penance on the part of Christ's followers. It is clear, however, that

Christian penance will only be authentic if it is inspired by love and not by mere fear; if it consists in a serious effort to crucify the "old man" so that the "new" can be born by the power of Christ; if it takes as its model Christ, who though he was innocent chose the path of poverty, patience, austerity and, one can say, the penitential life.

As the synod recalled, the pastors of the church are also expected to provide catechesis on conscience and its formation. This too is a very relevant topic in view of the fact that in the upheavals to which our present culture is subjected this interior sanctuary, man's innermost self, his conscience, is too often attacked, put to the test, confused and obscured. Valuable guidelines for a wise catechesis on conscience can be found both in the doctors of the church and in the theology of the Second Vatican Council, and especially in the documents on the church in the modern world[142] and on religious liberty.[143] Along these same lines, Pope Paul VI often reminded us of the nature and role of conscience in our life.[144] I myself, following his footsteps, miss no opportunity to throw light on this most lofty element of man's greatness and dignity,[145] this "sort of moral sense which leads us to discern what is good and what is evil . . . like an inner eye, a visual capacity of the spirit, able to guide our steps along the path of good." And I have reiterated the need to form one's conscience, lest it become "a force which is destructive of the true humanity of the person, rather than that holy place where God reveals to him his true good."[146]

On other points too, of no less relevance for reconciliation, one looks to the pastors of the church for catechesis.

On the sense of sin, which, as I have said, has become considerably weakened in our world.

On temptation and temptations: The Lord Jesus himself, the Son of God, "who in every respect has been tempted as we are, yet without sin,"[147] allowed himself to be tempted by the evil one[148] in order to show that, like himself, his followers too would be subjected to temptation, and in order to show how one should behave when subjected to temptation. For those who beseech the Father not to be tempted beyond their own strength[149] and not to succumb to temptation,[150] and for those who do not expose themselves to occasions of sin, being subjected to temptation does not mean that they have sinned; rather it is an opportunity for growing in fidelity and consistency through humility and watchfulness.

Catechesis is also expected on fasting: This can be practiced in old forms and new as a sign of conversion, repentance and personal mortification and, at the same time, as a sign of union with Christ crucified and of solidarity with the starving and suffering.

Catechesis on almsgiving: This is a means of making charity a practical thing by sharing what one possesses with those suffering the consequences of poverty.

Catechesis on the intimate connection which links the overcoming of divisions in the world with perfect communion with God and among people, which is the eschatological purpose of the church.

Catechesis on the concrete circumstances in which reconciliation has to be achieved (in the family, in the civil community, in social structures) and particularly catechesis on the four reconciliations which repair the four fundamental rifts; reconciliation of man with God, with self, with the brethren and with the whole of creation.

Nor can the church omit, without serious mutilation of her essential message, a constant catechesis on what the traditional Christian language calls the four last things of man: death, judgment (universal and particular), hell and heaven. In a culture which tends to imprison man in the earthly life at which he is more or less successful, the pastors of the church are asked to provide a catechesis which will reveal and illustrate with the certainties of faith what comes after the present life: beyond the mysterious gates of death, an eternity of joy in communion with God or the punishment of separation from him. Only in this eschatological vision can one realize the exact nature of sin and feel decisively moved to penance and reconciliation.

Pastors who are zealous and creative never lack opportunities for imparting this broad and varied catechesis, taking into account the different degrees of education and religious formation of those to whom they speak. Such opportunities are often given by the biblical readings and the rites of the Mass and the sacraments, as also by the circumstances of their celebration. For the same purpose many initiatives can be taken such as sermons, lectures, discussions, meetings, courses of religious education, etc., as happens in many places. Here I wish to point out in particular the importance and effectiveness of the old-style popular missions for the purposes of such catechesis. If adapted to the peculiar needs of the present time, such missions can be, today as yesterday, a useful instrument of religious education also regarding penance and reconciliation.

In view of the great relevance of reconciliation based on conversion in the delicate field of human relationships and social interaction at all levels, including the international level, catechesis cannot fail to inculcate the valuable contribution of the church's social teaching. The timely and precise teaching of my predecessors from Pope Leo XIII onward, to which was added the substantial contribution the pastoral constitution *Gaudium et Spes* of the Second Vatican Council and the contributions of the different episcopates elicited by various circumstances in their respective countries, has made up an ample and solid body of doctrine. This regards the many different needs inherent in the life of the human community, in relationships between individuals, families, groups in their different spheres and in the very constitution of a society that intends to follow the moral law, which is the foundation of civilization.

At the basis of this social teaching of the church there is obviously to be found the vision which the church draws from the word of God concerning the rights and duties of individuals, the family and the community; concerning the value of liberty and the nature of justice, concerning the primacy of charity, concerning the dignity of the human person and the exigencies of the common good to which politics and the economy itself must be directed. Upon these fundamental principles of the social magisterium, which confirm and repropose the universal dictates of reason and of the conscience of peoples, there rests in great part the hope for a peaceful solution to many social conflicts and, in short, the hope for universal reconciliation.

The Sacraments

27. The second divinely instituted means which the church offers for the pastoral activity of penance and reconciliation is constituted by the sacraments.

In the mysterious dynamism of the sacraments, so rich in symbolism and content, one can discern one aspect which is not always emphasized: Each sacrament, over and above its own proper grace, is also a sign of penance and reconciliation. Therefore in each of them it is possible to relive these dimensions of the spirit.

Baptism is of course a salvific washing which, as St. Peter says, is effective "not as a removal of dirt from the body but as an appeal to God for a clear conscience."[151] It is death, burial and resurrection with the dead, buried and risen Christ.[152] It is a gift of the Holy Spirit through Christ.[153] But this essential and original constituent of Christian baptism, far from eliminating the penitential element already present in the baptism which Jesus himself received from John "to fulfill all righteousness,"[154] in fact enriches it. In other words, it is a fact of conversion and of reintegration into the right order of relationships with God, of reconciliation with God, with the elimination of the original stain and the consequent introduction into the great family of the reconciled.

Confirmation likewise, as a ratification of baptism and together with baptism a sacrament of initiation, in conferring the fullness of the Holy Spirit and in bringing the Christian life to maturity, signifies and accomplishes thereby a greater conversion of the heart and brings about a more intimate and effective membership of the same assembly of the reconciled, which is the church of Christ.

The definition which St. Augustine gives of the eucharist as *"sacramentum pietatis, signum unitatis, vinculum caritatis"*[155] clearly illustrates the effects of personal sanctification (*pietas*) and community reconciliation (*unitas* and *caritas*) which derive from the very essence of the eucharistic mystery as an unbloody renewal of the sacrifice of the cross, the source of salvation and of reconciliation for all people.

However, it must be remembered that the church, guided by faith in this great sacrament, teaches that no Christian who is conscious of grave sin can receive the eucharist before having obtained God's forgiveness. This we read in the instruction *Eucharisticum Mysterium* which, duly approved by Paul VI, fully confirms the teaching of the Council of Trent: "The eucharist is to be offered to the faithful also 'as a remedy, which frees us from daily faults and preserves us from mortal sin' and they are to be shown the fitting way of using the penitential parts of the liturgy of the Mass. The person who wishes to receive holy communion is to be reminded of the precept: 'Let a man examine himself' (1 Cor 11:28). And the church's custom shows that such an examination is necessary, because no one who is conscious of being in mortal sin, however contrite he may believe himself to be, is to approach the holy eucharist without having first made a sacramental confession. If this person finds himself in need and has no means of going to confession, he should first make an act of perfect contrition."[156]

The sacrament of orders is intended to give to the church the pastors who, besides being teachers and guides, are called to be witnesses and workers of unity, builders of the family of God, and defenders and preservers of the communion of this family against the sources of division and dispersion.

The sacrament of matrimony, the exaltation of human love under the action of grace, is a sign of the love of Christ for the church. But it is also a sign of the victory which Christ grants to couples in resisting the forces which deform and destroy love, in order that the family born from this sacrament may be a sign also of the reconciled and reconciling church for a world reconciled in all its structures and institutions.

Finally, the anointing of the sick in the trial of illness and old age and especially at the Christian's final hour is a sign of definitive conversion to the Lord and of total acceptance of suffering and death as a penance for sins. And in this is accomplished supreme reconciliation with the Father.

However, among the sacraments there is one which, though it has often been called the sacrament of confession because of the accusation of sins which takes place in it, can more appropriately be considered by antonomasia the sacrament of penance, as it is in fact called. And thus it is the sacrament of conversion and reconciliation. The recent synod particularly concerned itself with this sacrament because of its importance with regard to reconciliation.

CHAPTER TWO:
THE SACRAMENT OF PENANCE
AND RECONCILIATION

28. In all its phases and at all its levels the synod considered with the greatest attention that sacramental sign which represents and at the same time accomplishes penance and reconciliation. This sacrament in itself certainly does not contain all possible ideas of conversion and reconciliation. From the very beginning, in fact, the church has recognized and used many and varying forms of penance. Some are liturgical or paraliturgical and include the penitential act in the Mass, services of atonement and pilgrimages; others are of an ascetical character, such as fasting. But of all such acts none is more significant, more divinely efficacious or more lofty and at the same time easily accessible as a rite than the sacrament of penance.

From its preparatory stage and then in the numerous interventions during the sessions, in the group meetings and in the final propositions, the synod took into account the statement frequently made with varying nuances and emphases, namely: The sacrament of penance is in crisis. The synod took note of this crisis. It recommended a more profound catechesis, but it also recommended a no less profound analysis of a theological, historical, psychological, sociological and juridical character of penance in general and of the sacrament of penance in particular. In all of this the synod's intention was to clarify the reasons for the crisis and to open the way to a positive solution for the good of humanity. Meanwhile, from the synod itself the church has received a clear confirmation of its faith regarding the sacrament which gives to every Christian and to the whole community of believers the certainty of forgiveness through the power of the redeeming blood of Christ.

It is good to renew and reaffirm this faith at a moment when it might be weakening, losing something of its completeness or entering into an area of shadow and silence, threatened as it is by the negative elements of the above-mentioned crisis. For the sacrament of confession is indeed being undermined, on the one hand by the obscuring of the mortal and religious conscience, the lessening of a sense of sin, the distortion of the concept of repentance and the lack of effort to live an authentically Christian life. And on the other hand, it is being undermined by the sometimes widespread idea that one can obtain forgiveness directly from God, even in a habitual way, without approaching the sacrament of reconciliation. A further negative influence is the routine of a sacramental practice sometimes lacking in fervor and real spontaneity, deriving perhaps from a mistaken and distorted idea of the effects of the sacrament.

It is therefore appropriate to recall the principal aspects of this great sacrament.

"Whose Sins You Shall Forgive"

29. The books of the Old and New Testament provide us with the first and fundamental fact concerning the Lord's mercy and forgiveness. In the Psalms and in the preaching of the prophets, the name merciful is perhaps the one most often given to the Lord, in contrast to the persistent cliché whereby the God of the Old Testament is presented above all as severe and vengeful. Thus in the Psalms there is a long sapiential passage drawing from the Exodus tradition, which recalls God's kindly action in the midst of his people. This action, though represented in an anthropomorphic way, is perhaps one of the most eloquent Old Testament proclamations of the divine mercy. Suffice it to quote the verse: "Yet he, being compassionate, forgave their iniquity and did not destroy them; he restrained his anger often, and did not stir up all his wrath. He remembered that they were but flesh, a wind that passes and comes not again."[157]

In the fullness of time the Son of God, coming as the lamb who takes away and bears upon himself the sin of the world,[158] appears as the one who has the power both to judge[159] and to forgive sins,[160] and who has come not to condemn but to forgive and save.[161]

Now this power to "forgive sins" Jesus confers through the Holy Spirit upon ordinary men, themselves subject to the snare of sin, namely his apostles: "Receive the Holy Spirit. Whose sins you shall forgive, they are forgiven; whose sins you shall retain, they are retained."[162] This is one of the most awe-inspiring innovations of the Gospel! He confers this power on the apostles also as something which they can transmit—as the church has understood it from the beginning—to their successors, charged by the same apostles with the mission and responsibility of continuing their work as proclaimers of the Gospel and ministers of Christ's redemptive work.

Here there is seen in all its grandeur the figure of the minister of the sacrament of penance who by very ancient custom is called the confessor.

Just as at the altar where he celebrates the eucharist and just as in each one of the sacraments, so the priest, as the minister of penance, acts "in persona Christi." The Christ whom he makes present and who accomplishes the mystery of the forgiveness of sins is the Christ who appears as the brother of man,[163] the merciful high priest, faithful and compassionate,[164] the shepherd intent on finding the lost sheep,[165] the physician who heals and comforts,[166] the one master who teaches the truth and reveals the ways of God,[167] the judge of the living and the dead,[168] who judges according to the truth and not according to appearances.[169]

This is undoubtedly the most difficult and sensitive, the most exhausting and demanding ministry of the priest, but also one of the most beautiful and consoling. Precisely for this reason and with awareness also of the strong recommendation of the synod, I will never grow weary of exhorting my brothers, the bishops and priests, to the faithful and diligent performance of ministry.[170] Before the consciences of the faithful, who open up to him with a mixture of fear and trust, the confessor is called to a lofty task which is one of service and penance and human reconciliation. It is a task of learning the weaknesses and falls of those faithful people, assessing their desire for renewal and their efforts to achieve it, discerning the action of the Holy Spirit in their hearts, imparting to them a forgiveness which God alone can grant, "celebrating" their reconciliation with the Father, portrayed in the parable of the prodigal son, reinstating these redeemed sinners in the ecclesial community with their brothers and sisters, and paternally admonishing these penitents with a firm, encouraging and friendly "Do not sin again."[171]

For the effective performance of this ministry, the confessor must necessarily have human qualities of prudence, discretion, discernment and a firmness tempered by gentleness and kindness. He must likewise have a serious and careful preparation, not fragmentary but complete and harmonious, in the different branches of theology, pedagogy and psychology, in the methodology of dialogue and above all in a living and communicable knowledge of the word of God. But it is even more necessary that he should live an intense and genuine spiritual life. In order to lead others along the path of Christian perfection the minister of penance himself must first travel this path. More by actions than by long speeches he must give proof of real experience of lived prayer, the practice of the theological and moral virtues of the Gospel, faithful obedience to the will of God, love of the church and docility to her magisterium.

All this fund of human gifts, Christian virtues and pastoral capabilities has to be worked for and is only acquired with effort. Every priest must be trained for the ministry of sacramental penance from his years in the seminary, not only through the study of dogmatic, moral, spiritual and pastoral theology (which are simply parts of a whole), but also through the study of the human sciences, training in dialogue and especially in how to deal with people in the pastoral context. He must then be guided and looked after in his first activities. He must always ensure his own improvement and updating by means of permanent study. What a wealth of grace, true life and spiritual radiation would be poured out on the church if every priest were careful never to miss through negligence or various excuses the appointment with the faithful in the confessional and if he were even more careful never to go to it unprepared or lacking the necessary human qualities and spiritual and pastoral preparation!

In this regard I cannot but recall with devout admiration those extraordinary apostles of the confessional such as St. John Nepomucene, St. John Vianney, St. Joseph Cafasso and St. Leopold of Castelnuovo, to mention only the best-known confessors whom the church has added to the list of her saints. But I also wish to pay homage to the innumerable host of holy and almost always anonymous confessors to whom is owed the salvation of so many souls who have been helped by them in conversion, in the struggle against sin and temptation, in spiritual progress and, in a word, in achieving holiness. I do not hesitate to say that even the great canonized saints are generally the fruit of those confessionals, and not only the saints but also the spiritual patrimony of the church and the flowering of a civilization permeated with the Christian spirit! Praise then to this silent army of our brothers who have served well and serve each day the cause of reconciliation through the ministry of sacramental penance!

The Sacrament of Forgiveness

30. From the revelation of the value of this ministry and power to forgive sins, conferred by Christ on the apostles and their successors, there developed in the church an awareness of the sign of forgiveness, conferred through the sacrament of penance. It is the certainty that the Lord Jesus himself instituted and entrusted to the church—as a gift of his goodness and loving kindness[172] to be offered to all—a special sacrament for the forgiveness of sins committed after baptism.

The practice of this sacrament, as regards its celebration and form, has undergone a long process of development as is attested to by the most ancient sacramentaries, the documents of councils and episcopal synods, the preaching of the fathers and the teaching of the doctors of the church. But with regard to the substance of the sacrament there has always remained firm and unchanged in the consciousness of the church the certainty that, by the will of Christ, forgiveness is offered to each individual by means of sacramental absolution given by the ministers of penance. It is a certainty reaffirmed with particular vigor both by the Council of Trent[173] and by the Second Vatican Council: "Those who approach the sacrament of penance obtain pardon from God's mercy for the offenses committed against him, and are, at the same time, reconciled with the church which they have wounded by their sins and which by charity, by example and by prayer works for their conversion."[174] And as an essential element of faith concerning the value and purpose of penance it must be reaffirmed that our savior Jesus Christ instituted in his church the sacrament of penance so that the faithful who have fallen into sin after baptism might receive grace and be reconciled with God.[175]

The church's faith in this sacrament involves certain other fundamental truths which cannot be disregarded. The sacramental rite of penance, in its evolution and variation of actual forms, has always preserved and highlighted these truths. When it recommended a reform of this rite, the Second Vatican Council intended to ensure that it would express these truths even more clearly,[176] and this has come about with the new Rite of Penance.[177] For the latter has made its own the whole of the teaching brought together by the Council of Trent, transferring it from its particular historical context (that of a resolute effort to clarify doctrine in the face of the serious deviations from the church's genuine teaching), in order to translate it faithfully into terms more in keeping with the context of our own time.

Some Fundamental Convictions

31. The truths mentioned above, powerfully and clearly confirmed by the synod and contained in the propositions, can be summarized in the following convictions of faith, to which are connected all the other affirmations of the Catholic doctrine on the sacrament of penance.

I. The first conviction is that for a Christian the sacrament of penance is the primary way of obtaining forgiveness and the remission of serious sin committed after baptism. Certainly the Savior and his salvific action are not so bound to a sacramental sign as to be unable in any period or area of the history of salvation to work outside and above the sacraments. But in the school of faith we learn that the same Savior desired and provided that the simple and precious sacraments of faith would ordinarily be the effective means through which his redemptive power passes and operates. It would therefore be foolish, as well as presumptuous, to wish arbitrarily to disregard the means of grace and salvation which the Lord has provided and, in the specific case, to claim to receive forgiveness while doing without the sacrament which was instituted by Christ precisely for forgiveness. The renewal of the rites carried out after the council does not sanction any illusion or alteration in this direction. According to the church's intention, it was and is meant to stir up in each one of us a new impulse toward the renewal of our interior attitude; toward a deeper understanding of the nature of the sacrament of penance; toward a reception of the sacrament which is more filled with faith, not anxious but trusting; toward a more frequent celebration of the sacrament which is seen to be completely filled with the Lord's merciful love.

II. The second conviction concerns the function of the sacrament of penance for those who have recourse to it. According to the most ancient traditional idea, the sacrament is a kind of judicial action; but this takes place before a tribunal of mercy rather than of strict and rigorous justice, which is comparable to human tribunals only by analogy,[178] namely insofar as sinners reveal their sins and their condition as creatures subject to sin; they commit themselves to renouncing and combating sin; accept the punishment (sacramental penance) which the confessor imposes on them and receive absolution from him.

But as it reflects on the function of this sacrament, the church's consciousness discerns in it, over and above the character of judgment in the sense just mentioned, a healing of a medicinal character. And this is linked to the fact that the Gospel frequently presents Christ as healer,[179] while his redemptive work is often called, from Christian antiquity, *medicina salutis.* "I wish to heal, not accuse," St. Augustine said, referring to the exercise of the pastoral activity regarding penance,[180] and it is thanks to the medicine of confession that the experience of sin does not degenerate into despair.[181] The Rite of Penance alludes to this healing aspect of the sacrament,[182] to which modern man is perhaps more sensitive, seeing as he does in sin the element of error but even more the element of weakness and human frailty.

Whether as a tribunal of mercy or a place of spiritual healing, under both aspects the sacrament requires a knowledge of the sinner's heart in order to be able to judge and absolve, to cure and heal. Precisely for this reason the sacrament involves on the part of the penitent a sincere and complete confession of sins. This therefore has a raison d'être not only inspired by ascetical purposes (as an exercise of humility and mortification), but one that is inherent in the very nature of the sacrament.

III. The third conviction, which is one that I wish to emphasize, concerns the realities or parts which make up the sacramental sign of forgiveness and reconciliation. Some of these realities are acts of the penitent, of varying importance but each indispensable either for the validity, the completeness or the fruitfulness of the sign.

First of all, an indispensable condition is the rectitude and clarity of the penitent's conscience. People cannot come to true and genuine repentance until they realize that sin is contrary to the ethical norm written in their inmost being;[183] until they admit that they have had a personal and responsible experience of this contrast; until they say not only that "sin exists" but also "I have sinned;" until they admit that sin has introduced a division into their consciences which then pervades their whole being and separates them from God and from their brothers and sisters. The sacramental sign of this clarity of conscience is the act traditionally called the examination of conscience, an act that must never be one of anxious psychological introspection, but a sincere and calm comparison with the interior moral law, with the evangelical norms proposed by the church, with Jesus Christ himself, who is our teacher and model of life, and with the heavenly Father, who calls us to goodness and perfection.[184]

But the essential act of penance, on the part of the penitent, is contrition, a clear and decisive rejection of the sin committed, together with a resolution not to commit it again,[185] out of the love which one has for God and which is reborn with repentance. Understood in this way, contrition is therefore the beginning and the heart of conversion, of that evangelical *metanoia* which brings the person back to God like the prodigal son returning to his father, and which has in the sacrament of penance its visible sign and which perfects attrition. Hence "upon this contrition of heart depends the truth of penance."[186]

While reiterating everything that the church, inspired by God's word, teaches about contrition, I particularly wish to emphasize here just one aspect of this doctrine. It is one that should be better known and considered. Conversion and contention are often considered under the aspect of the undeniable demands which they involve and under the aspect of the mortification which they impose for the purpose of bringing about a radical change of life. But we all do well to recall and emphasize the fact that contrition and conversion are even more a drawing near to the holiness of God, a rediscovery of one's true identity, which has been upset and disturbed by sin, a liberation in the very depth of self and thus a regaining of lost joy, the joy of being saved,[187] which the majority of people in our time are no longer capable of experiencing.

We therefore understand why, from the earliest Christian times, in line with the apostles and with Christ, the church has included in the sacramental sign of penance the confession of sins. This latter takes on such importance that for centuries the usual name of the sacrament has been and still is that of confession. The confession of sins is required, first of all, because the sinner must be known by the person who in the sacrament exercises the role of judge. He has to evaluate both the seriousness of the sins and the repentance of the penitent; he also exercises the role of the healer and must acquaint himself with the condition of the sick person in order to treat and heal him. But the individual confession also has the value of a sign: a sign of the meeting of the sinner with the mediation of the church in the person of the minister, a sign of the person's revealing of self as a sinner in the sight of God and the church, of facing his own sinful condition in the eyes of God. The confession of sins therefore cannot be reduced to a mere attempt at psychological self-liberation even though it corresponds to that legitimate and natural need, inherent in the human heart, to open oneself to another. It is a liturgical act, solemn in its dramatic nature, yet humble and sober in the grandeur of its meaning. It is the act of the prodigal son who returns to his Father and is welcomed by him with the kiss of peace. It is an act of honesty and courage. It is an act of entrusting oneself, beyond sin, to the mercy that forgives.[188] Thus we understand why the confession of sins must ordinarily be individual not collective, just as sin is a deeply personal matter. But at the same time this confession in a way forces sin out of the secret of the heart and thus out of the area of pure individuality, emphasizing its social character as well, for through the minister of penance it is the ecclesial community, which has been wounded by sin, that welcomes anew the repentant and forgiven sinner.

The other essential stage of the sacrament of penance this time along to the confessor as judge and healer, a figure of God the Father welcoming and forgiving the one who returns: This is the absolution. The words which express it and the gestures that accompany it in the old and in the new Rite of Penance are significantly simple in their grandeur. The sacramental formula "I absolve you" and the imposition of the hand and the Sign of the Cross made over the penitent show that at this moment the contrite and converted sinner comes into contact with the power and mercy of God. It is the moment at which, in response to the penitent, the Trinity becomes present in order to blot out sin and restore innocence. And the saving power of the passion, death and resurrection of Jesus is also imparted to the penitent as the "mercy stronger than sin and offense," as I defined it in my encyclical *Dives in Misericordia*. God is always the one who is principally offended by sin—"*Tibi soli peccavi!*"—and God alone can forgive. Hence the absolution that the priest, the minister of forgiveness, though himself a sinner, grants to the penitent is the effective sign of the intervention of the Father in every absolution and the sign of the "resurrection" from "spiritual death" which is renewed each time that the sacrament of penance is administered. Only faith can give us certainty that at that moment every sin is forgiven and blotted out by the mysterious intervention of the Savior.

Satisfaction is the final act which crowns the sacramental sign of penance. In some countries the act which the forgiven and absolved penitent agrees to perform after receiving absolution is called precisely the penance. What is the meaning of this satisfaction that one makes or the penance that one performs? Certainly it is not a price that one pays for the sin absolved and for the forgiveness obtained: No human price can match what is obtained, which is the fruit of Christ's precious blood. Acts of satisfaction—which, while remaining simple and humble, should be made to express more clearly all that they signify—mean a number of valuable things: They are the sign of the personal commitment that the Christian has made to God in the sacrament to begin a new life (and therefore they should not be reduced to mere formulas to be recited, but should consist of acts of worship, charity, mercy or reparation). They include the idea that the pardoned sinner is able to join his own physical and spiritual mortification—which has been sought after or at least accepted—to the passion of Jesus, who has obtained the forgiveness for him. They remind us that even after absolution there remains in the Christian a dark area due to the wound of sin, to the imperfection of love in repentance, to the weakening of the spiritual faculties. It is an area in which there still operates an infectious source of sin which must always be fought with mortification and penance. This is the meaning of the humble but sincere act of satisfaction.[189]

IV. There remains to be made a brief mention of other important convictions about the sacrament of penance.

First of all, it must be emphasized that nothing is more personal and intimate that this sacrament, in which the sinner stands alone before God with his sin, repentance and trust. No one can repent in his place or ask forgiveness in his name. There is a certain solitude of the sinner in his sin, and this can be seen dramatically represented in Cain with sin "crouching at his door," as the Book of Genesis says so effectively, and with the distinctive mark on his forehead;[190] in David, admonished by the prophet Nathan;[191] or in the prodigal son when he realizes the condition to which he has reduced himself by staying away from his father and decides to return to him.[192] Everything takes place between the individual alone and God. But at the same time one cannot deny the social nature of this sacrament, in which the whole church—militant, suffering and glorious in heaven—comes to the aid of the penitent and welcomes him again into her bosom, especially as it was the whole church which had been offended and wounded by his sin. As the minister of penance, the priest by virtue of his sacred office appears as the witness and representative of this ecclesial nature of the sacrament. The individual nature and ecclesial nature are two complementary aspects of the sacrament which the progressive reform of the Rite of Penance, especially that contained in the *Ordo Paenitentiae* promulgated by Paul VI, has sought to emphasize and to make more meaningful in its celebration.

V. Second, it must be emphasized that the most precious result of the forgiveness obtained in the sacrament of penance consists in reconciliation with God, which takes place in the inmost heart of the son who was lost and found again, which every penitent is. But it has to be added that this reconciliation with God leads, as it were, to other reconciliations which repair the breaches caused by sin. The forgiven penitent is reconciled with himself in his inmost being, where he regains his own true identity. He is reconciled with his brethren whom he has in some way attacked and wounded. He is reconciled with the church. He is reconciled with all creation.

As a result of an awareness of this, at the end of the celebration there arises in the penitent a sense of gratitude to God for the gift of divine mercy received, and the church invites the penitent to have this sense of gratitude.

Every confessional is a special and blessed place from which, with divisions wiped away, there is born new and uncontaminated a reconciled individual—a reconciled world!

VI. Last, I particularly wish to speak of one final consideration, one which concerns all of us priests, who are the ministers of the sacrament of penance.[193] The priest's celebration of the eucharist and administration of the other sacraments, his pastoral zeal, his relationship with the faithful his communion with his brother priests, his collaboration with his bishop, his life of prayer—in a word, the whole of his priestly existence, suffers an inexorable decline if by negligence or for some other reason he fails to receive the sacrament of penance at regular intervals and in a spirit of genuine faith and devotion. If a priest were no longer to go to confession or properly confess his sins, his priestly being and his priestly action would feel its effects very soon and this would also be noticed by the community of which he was the pastor.

But I also add that even in order to be a good and effective minister of penance the priest needs to have recourse to the source of grace and holiness present in this sacrament. We priests, on the basis of our personal experience, can certainly say that the more careful we are to receive the sacrament of penance and to approach it frequently and with good dispositions, the better we fulfill our own ministry as confessors and ensure that our penitents benefit from it. And on the other hand, this ministry would lose much of its effectiveness if in some way we were to stop being good penitents. Such is the internal logic of this great sacrament. It invites all of us priests of Christ to pay renewed attention to our personal confession.

Personal experience in its turn becomes and must become today an incentive for the diligent, regular, patient and fervent exercise of the sacred ministry of penance, to which we are committed by the very fact of our priesthood and our vocation as pastors and servants of our brothers and sisters. Also with this present exhortation I therefore address an earnest invitation to all the priests of the world, especially to my brothers in the episcopacy and to pastors of souls, an invitation to make every effort to encourage the faithful to make use of this sacrament. I urge them to use all possible and suitable means to ensure that the greatest possible number of our brothers and sisters receive the "grace that has been given to us" through penance for the reconciliation of every soul and of the whole world with God in Christ.

Forms of Celebration

32. Following the suggestions of the Second Vatican Council, the *Ordo Paenitentiae* provided three rites which, while always keeping intact the essential elements, make it possible to adapt the celebration of the sacrament of penance to particular pastoral circumstances.

The first form—reconciliation of individual penitents—is the only normal and ordinary way of celebrating the sacrament, and it cannot and must not be allowed to fall into disuse or be neglected. The second form—reconciliation of a number of penitents with individual confession and absolution—even though in the preparatory acts it helps to give greater emphasis to the community aspects of the sacrament, is the same as the first form in the culminating sacramental act, namely individual confession and individual absolution of sins. It can thus be regarded as equal to the first form as regards the normality of the rite. The third form however—reconciliation of a number of penitents with general confession and absolution—is exceptional in character. It is therefore not left to free choice but is regulated by a special discipline.

The first form makes possible a highlighting of the more personal—and essential—aspects which are included in the penitential process. The dialogue between penitent and confessor, the sum of the elements used (the biblical texts, the choice of the forms of "satisfaction," etc.), make the sacramental celebration correspond more closely to the concrete situation of the penitent. The value of these elements are perceived when one considers the different reasons that bring a Christian to sacramental penance: a need for personal reconciliation and readmission to friendship with God by regaining the grace lost by sin; a need to check one's spiritual progress and sometimes a need for a more accurate discernment of one's vocation; on many other occasions a need and a desire to escape from a state of spiritual apathy and religious crisis. Thanks then to its individual character, the first form of celebration makes it possible to link the sacrament of penance with something which is different but readily linked with it: I am referring to spiritual direction. So it is certainly true that personal decision and commitment are clearly signified and promoted in this first form.

The second form of celebration, precisely by its specific dimension, highlights certain aspects of great importance: The word of God listened to in common has remarkable effect as compared to its individual reading and better emphasizes the ecclesial character of conversion and reconciliation. It is particularly meaningful at various seasons of the liturgical year and in connection with events of special pastoral importance. The only point that needs mentioning here is that for celebrating the second form there should be an adequate number of confessors present.

It is therefore natural that the criteria for deciding which of the two forms of celebration to use should be dictated not by situational and subjective reasons, but by a desire to secure the true spiritual good of the faithful in obedience to the penitential discipline of the church.

We shall also do well to recall that, for a balanced spiritual and pastoral orientation in this regard, great importance must continue to be given to teaching the faithful also to make use of the sacrament of penance for venial sins alone, as is borne out by a centuries-old doctrinal tradition and practice.

Though the church knows and teaches that venial sins are forgiven in other ways too—for instance, by acts of sorrow, works of charity, prayer, penitential rites—she does not cease to remind everyone of the special usefulness of the sacramental moment for these sins too. The frequent use of the sacrament—to which some categories of the faithful are in fact held—strengthens the awareness that even minor sins offend God and harm the church, the body of Christ. Its celebration then becomes for the faithful "the occasion and the incentive to conform themselves more closely to Christ and to make themselves more docile to the voice of the Spirit."[194] Above all it should be emphasized that the grace proper to the sacramental celebration has a great remedial power and helps to remove the very roots of sin.

Attention to the actual celebration,[195] with special reference to the importance of the word of God which is read, recalled and explained, when this is possible and suitable, to the faithful and with them, will help to give fresh life to the practice of the sacrament and prevent it from declining into a mere formality and routine. The penitent will be helped rather to discover that he or she is living a salvific event capable of inspiring fresh life and giving true peace of heart. This careful attention to the celebration will also lead the individual churches to arrange special times for the celebration of the sacrament. It will also be an incentive to teaching the faithful, especially children and young people, to accustom themselves to keeping to these times except in cases of necessity, when the parish priest must always show a ready willingness to receive whoever comes to him.

Celebration of the Sacrament with General Absolution

33. The new liturgical regulation and, more recently, the Code of Canon Law,[196] specify the conditions which make it lawful to use "the rite of reconciliation of a number of penitents with general confession and absolution." The norms and regulations given on this point, which are the result of mature and balanced consideration, must be accepted and applied in such a way as to avoid any sort of arbitrary interpretation.

It is opportune to reflect more deeply on the reasons which order the celebration of penance in one of the first two forms and permit the use of the third form. First of all, there is the reason of fidelity to the will of the Lord Jesus, transmitted by the doctrine of the church, and also the reason of obedience to the church's laws. The synod repeated in one of its propositions the unchanged teaching which the church has derived from the most ancient tradition, and it repeated the law with which she has codified the ancient penitential practice: The individual and integral confession of sins with individual absolution constitutes the only ordinary way in which the faithful who are conscious of serious sin are reconciled with God and with the church. From this confirmation of the church's teaching it is clear that every serious sin must always be stated, with its determining circumstances, in an individual confession.

Then there is a reason of the pastoral order. While it is true that, when the conditions required by canonical discipline occur, use may be made of the third form of celebration, it must not be forgotten that this form cannot become an ordinary one, and it cannot and must not be used—as the synod repeated—except "in cases of grave necessity." And there remains unchanged the obligation to make an individual confession of serious sins before again having recourse to another general absolution. The bishop therefore, who is the only one competent in his own diocese to assess whether the conditions actually exist which canon law lays down for the use of the third form, will give this judgment with a grave obligation on his own conscience, with full respect for the law and practice of the church and also taking into account the criteria and guidelines agreed upon—on the basis of the doctrinal and pastoral considerations explained above—with the other members of the episcopal conference. Equally it will always be a matter of genuine pastoral concern to lay down and guarantee the conditions that make recourse to the third form capable of producing the spiritual fruits for which it is meant. The exceptional use of the third form of celebration must never lead to a lesser regard for, still less an abandonment of, the ordinary forms nor must it lead to this form being considered an alternative to the other two forms. It is not in fact left to the freedom of pastors and the faithful to choose from among these forms the one considered most suitable. It remains the obligation of pastors to facilitate for the faithful the practice of integral and individual confession of sins, which constitutes for them not only a duty but also an inviolable and inalienable right, besides being something needed by the soul. For the faithful, the use of the third form of celebration involves the obligation of following all the norms regulating its exercise, including that of not having recourse again to general absolution before a normal integral and individual confession of sins, which must be made as soon as possible. Before granting absolution the priest must inform and instruct the faithful about this norm and about the obligation to observe it.

With this reminder of the doctrine and the law of the church I wish to instill into everyone the lively sense of responsibility which must guide us when we deal with sacred things like the sacraments, which are not our property, or like consciences, which have a right not to be left in uncertainty and confusion. The sacraments and consciences, I repeat, are sacred, and both require that we serve them in truth.

This is the reason for the church's law.

Some More Delicate Cases

34. I consider it my duty to mention at this point, if very briefly, a pastoral case that the synod dealt with—insofar as it was able to do so—and which it also considered in one of the propositions. I am referring to certain situations, not infrequent today, affecting Christians who wish to continue their sacramental religious practice, but who are prevented from doing so by their personal condition, which is not in harmony with

the commitments freely undertaken before God and the church. These are situations which seem particularly delicate and almost inextricable.

Numerous interventions during the synod, expressing the general thought of the fathers, emphasized the coexistence and mutual influence of two equally important principles in relation to these cases. The first principle is that of compassion and mercy, whereby the church, as the continuer in history of Christ's presence and work, not wishing the death of the sinner but that the sinner should be converted and live,[197] and careful not to break the bruised reed or to quench the dimly burning wick,[198] ever seeks to offer, as far as possible, the path of return to God and of reconciliation with him. The other principle is that of truth and consistency, whereby the church does not agree to call good evil and evil good. Basing herself on these two complementary principles, the church can only invite her children who find themselves in these painful situations to approach the divine mercy by other ways, not however through the sacraments of penance and the eucharist until such time as they have attained the required dispositions.

On this matter, which also deeply torments our pastoral hearts, it seemed my precise duty to say clear words in the apostolic exhortation *Familiaris Consortio*, as regards the case of the divorced and remarried,[199] and likewise the case of Christians living together in an irregular union.

At the same time and together with the synod, I feel that it is my clear duty to urge the ecclesial communities and especially the bishops to provide all possible assistance to those priests who have fallen short of the grave commitments which they undertook at their ordination and who are living in irregular situations. None of these brothers of ours should feel abandoned by the church.

For all those who are not at the present moment in the objective conditions required by the sacrament of penance, the church's manifestations of maternal kindness, the support of acts of piety apart from sacramental ones, a sincere effort to maintain contact with the Lord, attendance at Mass and the frequent repetition of acts of faith, hope, charity and sorrow made as perfectly as possible can prepare the way for full reconciliation at the hour that providence alone knows.

Concluding Expression of Hope

35. At the end of this document I hear echoing within me and I desire to repeat to all of you the exhortation which the first bishop of Rome, at a critical hour of the beginning of the church, addressed "to the exiles of the dispersion . . . chosen and destined by God the Father . . . : Have unity of spirit, sympathy, love of the brethren, a tender heart and a humble mind."[200] The apostle urged: "Have unity of spirit." But

he immediately went on to point out the sins against harmony and peace which must be avoided: "Do not return evil for evil or reviling for reviling; but on the contrary bless, for to this you have been called, that you may obtain a blessing." And he ended with a word of encouragement and hope: "Who is there to harm you if you are zealous for what is right?"[201]

At an hour of history which is no less critical, I dare to join my exhortation to that of the prince of the apostles, the first to occupy this See of Rome as a witness to Christ and as pastor of the church, and who here "presided in charity" before the entire world. In communion with the bishops who are the successors of the apostles and supported by the collegial reflection that many of them, meeting in the synod, devoted to the topics and problems of reconciliation, I too wish to speak to you with the same spirit of the fisherman of Galilee when he said to our brothers and sisters in the faith, distant in time but so closely linked in heart: "Have unity of spirit. . . . Do not return evil for evil. . . . Be zealous for what is right."[202] And he added: "It is better to suffer for doing right, if that should be God's will, than for doing wrong."[203]

This exhortation is completely permeated by words which Peter had heard from Jesus himself and by ideas which formed part of his "good news": the new commandment of love of neighbor; the yearning for and commitment to unity; the beatitudes of mercy and patience in persecution for the sake of justice; the repaying of evil with good; the forgiveness of offenses; the love of enemies. In these words and ideas is the original and transcendent synthesis of the Christian ethic or, more accurately and more profoundly, of the spirituality of the new covenant in Jesus Christ.

I entrust to the Father, rich in mercy, I entrust to the Son of God, made man as our redeemer and reconciler, I entrust to the Holy Spirit, source of unity and peace, this call of mine, as father and pastor, to penance and reconciliation. May the most holy and adorable Trinity cause to spring up in the church and in the world the small seed which at this hour I plant in the generous soil of many human hearts.

In order that in the not too distant future abundant fruits may come from it, I invite you all to join me in turning to Christ's heart, the eloquent sign of the divine mercy, the "propitiation for our sins," "our peace and reconciliation,"[204] that we may draw from it an interior encouragement to hate sin and to be converted to God, and find in it the divine kindness which lovingly responds to human repentance.

I likewise invite you to turn with me to the immaculate heart of Mary, mother of Jesus, in whom "is effected the reconciliation of God with humanity . . . , is accomplished the work of reconciliation, because she has received from God the fullness of grace in virtue of the redemptive sacrifice of Christ."[205] Truly Mary has been associated with God, by virtue of her divine motherhood, in the work of reconciliation.[206]

Into the hands of this mother, whose *fiat* marked the beginning of that "fullness of time" in which Christ accomplished the reconciliation of humanity with God, to her immaculate heart—to which we have repeatedly entrusted the whole of humanity, disturbed by sin and tormented by so many tensions and conflicts—I now in a special way entrust this intention: that through her intercession humanity may discover and travel the path of penance, the only path that can lead it to full reconciliation.

To all of you who in a spirit of ecclesial communion in obedience and faith[207] receive the indications, suggestions and directives contained in this document and seek to put them into living pastoral practice, I willingly impart my apostolic blessing.

Given in Rome at St. Peter's on December 2, the first Sunday of Advent, in the year 1984, the seventh of my pontificate.

Joannes Paulus PP. II

NOTES

1. Mk 1:15.
2. Cf. Pope John Paul II, opening speech at the Third General Conference of the Latin American Episcopate: AAS 71 (1979), 198-204.
3. The idea of a "shattered world" is seen in the works of numerous contemporary writers, both Christian and non-Christian, witnesses of man's condition in this tormented period of history.
4. Cf. Pastoral Constitution on the Church in the Modern World *Gaudium et Spes*, nos. 3, 43 and 44; Decree on the Ministry and Life of Priests *Presbyterorum Ordinis*, no. 12; Pope Paul VI, encyclical *Ecclesiam Suam*: AAS 56 (1964), 609-659. ˙
5. At the very beginning of the church, the apostle Paul wrote with words of fire about division in the body of the church, in the famous passage 1 Cor 1:10-16. Years later, St. Clement of Rome was also to write to the Corinthians, to condemn the wounds inside that community: cf. Letter to the Corinthians, III-VI; LVII: *Patres Apostolici*, ed. Funk, I, 103-109; 171-173. We know that from the earliest fathers onward Christ's seamless robe, which the soldiers did not divide, became an image of the church's unity: cf. St. Cyprian, *De Ecclesiae Catholicae Unitate*, 7: CCL 3/1, 254f; St. Augustine, *In Ioannis Evangelium Tractatus*, 118, 4: CCL 36, 656f; St. Bede the Venerable, *In Marci Evangelium Expositio*, IV, 15: CCL 120, 630i *In Lucae Evangelium Expositio*, VI, 23: CCL 120, 403; *In S. Ioannis Evangelium Expositio*, 19: PL 92, 911f.
6. The encyclical *Pacem in Terris*, John XXIII's spiritual testament, is often considered a "social document" and even a "political message," and in fact it is if these terms are understood in their broadest sense. As is evident more than twenty years after its publication, the document is in fact more than a strategy for the peaceful coexistence of people and nations; it is a pressing reminder of the higher values without which peace on earth becomes a mere dream. One of these values is precisely that of reconciliation among people, and John XXIII often referred to this subject. With regard to Paul VI, it will suffice to recall that in calling the church and the world to celebrate the Holy Year of 1975, he wished "renewal and reconciliation" to be the central idea of that important event. Nor can one forget the catechesis which he devoted to this key theme, also in explaining the jubilee itself.
7. As I wrote in the bull of indiction of the Jubilee Year of the Redemption: "This special time, when all Christians are called upon to realize more profoundly their vocation to reconciliation with the Father in the Son, will only reach its full achievement if it leads to a fresh commitment by each and every person to the service of reconciliation, not only among all the disciples of Christ but also among all men and women": bull *Aperite Portas Redemptori*, 3: AAS 75 (1983), 93.
8. The theme of the synod was, more precisely, "Reconciliation and Penance in the Mission of the Church."
9. Cf. Mt 4:17; Mk 1:15.
10. Cf. Lk 3:8.
11. Cf. Mt 16:24-26; Mk 8:34-36; Lk 9:23-25.
12. Eph 4:23f.
13. Cf. 1 Cor 3:1-20.
14. Cf. Col 3:1f.

15   "We beseech you on behalf of Christ, be reconciled to God": 2 Cor 5:20.

16   "We also rejoice in God through our Lord Jesus Christ, through whom we have now received our reconciliation": Rom 5:11; cf. Col 1:20.

17   The Second Vatican Council noted: "The dichotomy affecting the modern world is, in fact, a symptom of the deeper dichotomy that is in man himself. He is the meeting point of many conflicting forces. In his condition as a created being he is subject to a thousand shortcomings, but feels untrammeled in his inclinations and destined for a higher form of life. Torn by a welter of anxieties he is compelled to choose between them and repudiate some among them. Worse still, feeble and sinful as he is, he often does the very thing he hates and does not do what he wants (cf. Rom 7:14ff). And so he feels himself divided, and the result is a host of discords in social life": *Gaudium et Spes*, 10.

18   Cf. Col 1:19f.

19   Cf. Pope John Paul II, encyclical *Dives in Misericordia*, 5-6: AAS 72 (1980), 1193-1199.

20   Cf. Lk 15:11-32.

21   In the Old Testament, the Book of Jonah is a wonderful anticipation and figure of this aspect of the parable. Jonah's sin is that he was "displeased . . . exceedingly and he was angry" because God is "a gracious God and merciful, slow to anger, and abounding in steadfast love, and repentest of evil." His sin is also that of pitying a castor oil plant "which came into being in a night and perished in a night" and not understanding that the Lord pities Nineveh. Cf. Jon 4.

22   Cf. Rom 5:10f; cf. Col 1:20-22.

23   Cf. 2 Cor 5:18, 20.

24   Jn 11:52.

25   Cf. Col 1:20.

26   Cf. Sir 44:17.

27   Eph 2:14.

28   Eucharistic Prayer 3.

29   Cf. Mt 5:23f.

30   *Ibid.*, 27:46; Mk 15:34, Ps 22(21):2.

31   Cf. Eph 2:14-16.

32   St. Leo the Great, Tractatus 63 (*De Passione Domini*, 12), 6: CCL 138/A, 386.

33   Cf. 2 Cor 5:18f.

34   Dogmatic Constitution on the Church *Lumen Gentium*, 1.

35   "The church is also by her nature always reconciling, handing on to others the gift that she herself has received, the gift of having been forgiven and made one with God": Pope John Paul II, Homily at Liverpool, May 30, 1982: *Insegnamenti*, V, 2 (1982), 1992.

36   Cf. Acts 15:2-33.

37   Cf. Apostolic exhortation *Evangelii Nuntiandi*, 13: AAS 68 (1976), 12f.

38   Cf. Pope John Paul II, apostolic exhortation *Catechesi Tradendae*, 24: AAS 71 (1979), 1297.

39   Cf. Pope Paul VI, encyclical *Ecclesiam Suam*: AAS 56 (1964), 609-659.

40   Cf. 2 Cor 5:20.

41   Cf. 1 Jn 4:8.

42   Cf. Wis 11:23-26; Gn 1:27; Ps 8:4-8.

43   Cf. Wis 2:24.

44   Cf. Gn 3:12f; 4:1-16.

45   Cf. Eph 2:4.

46   Cf. *ibid.*, 1:10.

47   Jn 13:34.

48   Cf. Second Vatican Council, Pastoral Constitution on the Church in the Modern World *Gaudium et Spes*, 38.

49   Cf. Mk 1:15.

50   Cf. 2 Cor 5:20.

51   Cf. Eph 2:14-16.

52   Cf. St. Augustine, *De Civitate Dei*, XXII 17: CCL 48, 835f; St. Thomas Aquinas, *Summa Theologiae*, III pars, q. 64, art. 2 ad tertium.

53   Cf. Pope Paul VI, Allocution at the Closing of the Third Session of the Second Vatican Ecumenical Council, November 21, 1964: ASS 56 (1964), 1015-1018.

54   Second Vatican Council, Dogmatic Constitution on the Church *Lumen Gentium*, 39.

55   *Ibid.*, Decree on Ecumenism *Unitatis Redintegratio*, 4.

56   1 Jn 1:8-9.

57   1 Jn 3:20; cf. my reference to this passage in my address at the general audience of March 14, 1984: *Insegnamenti*, VII, 1 (1984) 683.

58   Cf. 2 Sm 11-12.

59   Cf. Ps 50(51):3-4.

60   Cf. Lk 15:18, 21.

61   Lettere, Florence 1970, I, pp. 3f; II *Dialogo della Divina Providenza*, Rome 1980, passim.

62   Cf. Rom 3:23-26.

63   Cf. Eph 1:18.

64   Cf. Gn 11:1-9.

65   Cf. Ps 127 (126):1.

66   Cf. 2 1 Thes 2:7.

67   Cf. Rom 7:7-25; Eph 2:2, 6:12.

68   The terminology used in the Septuagint Greek translation and in the New Testament for sin is significant. The most common term for sin is *hamartia*, with its various derivatives. It expresses the concept of offending more or less gravely against a norm or law, or against a person or even a divinity. But sin is also called *adikia*, and the concept here is of acting unjustly. The Bible also speaks of *parabasis* (transgression), *asebeis* (impiety) and other concepts. They all convey the image of sin.

69   Gn 3:5: "And you will be like God, knowing good and evil"; cf. also v. 22.

70   Cf. *ibid.*, 3:12.

71   Cf. *ibid.*, 4:2-16.

72   The expression from the French writer Elizabeth Leseur, *Journal et Pensees de Chaque Jour*, Paris 1918, p. 31.

73   Cf. Mt 22:39; Mk 12:31; Lk 10:27f.

74   Cf. Sacred Congregation for the Doctrine of the Faith, Instruction on Certain Aspects of the Theology of Liberation *Libertatis Nuntius*; August 6, 1984, IV, 14-15: AAS 76 (1984), 885f.

75   Cf. Nm 15:30.

76   Cf. Lv 18:26-30.

77   Cf. *ibid.*, 19:4.

78   Cf. *ibid.*, 20:1-7.

79 Cf. Ex 21:17.
80 Cf. Lv 4:2ff; 5:1ff; Nm 15:22-29.
81 Cf. Mt 5:28; 6:23; 12:31f; 15:19; Mk 3:28-30; Rom 1:29-31; 13:13; Jas 4.
82 Cf. Mt 5:17; 15:1-10; Mk 10:19; Lk 18:20.
83 Cf. 1 Jn 5:16f.
84 Cf. 1 Jn 17:3.
85 Cf. 1 Jn 2:22.
86 Cf. 1 Jn 5:21.
87 Cf. 1 Jn 5:16-21.
88 Cf. Mt 12:31f.
89 Cf. St. Thomas Aquinas, *Summa Theologiae*, II-II, q. 14, aa. 1-8.
90 Cf. 1 Jn 3:20.
91 St. Thomas Aquinas, *Summa Theologiae*, II-II, q. 14, a. 3, ad primum.
92 Cf. Phil 2:12.
93 Cf. St. Augustine, *De Spintu et Littera*, XXVIII: CSEL 60, 202f; *Enarrat. in ps.* 39, 22: CCL 38, 441; *Enchiridion ad Laurentium de Fide et Spe et Cantate*, XIX, 71: CCL 46, 88; *In Ioannis Evangelium Tractatus*, 12, 3,14: CCL 36, 129.
94 St. Thomas Aquinas, *Summa Theologiae*, I-II, q. 72, a. 5.
95 Cf. Council of Trent, Session VI, *De Iustificatione*, Chap. 2 and Canons 23, 25, 27: *Conciliorum Oecumenicorum Decreta*, Bologna 1973, 671 and 680f (DS 1573, 1575, 1577).
96 Cf. Council of Trent, Session IV *De Iustificatione*, Chapt. 15: *Conciliorum Oecumenicorum Decreta*, ed. dt. 677 (DS 1544).
97 Pope John Paul II, Angelus Message of March 14, 1982: *Insegnamenti* V, 1 (1982),861.
98 *Gaudium et Spes*, 16.
99 Pope John Paul II, Angelus Message of March 14, 1982: *Insegnamenti* V, 1 (1982),860.
100 Pope Pius XII, Radio Message to the U.S. National Catechetical Congress in Boston (October 26, 1946): *Discorsi e Radiomessaggi* VIII (1946) 288.
101 Cf. Pope John Paul II, encyclical *Redemptor Hominis*, 15: AAS 71 (1979), 286-289.
102 Cf. *Gaudium et Spes*, 3; cf. 1 Jn 3:9.
103 Pope John Paul II, Address to the Bishops of the Eastern Region of France (April 1,1982), 2: *Insegnamenti* V, 1 (1982), 1081.
104 1 Tm 3:15f.
105 The text presents a certain difficulty, since the relative pronoun which opens the literal translation does not agree with the neuter *mysterion*. Some late manuscripts have adjusted the text in order to correct the grammar. But it was Paul's intention merely to put next to what he had written a venerable text which for him was fully explanatory.
106 The early Christian community expresses its faith in the crucified and glorified Christ, whom the angels adore and who is the Lord. But the striking element of this message remains the phrase "manifested in the flesh": that the eternal Son of God became man is the "great mystery."
107 1 Jn 5:18f.
108 *Ibid.*, 3:9.
109 1 Tm 3:15.
110 1 Jn 1:8.
111 *Ibid.*, 5:19.
112 Cf. Ps. 51(50):5.

113   Cf. Eph. 2:4.
114   Cf. Pope John Paul II, *Dives in Misericordia*, 8; 15: AAS 72 (1980), 1203-1207; 1231.
115   2 Sm 12:13.
116   Ps 51(50):3.
117   *Ibid.*, 51(50):7.
118   2 Sm 12:13.
119   Cf. 2 Cor 5:18.
120   Cf. 2 Cor 5:19.
121   *Gaudium et Spes*, 92.
122   Decree on the Pastoral Office of Bishops in the Church *Christus Dominus*, 13; cf. Declaration on Christian Education *Gravissimum Educationis*, 8; Decree on the Church's Missionary Activity *Ad Gentes*, 11-12.
123   Cf. Pope Paul VI, *Ecclesiam Suam*, III: AAS 56 (1964), 639-659.
124   *Lumen Gentium*, 1, 9,13.
125   Pope Paul VI, apostolic exhortation *Paterna Cum Benevolentia*: AAS 67 (1975), 5-23.
126   Cf. *Unitatis Redintegratio*, 7-8.
127   *Ibid.*, 4.
128   St. Augustine, *Sermo* 96, 7: PL 38, 588.
129   Pope John Paul II, Speech to Members of the Diplomatic Corps Accredited to the Holy See (January 15, 1983), 4, 6, 1 1: AAS 75 (1983), 376, 378f, 381.
130   Pope John Paul II, Homily at the Mass for the 16th World Day of Peace (January 1, 1983), 6: *Insegnamenti* VI, 1 (1983), 7.
131   Pope Paul VI, apostolic exhortation *Evangelii Nuntiandi*, 70: AAS 68 (1976), 59f.
132   1 Tm 3:15.
133   Cf. Mt 5:23f.
134   Cf. *ibid.*, 5:38-40.
135   Cf. *ibid.*, 6:12.
136   Cf. *ibid.*, 5:43ff.
137   Cf. *ibid.*, 18:21f.
138   Cf. Mk 1:14; Mt 3:2; 4:17; Lk 3:8.
139   Cf. Lk 15:17.
140   *Ibid.*, 17:3f.
141   Cf. Mt 3:2; Mk 1:2-6; Lk 3:1-6.
142   Cf. *Gaudium et Spes*, 8, 16, 19, 26, 41, 48.
143   Cf. Declaration on Religious Liberty *Dignitatis Humanae*, 2, 3, 4.
144   Cf. among many others the addresses at the general audiences of March 28, 1973: *Insegnamenti* XI (1973), 294ff; August 8,1973: *ibid.*, 772ff, November 7, 1973: *ibid.*, 1054ff; March 13, 1974: *Insegnamenti* XII (1974), 230ff; May 8, 1974: *ibid.*, 402ff; February 12, 1975: *Insegnamenti* XIII (1975), *ibid.*, 290ff; July 13, 1977: *Insegnamenti* XV (1977), 710ff.
145   Cf. Pope John Paul II, Angelus Message of March 17, 1982: *Insegnamenti* V, 1 (1982), 860f.
146   Cf. Pope John Paul II, General Audience Address of August 17, 1983, 1-3: *Insegnamenti* VI, 2 (1983), 256f.
147   Heb 4:15.
148   Cf. Mt 4:1-11; Mk 1:12f; Lk 4:1-13.
149   Cf. 1 Cor 10:13.

150   Cf. Mt 6:13; Lk 11:4.

151   1 Pt 3:21.

152   Cf. Rom 6:3f; Col 2:12.

153   Cf. Mt 3:11; Lk 3:16; Jn 1:33; Acts 1:5; 11:16.

154   Cf. Mt 3:15.

155   St. Augustine, *In Ioannis Evangelium Tractatus*, 26, 13: CCL 36, 266.

156   Sacred Congregation of Rites, Instruction on the Worship of the Eucharistic Mystery *Eucharisticum Mysterium* (May 25, 1967) 35, AAS 59 (1967), 560f.

157   Ps 78(77):38f.

158   Cf. Jn 1:29; Is 53:7-12.

159   Cf. Jn 5:27.

160   Cf. Mt 9:2-7; Lk 5.-18-25; 7:47-49; Mk 2:3-12.

161   Cf. Jn 3:17.

162   Jn 20:22; Mt 18:18; cf. also, as regards Peter, Mt 16:19. Blessed Isaac of Stella in one of his talks emphasizes the full communion of Christ with the church in the forgiveness of sins: "The church can forgive nothing without Christ and Christ does not wish to forgive anything without the church. The church can forgive nothing except to a penitent, that is to say, to a person whom Christ has touched with his grace: Christ does not wish to consider anything forgiven in a person who despises the church": *Sermo 11* (*In Dominica II Post Epiphaniam*, 1): PL 194, 1729.

163   Cf. Mt 12:49f; Mk 3:33f; Lk 8:20f; Rom 8:29: "the firstborn among many brethren."

164   Cf. Heb 2:17; 4:15.

165   Cf. Mt 18:12f; Lk 15:4-6.

166   Cf. Lk 5:31f.

167   Cf. Mt 22:16.

168   Cf. Acts 10:42.

169   Cf. Jn 8:16.

170   Cf. the address to the penitentiaries of the Roman patriarchal basilicas and to the priest confessors at the closing of the Jubilee of the Redemption July 9, 1984): *L'Osservatore Romano*, July 9-10, 1984.

171   Jn 8:11.

172   Cf. Ti 3:4.

173   Cf. Council of Trent, Session XIV *De Sacramento Poenitentiae*, Chap. 1 and Canon 1: *Conciliorum Oecumenicorum Decreta*, 703f, 711 (DS 1668-1670, 1701).

174   *Lumen Gentium*, 11.

175   Cf. Council of Trent, Session XIV, *De Sacramento Poenitentiae*, Chap. 1 and Canon 1: *Conciliorum Oecumenicorum Decreta*, ed. cit.,703f, 711 (DS 1668-1670, 1701).

176   Cf. Constitution on the Sacred Liturgy *Sacrosanctum Concilium*, 72.

177   Cf. *Rituale Romanum ex Decreto Sacrosancti Conalii Oecumenici Vaticani II Instauratum, Auctoritate Pauli VI Promulgatum: Ordo Paenitentiae*, Vatican Polyglot Press, 1974.

178   The Council of Trent uses the attenuated expression "ad instar actus iudicialis" (Session XIV, *De Sacramento Poenitentiae*, Chap. 6: *Conciliorum Oecumenicorum Decreta*, ed. dt., 707 (DS 1685), in order to emphasize the difference from human tribunals. The new *Rite of Penance* makes reference to this function, Nos. 6b and 10a.

179   Cf. Lk 5:31f: "Those who are well have no need of a physician, but those who are sick" concluding: "I have . . . come to call . . . sinners to repentance"; Lk 9:2: "And he sent them out to preach the kingdom of God and to heal." The image of Christ the physician

takes on new and striking elements if we compare it with the figure of the Servant of Yahweh, of whom the Book of Isaiah prophesies that "he has borne our griefs and carried our sorrows" and that "with his stripes we are healed" (Is 53:4f).

[180] St. Augustine, *Sermo* 82, 8: PL 38, 511.

[181] *Ibid.*, *Sermo* 352, 3, 8:9: PL 39, 1558f.

[182] Cf. *Ordo Paenitentiae*, 6c.

[183] Even the pagans recognized the existence of "divine" moral laws which have "always" existed and which are written in the depths of the human heart, cf. Sophocles (Antigone, w. 450-460) and Aristotle (Rhetor., Book I, Chap.15, 1375 a-b).

[184] On the role of conscience cf. what I said at the general audience of March 14, 1984, 3: *Insegnamenti* VII, 1 (1984), 683.

[185] Cf. Council of Trent, Session XIV *De Sacramento Poenitentiae*, Chap. 4, *De Contritione: Conciliorum Oecumenicorum Decreta*, ed. cit., 705 (DS 1676-1677). Of course, in order to approach the sacrament of penance it is sufficient to have attrition, or imperfect repentance, due more to fear than to love. But in the sphere of the sacrament, the penitent, under the action of the grace that he receives, "ex attrito fit contus," since penance really operates in the person who is well disposed to conversion in love: cf. Council of Trent, *ibid.*, ed. cit., 705 (DS 1678).

[186] *Ordo Paenitentiae*, 6c.

[187] Cf. Ps 51(50):12.

[188] I had occasion to speak of these fundamental aspects of penance at the general audiences of May 19, 1982: *Insegnamenti* V, 2 (1982), 1758ff; February 28, 1979: *Insegnamenti* II (1979), 475-478; March 21, 1984: *Insegnamenti* VII, 1 (1984), 720-722. See also the norms of the *Code of Canon Law* concerning the place for administering the sacrament and concerning confessionals (Canon 964, 2-3)

[189] I dealt with this subject concisely at the general audience of March 7, 1984: *Insegnamenti* VII, 1 (1984), 631-633.

[190] Cf. Gn 4:7, 15.

[191] Cf. 2 Sm 12.

[192] Cf. Lk 15:17-21.

[193] Cf. *Presbyterorum Ordinis*, 18.

[194] *Ordo Paenitentiae*, 7b.

[195] Cf. *ibid.*, 17.

[196] Canons 961-963.

[197] Cf. Ez 18:23.

[198] Cf. Is 42:3; Mt 12:20.

[199] Cf. *Familiaris Consortio*, 84: AAS 74 (1982), 184-186.

[200] Cf. 1 Pt 1:1f; 3:8.

[201] *Ibid.*, 3:9, 13.

[202] *Ibid.*, 3:8, 9, 13.

[203] *Ibid.*, 3:17.

[204] Litany of the Sacred Heart, cf. 1 Jn 2:2; Eph 2:14; Rom 3:25; 5:11.

[205] Pope John Paul II, General Audience Address of December 7, 1983, no. 2: *Insegnamenti*, VI, 2 (1983), 1264.

[206] *Ibid.*, General Audience Address of January 4, 1984: *Insegnamenti*, VII, 1 (1984), 16-18.

[207] Cf. Rom 1:5; 16:26.

BIBLIOGRAPHY

Champlin, Joseph M., Elizabeth Drotar, and Thomas Likona. *With Hearts Light as Feathers: The First Reconciliation of Children*. New York: Crossroad, 1995.

Clendenen, Avis, and Troy Martin. *Forgiveness: Finding Freedom Through Reconciliation*. New York: Crossroad, 2002.

Code of Canon Law: Latin-English Edition: New English Translation (*Codex Iuris Canonici*). Washington, DC: Canon Law Society of America, 1998.
- Book IV: The Sanctifying Function of the Church (cc. 834-839)
- Part I: The Sacraments (cc. 840-848)
- Title IV: The Sacrament of Penance (cc. 960-997)

Coffey, David M̄. *The Sacrament of Reconciliation*. Collegeville, MN: The Liturgical Press, 2001.

Dallen, James. *The Reconciling Community: The Rite of Penance*. New York: Pueblo Publishing Company, 1986.

Dallen, James, and Joseph Favazza. *Removing the Barriers: The Practice of Reconciliation*. Chicago: Liturgy Training Publications, 1991.

Enright, Robert D., and Joanna North, eds. *Exploring Forgiveness*. Madison, WI: University of Wisconsin Press, 1998.

Forest, Jim. *Confession: Doorway to Forgiveness*. Maryknoll, NY: Orbis, 2002.

Gula, Richard M. *To Walk Together Again: The Sacrament of Reconciliation*. New York: Paulist Press, 1984.

Hahn, Scott. *Lord, Have Mercy: The Healing Power of Confession*. New York: Doubleday, 2003.

Hellwig, Monika. *Sign of Reconciliation and Conversion: The Sacrament of Penance for Our Times*. Wilmington, DE: M. Glazier, 1982.

Hughes, Kathleen. *Saying Amen: A Mystagogy of Sacrament*. Chicago: Liturgy Training Publications, 1999.

Hughes, Kathleen, and Joseph Favazza. *A Reconciliation Sourcebook*. Chicago: Liturgy Training Publications, 1997.

Kennedy, Robert J., ed. *Reconciliation: The Continuing Agenda*. Collegeville, MN: The Liturgical Press, 1987.

———. *Reconciling Embrace: Foundations for the Future of Sacramental Reconciliation*. Chicago: Liturgy Training Publications, 1998.

Kidder, Annmarie. *Making Confession, Hearing Confession: The History of the Cure of Souls*. Collegeville, MN: The Liturgical Press, 2010.

McCullough, Michael E., Kenneth I. Pargament, and Carl E. Thorsen. *Forgiveness: Theory, Research, and Practice*. New York: The Guilford Press, 2000.

Morneau, Robert F. *Reconciliation*. Maryknoll, NY: Orbis Books, 2007.

O'Loughlin, Frank. *The Future of the Sacrament of Penance*. New York: Paulist Press, 2009.

Rahner, Karl. "Some Forgotten Truths Concerning the Sacrament of Penance." In *Theological Investigations*, vol. 2. Baltimore: Darton, Longman and Todd, 1964.

———. *Theological Investigations*, vol. 15. New York: Crossroad, 1982.

Schillebeeckx, Edward, ed. "Sacramental Reconciliation." *Concilium* 61 (1971).

United States Conference of Catholic Bishops (USCCB), Bishops' Committee on the Liturgy. "Rereading the Constitution on the Liturgy (Art. 72)." *BCL Newsletter* 28 (June/July 1992): 22-26. Reprinted in *Thirty-Five Years of the BCL Newsletter* (Washington, DC: USCCB, 2004), 1302-1306.

Upton, Julia. *A Time for Embracing: Reclaiming Reconciliation*. Collegeville, MN: The Liturgical Press, 1999.

USCCB Committee for Pastoral Research and Practices. *Reflections on the Sacrament of Penance in Catholic Life Today: A Study Document*. Washington, DC: USCCB, 1990.

Weinandy, Thomas. *Sacrament of Mercy: A Spiritual and Penitential Guide to Confession*. Boston, MA: Pauline Books, 1997. Republished, Lima, OH: Academic Renewal Press, 2005.